THE HISTORIES OF
RAPHAEL SAMUEL
A PORTRAIT OF A PEOPLE'S HISTORIAN

THE HISTORIES OF
RAPHAEL SAMUEL
A PORTRAIT OF A PEOPLE'S HISTORIAN

SOPHIE SCOTT-BROWN

PRESS

Published by ANU Press
The Australian National University
Acton ACT 2601, Australia
Email: anupress@anu.edu.au
This title is also available online at press.anu.edu.au

National Library of Australia Cataloguing-in-Publication entry

Creator:	Scott-Brown, Sophie, author.
Title:	The histories of Raphael Samuel : a portrait of a people's historian / Sophie Scott-Brown.
ISBN:	9781760460365 (paperback) 9781760460372 (ebook)
Series:	ANU lives series in biography.
Subjects:	Samuel, Raphael. Historians--Great Britain--Biography. Marxian historiography. Historical materialism. Social history.
Dewey Number:	907.202

All rights reserved. No part of this publication may be reproduced, stored in a retrieval system or transmitted in any form or by any means, electronic, mechanical, photocopying or otherwise, without the prior permission of the publisher.

The ANU.Lives Series in Biography is an initiative of the National Centre of Biography at The Australian National University, ncb.anu.edu.au.

Cover design and layout by ANU Press. Portrait of Raphael Samuel by Lucinda Douglas-Menzies.

This edition © 2017 ANU Press

Contents

Acknowledgements vii

Abbreviations ix

Introduction 1

1. The Ingrained Activist: Communism as a Way of Life, the Communist Party Historians' Group and Oxford Student Politics 17

2. Reinventing the Organiser: Anti-authoritarianism, Activist Politics and the First New Left 55

3. The Workshop Historian: Ruskin College and the Early Years of the History Workshop. .95

4. The Secret Life of Headington Quarry: People's History in the Field 131

5. The Socialist Historian? 163

6. Stranger Memories of Who We Really Are: History, the Nation and the Historian. 201

Afterword: The Historian's Work in Progress 231

Select Bibliography. 235

Acknowledgements

Like many before me, I was heading somewhere else entirely when I was waylaid, detained and generally derailed by Raphael Samuel. I found myself intrigued by the paradoxical nature and provocative writing of this unusual historian. Curious to know more about how he developed his imaginative approach to history, I set out to research his life and thought. This proved to be a difficult journey that could not have been done without a tremendous amount of help and support from a large number of people.

I would like to thank Sally Alexander, Jonathan Clark, Paul Connell, Anna Davin, Dave Douglass, David Goodway, Alun Howkins, Ken Jones, Hilda Kean, Ian Manborde, Paul Martin, Gareth Stedman Jones, Carolyn Steedman and Barbara Taylor, who all very kindly shared their memories of Raphael, patiently fielding vague, occasionally clumsy and sometimes repetitive questions. I am also grateful to Stefan Dickers, the archivist at the Bishopsgate Institute, London, for his continual help and cheerful encouragement with the project, to Alison Light for her kind interest and valuable insights, and to Brian Harrison for allowing me to use the transcripts of his own interviews with Raphael.

This project was facilitated by an international scholarship from The Australian National University (ANU) and was conducted with the support of ANU School of History. Marnie Hughes-Warrington was instrumental early on in helping to identify key themes. Lawrence Goldman gave me support and encouragement during his visit to ANU in 2012 and again on my visit to Oxford in 2014. Karen Fox provided sympathetic and patient mentorship. Melanie Nolan offered unflagging and generous support, energetic interest and rigorous critique. It has been a privilege to work with her.

I would also like to acknowledge Alastair MacLachlan for discussing, at length, different aspects of the project with me, Tom MacLachlan for timely technological wizardry and Geoff Hunt for his sharp eyes and discerning guidance. Part of my research was carried out as a visiting fellow at Wolfson College, Oxford. I am grateful to Hermione Lee for her comments on an earlier draft of the project. My thanks also to Hilda Kean and the anonymous readers of the completed manuscript for their thought-provoking comments, which have proved invaluable.

Love and thanks are due to Lesley, Steven and Tom Scott-Brown. And to Matt who shared in every trial, trouble and footnote.

In memory of Geoffrey Bolton, another Balliol boy, historian and biographer, whose gentle guidance was much valued.

Abbreviations

BUF	British Union of Fascists
CCCS	Centre for Contemporary Cultural Studies
CND	Campaign for Nuclear Disarmament
CPGB	Communist Party of Great Britain
CPHG	Communist Party Historians' Group
HW	History Workshop
HWJ	*History Workshop Journal*
ICS	Institute of Community Studies
KAS	King Alfred School
LBC	Left Book Club
NLR	*New Left Review*
NR	*The New Reasoner*
P&P	*Past and Present*
RSA	Raphael Samuel Archive
SDP	Social Democratic Party
SH	*Social History*
TW	Theatre Workshop
ULR	*Universities and Left Review*
WEA	Workers' Educational Association

Introduction

A man of paradox?

For the British historian Raphael Samuel (1934–1996), the making of history was inextricably linked with politics. Best known as the moving force behind the History Workshop (HW) and as a founder editor of the *History Workshop Journal* (*HWJ*), Samuel's self-identified objective was the democratisation of history-making. Yet accounts of him and reactions to his approach to history are characterised by paradox: a born organiser renowned for the chaotic nature of his activities; a trained historian who attacked professional history-making; a lifelong socialist whose relationship to the wider left was often strained; a thinker celebrated for originality and condemned for conceptual confusion. His long-term legacy is no less conflicted. Dismissed by some as a relatively obscure figure, for others he has assumed almost mythical properties as a far-sighted 'prophet' with a vision ahead of his times. Taking these incongruities as a point of departure, this book illuminates Samuel as a neglected but important thinker and asks what, if any, significance he has for modern historiography.

Born into an extended Jewish family in London, Samuel, in his youth, was a devoted Communist Party activist. Like many others, he left the party in 1956; becoming a key figure in the first British New Left movement (1956–62) and later an adult education tutor at the trade union–affiliated Ruskin College. Here, he became the key organiser and, for some, the living personification of the HW's moral, political and methodological agenda.[1] Later, he was instrumental in the creation

---

1   David Feldman and Jon Lawrence, 'Introduction: Structures and Transformations in British Historiography', in Feldman and Lawrence, eds, *Structures and Transformations in Modern British History* (Cambridge: Cambridge University Press, 2011), 11.

of the *HWJ*. Towards the end of his life, he was a prominent voice in the British history wars, the national curriculum debates and a seemingly unlikely champion of the heritage industry. In different guises, the one consistent motif of his working life was a sustained attempt to recognise history-making as common social activity.

For all this activity, much of it in the public eye, he is an elusive figure in the existing literature surrounding contemporary British historiography, a passing mention or footnote at most.[2] There are several possible reasons for this. His work lacked 'scholarly' impact within the profession, he produced only one sole-authored monograph, *Theatres of Memory* (1994), in his lifetime, which he published through a political press (Verso, formerly New Left Books). Despite its ambitions, the book did not set out a clear theoretical position or advance a specific argument about the British past. Further, his career had few of the traditional markers of professional success: he did not gain a doctoral qualification, he worked mostly in a further (rather than higher) education institution and only in the year of his death was he appointed to a professorship and given a prominent chair at a university (University of East London).

---

2   Existing engagements with his life and work include the following: Robin Blackburn, 'Raphael Samuel: The Politics of Thick Description', *New Left Review* (*NLR*), I/221, Jan–Feb (1997), 133–38; Alison Light, 'Preface', in Raphael Samuel, *The Lost World of British Communism* (London: Verso, 2006); Sally Alexander, Alison Light and Gareth Stedman Jones, 'Editorial Preface', in Raphael Samuel, *Island Stories: Unravelling Britain* (London: Verso, 1998); Ken Jones, 'Raphael Samuel: Against Conformity', *Changing English: Studies in Culture and Education*, 5, 1 (1998), 17–26; Bill Schwarz, 'Foreword', in Raphael Samuel, *Theatres of Memory: The Past in Contemporary Culture* (London: Verso, 2012).

INTRODUCTION

Raphael Samuel, Ruskin College, Oxford, 1993
Source: Photographer Stefan Wallgren. Picture from Raphael Samuel Archive,
Bishopsgate Institute, London, courtesy of Alison Light and the Raphael Samuel Estate.

Not only did he lack these attributes, he also spent much of life openly criticising them, prompting those with a vested interest in identifying the discipline's innovators (namely, professional historians) to dismiss him as inconsequential, a minor figure embedded within a minority culture of radical left-wing British intellectuals. Even here, his position appears tenuous. He is far less prominent and celebrated than his close contemporaries E.P. Thompson, Stuart Hall and Perry Anderson.[3] Compared to the narrative power and historical vision of Thompson, or the theoretical might and imagination of Hall and Anderson, Samuel seems a man condemned to the margins.

Yet what engagement with him and his work as exists is far from indifferent, but deeply conflicted and emotive. This minor figure was a deeply divisive character, attracting both strong adulation and equally strong critique. His critics, notably figures on the hard intellectual left or professional historians, ranged in their positions. Some lamented that his romanticism and sentimentality had clouded his judgement, squandered his talents and resulted in missed opportunities. Take, for example, this from his former comrade and fellow historian Eric Hobsbawm:

> [H]is history had neither structure nor limits. It was an unending and astonishingly learned perambulation round the wonderful landscapes, of memory and the lives of common people, with an occasional intellectual pounce suggested by some particularly fascinating insight glimpsed along the way.[4]

Although charmingly phrased, 'an occasional intellectual pounce' is not a consistent body of work and a 'perambulation', no matter how learned, is still an aimless walk (rather than a forward march). Harvey Kaye, in his

---

3   On E.P. Thompson: Perry Anderson, *Arguments within English Marxism* (London: Verso Editions, 1980); Scott Hamilton, *The Crisis of Theory: E.P. Thompson, the New Left and Post War British Politics* (Manchester: Manchester University Press, 2012); Bryan Palmer, *E.P. Thompson: Objections and Oppositions* (London: Verso, 1994); Harvey Kaye and Keith McCelland, eds, *E. P. Thompson: Critical Perspectives* (Philadelphia: Temple University Press, 1990). On Perry Anderson: Gregory Elliot, *Perry Anderson: The Merciless Laboratory of History* (Minneapolis: University of Minnesota Press, 1998); Paul Blackledge, *Perry Anderson, Marxism and the New Left* (London: Merlin, 2004).
4   Eric Hobsbawm, *Interesting Times: A Twentieth Century Life* (London: Abacus, 2002), 212.

study of British Marxist historians, reinforced the point and extended it across the wider HW movement suggesting that the eclecticism of its research often caused it to lose focus on *class* struggle.⁵

Others took a darker view, not only condemning Samuel for lack of rigour but for inconsistency and inauthenticity as well. The former Ruskin tutor David Selbourne advanced this critique of his one-time colleague:

> Samuel embodied a peculiar style of privileged patronisation of working people … He often seemed a kind of vicarious proletarian himself, romanticising the lives and labours of the industrial working class whilst flattering as well as encouraging his students. This often silly class condescension was an uncomfortable thing to observe.⁶

Richard Hoggart, reviewing *Theatres of Memory*, went further, arguing that Samuel's openness was the product of a 'traumatised Marxist' struggling (and unable) to come to terms with the breakdown of his earlier communist identity amidst the wider disintegration of the political left.⁷ Patrick Wright, also reviewing *Theatres* (in which his own book had been subject to strong critique), substituted trauma for vanity, arguing that Samuel's impassioned defence of the popular was part of his desire to 'play the part' of the people's historian.⁸ Stefan Collini, whilst not putting the case as bluntly, followed in seeing a lack of sincerity in Samuel's attack on professional historians given that, as Collini argued, the book's best passages were unmistakably those of a professionally trained historian.⁹

By contrast, his supporters, many of whom were former students or colleagues closely involved in the HW, transformed romanticism, lack of structure and inconsistency into kindness, intellectual openness and creativity. For Gareth Stedman Jones, a friend and journal co-founder:

---

5   Harvey Kaye, *The Education of Desire: Marxists and the Writing of History* (London: Routledge, 1992), 122. See also: Dennis Dworkin, *Cultural Marxism in Postwar Britain: History, the New Left, and the Origins of Cultural Studies* (Durham and London: Duke University Press, 1997), 187; Kynan Gentry, 'Ruskin, Radicalism and Raphael Samuel: Politics Pedagogy and the Origins of the History Workshop', *History Workshop Journal*, 76 (2013), 187–211.
6   David Selbourne, 'The Last Comrade', *The Observer*, 15 December 1996, 24.
7   Richard Hoggart, 'Review: Theatres of Memory', *Political Quarterly*, 66, 3 (1995), 215–16.
8   Patrick Wright, 'Review of Theatres of Memory', *The Guardian*, 5 February 1995.
9   Stefan Collini, 'Speaking with Authority: The Historian as Social Critic', in *English Pasts: Essays in History and Culture* (Oxford: Oxford University Press, 1999), 95–102.

He was also an inspired teacher and the author of books and essays, which have expanded beyond recognition the intellectual and imaginative ranges both of English history and of the writing of history itself. But he was not a teacher and a writer; he was also an organiser and a prophet, a close and sometimes uncanny reader of 'the signs of the times.'[10]

An 'inspired teacher' was also how a former student (and later deputy British Prime Minister) recalled him, saying: 'He made me do something I thought I'd never do. Not just write an essay – that was difficult enough for me – but use the experience of poetry to illustrate a point'.[11]

Samuel's mercurial qualities have also been re-visioned. Ken Jones recast 'insincerity' into 'non-conformity', contending that he did not easily align with the orthodoxies of the wider political and intellectual left. This view was echoed by Robin Blackburn, a former editor of the *New Left Review*, who pointed out that his distinctive approach to history often posed a challenge to many of the settled concepts and categories of left-wing political thought.[12] Sheila Rowbotham, an early HW participant, developed this, adding that:

> While Raphael the organiser was a benign despot, his creative imaginative leaps and his interest in all and sundry made space: for people, for cultural insights and for original approaches to history.[13]

And elsewhere:

> Raphael was not simply a writer but a renowned organiser, the kind who was an initiator of great projects with the capacity to yoke his fellow to the concept and carry them on regardless of grizzles and groans ... He was the world's most adept hooker, and ruthless behind the charm.[14]

Rowbotham's insight tacitly acknowledged his role as a *teacher* as well as researcher of history, an aspect underplayed or misunderstood by the critics. Hilda Kean also stressed the importance of the pedagogical (as much as historiographical) significance of the HW method. She traced its connections to older traditions of democratic education in which the

---

10 Gareth Stedman Jones, 'Obituary: Raphael Samuel', *The Independent*, 11 December 1996.
11 John Prescott, 'Genuine Love for Others', *The Guardian*, 11 December 1996.
12 Jones, 'Raphael Samuel: Against Conformity', 17–26; Blackburn, 'Raphael Samuel: The Politics of Thick Description', 133–34.
13 Sheila Rowbotham, *Promises of a Dream: Remembering the Sixties* (London: Penguin, 2000), 142.
14 Sheila Rowbotham, 'Some Memories of Raphael', *NLR*, I/221, Jan–Feb (1997), 128–32.

authority of the tutor to determine the historical agenda was broken down and the student placed in a more active, directing role in the learning process.[15]

Despite interpretive differences, there are recurrent and common themes relating to Samuel as an individual. These include his intimate and empathetic style of teaching, his heterogeneous range of historical interests, and his fluidity in conceptual, political and personal positioning. Undeniably, he was a distinctive personality. It is this strange combination of obscurity, emotive critique and heated controversy that makes a study of his life worthwhile: what was it that so dramatically divided interpretations of him or that simply went unrecognised?

This study contends that the most significant aspect of Samuel was his entire way of being a historian. For him, democratising history implied more than changing the content or epistemological structure of history, it required that he, as a historian, 'concede the practice of democracy'.[16] The practical impact of this not only affected his personal conception of history but implied a larger shift in his working values, behaviour and practices. It meant a move away from determining the object of study towards enabling the emergence of a common discursive framework, capable of accommodating a diverse range of history-making activities and perspectives.

I further argue that his life and work has an enduring contemporary relevance by offering an insight into a response, at the level of practice, to history in the plural, without succumbing to unexamined relativism. In *Making History: Historians and the Uses of the Past* (2012), Jorma Kalela addressed this within a theoretical context. Kalela contended that, at a time when we have become more accustomed to thinking of histories instead of 'History', the impact of this on the day-to-day work of professional historians has been left relatively unexamined.[17] He proposed that such an epistemological transition challenged historians to abandon their traditional, authoritative position of deciding what

---

15 Hilda Kean, 'Public History and Raphael Samuel: A Forgotten Radical Pedagogy?', *Public History Review*, 11 (2004), 51–62; Hilda Kean, 'People, Historians and Public History; De-mystifying the Process of History Making', *Public Historian*, 32, 3 (2010), 25–38.
16 A phrase taken from Raymond Williams, Samuel's New Left contemporary, in: *Culture and Society 1780–1950* (London: Chatto and Windus, 1958), 341.
17 Jorma Kalela, *Making History: Historians and the Uses of the Past* (Basingstoke: Palgrave Macmillan, 2012).

was or was not of historical significance and adopt a facilitating role, enabling popular participation in historical research. This did not mean perpetuating academic conventions across a wider constituency, but lay in propagating the critical-analytical skills that characterised professionalism across a broader spectrum of subjects, sources and mediums. Such a move, he insisted, would mean 'an attitudinal change amongst scholars in giving respect and creating trust'.[18]

In the opening to *Making History*, Kalela drew on Samuel as a supporting point of reference. As both admirers and critics acknowledged, Samuel consciously styled himself as a people's historian and deliberately attempted to reflect this choice in his work as a historian-educator. As well as providing the first overview of his life in relation to his work, this book also uses him as a lens to examine history-making as a politics of personal disposition and practice.

In doing this, a biographical approach provides an indispensable tool of analysis and methodological approach. The philosopher and biographer Ray Monk, in a provocatively revisionist argument, made the case for biography as a 'non-theoretical activity' that, rather than privileging one or other explanatory model of human life (social, cultural, historical or biological), reconstructs the individual within a constellation of interwoven relationships.[19] Arguably, Monk's 'non-theoretical activity' can equally be construed as a *multi*-theoretical one without damaging the integrity of his main point: the study of a life both accommodates and requires a range of critical insights acting upon an eclectic array of empirical evidence.

To fully comprehend Samuel and his approach to history, it is necessary to understand the nature of his life, the interplay of all his histories. This approach offers three particular benefits. Firstly, bringing the social role of the historian into focus requires sensitivity to personality as performed politics. As Kalela indicated, democratising the teaching of history is dependent on an 'attitudinal change' in cultivating relationships of trust. Samuel's personal behaviour as a historian was as important to

---

18   Ibid., 162. For a sociohistorical discussion on the changing role of the contemporary intellectual see Zygmunt Bauman, *Legislators and Interpreters: On Modernity, Postmodernity and Intellectuals* (Cambridge: Polity Press, 1989).
19   Ray Monk, 'Life without Theory: Biography as an Exemplar of Philosophical Understanding', *Poetics Today*, 28, 3 (2007), 527–70.

'read' as his historical writing. His thinking was performed physically, through social interactions, as much as it was on the page. Discerning and defining these requires the intimate perspective that biography can offer.

Secondly, 'democratising' the role of the historian-educator by making them more accountable to their students (rather than the other way around) demands that the scholar responds to the conditions created within a given context. In this case, democratic practice is not defined by a set of static prescriptions on behaviour but by the adaptive application of ethical values (such as equality and inclusivity). The methodological impact for this study is a close consideration of the implications prompted by the specific social structures and environments in which he worked. For example, as indicated by Kean, Samuel's pedagogical priorities alongside the practical implications of Ruskin's worker student body were influential factors in determining the HW's research approach, a factor often overlooked by critics.[20]

Finally, biography allows these personal and social contexts to be brought into dialogue with the larger intellectual and cultural history of late twentieth-century Britain. This period is typically defined by the sense of dramatic and complex change across every area of social life. On the one hand, Britain's position as a political and economic world power declined, on the other a flurry of 'modernisation' ushered in the welfare state, expanded the public sphere and bolstered the perception of Britain as an affluent society.[21] Politically, concepts such as class, socialism and democratisation came under scrutiny, losing some of their cohesion in the face of emerging social movements (in particular, the women's

---

20 See also Sophie Scott-Brown, 'The Art of the Organiser: Raphael Samuel and the Origins of the History Workshop', *History of Education: The Journal of the History of Education*, 45, 3 (2016), 372–90, www.tandfonline.com/doi/full/10.1080/0046760X.2015.1103907 (accessed 15 December 2015).
21 For overviews on different aspects of postwar Britain see: Boris Ford, ed., *Modern Britain: The Cambridge Cultural History* (Cambridge: Cambridge University Press, 1992); Kenneth Morgan, *Britain since 1945: The People's Peace* (Oxford: Oxford University Press, 2001); Paul Addison and Harriet Jones, eds, *A Companion to Contemporary Britain 1939–2000* (Oxford: Blackwell, 2005).

movement). Intellectually, the confidence of the modern sciences was subject to interrogation and challenge from the so-called 'linguistic and cultural turn'.[22]

In fact, Samuel offers a particularly unique insight here. As Stedman Jones noted, as well as being a product of his times, he was also an 'uncanny reader' and responsive participant in them.[23] The cornerstone of his historiographical thought was an emphasis on the role of the present in shaping consciousness of the past and he took an active interest in the turbulent debates surrounding the nature of knowledge. Further, his individual life course, his journey from the settled convictions of a young communist activist to the unabashed pluralism of *Theatres of Memory*, offers an insight into the fragmentation of epistemological certainties and the range of responses to that process.

It should be stressed, however, that this study is not a full biography of Samuel; that is yet to be written. What is offered here is a portrait of him as a 'people's historian' who cultivated a deliberately conscious politics of performance, shaped by his times and continually reshaped by the particular contexts of his life and work.

---

22   For overviews of political thought in late twentieth-century Europe see: Geoff Eley, *Forging Democracy: The History of the Left in Europe 1850–2000* (New York: Oxford University Press, 2002). For more specific studies on the question of political consensus see: Jim Tomlinson, *The Politics of Decline: Understanding Post War Britain* (Abingdon: Routledge, 2014). For a contrasting interpretation see: Peter Kerr, *Postwar British Politics: From Conflict to Consensus* (London: Routledge, 2005). For an optimistic perspective on the breakdown of class-based politics see: Sheila Rowbotham, Lynne Segal and Hillary Wainwright, *Beyond the Fragments: Feminism and the Making of Socialism* (London: Merlin Press, 1979). For general overviews of postwar historiography see: David Cannadine, 'Viewpoint British History: Past, Present – and Future?', *Past and Present*, 116, 1 (1987), 169–91; Eric Hobsbawm, *On History* (London: Wiedenfield and Nicholson, 1997), see in particular chapters 6 'From Social History to the History of Society' and 16 'On History From Below'; Perry Anderson, 'A Culture in Contraflow II', *NLR*, I/182, Jul–Aug (1990), 85–137; Ioan Davies, 'British Cultural Marxism', *International Journal of Politics, Culture and Society*, 4, 3 (1991), 323–43; Jim Obelkevich, 'New Developments in History in the 1950s and 1960s', *Contemporary British History*, 14, 4 (2000), 125–42; Peter Lambert and Phillipp Schofield, eds, *Making History: An Introduction to the History and Practices of a Discipline* (Abingdon: Routledge, 2004); Elizabeth A. Clark, *History, Theory, Text: Historians and the Linguistic Turn* (Cambridge, MA: Harvard University Press, 2004); Georg G. Iggers, *Historiography in the Twentieth Century: From Scientific Objectivity to the Postmodern Challenge* (Hanover: Wesleyan University Press, 2005); Geoff Eley, *The Crooked Line: Social History to Cultural History* (Michigan: University of Michigan Press, 2005); Geoff Eley and Keith Nield, *The Future of Class in History: What's Left of the Social?* (Michigan: University of Michigan, 2007); Georg G. Iggers and Q. Edward Wang, eds, *A Global History of Modern Historiography* (London: Routledge, 2013).
23   Stedman Jones, 'Obituary: Raphael Samuel'.

In undertaking this study, I have drawn on various sources and modes of analysis. Given that the focus of this study is on Samuel as an intellectual personality, his published texts provide a major source for analysing both his ideas and his politics of practice. As an intellectual, his written work – articles, editorials, essays and monographs – constituted the main means by which he performed such a role in the public sphere. The argument presented here, that this performance posed a challenge to the traditional or conventional practices of a professional historian, assumes that, naturally, his published texts were a crucial part of this. The study, therefore, approaches his writing not only for descriptions of his ideas but also for the way in which it embodied and performed them.

Given that one of his principal objectives was to use history as part of a battle of ideas and that he was also an experienced political activist, I have placed his writing and activities in relation to the wider issues that they referenced, taking into consideration other individuals involved, the intended audience and the mediums through which different views were aired. This allows a sense of the choices he made in positioning himself and how he deliberately adapted this in accordance with the occasion. So, for example, the heated epistemological debates that raged across the pages of the *HWJ* and in the HW 13 meeting elicited from him a conciliatory response in those outlets but a more heated one in *New Left Review*, which he felt to be responsible for fuelling the drift towards theory.

In order to explore the deeper political and conceptual structures of his thinking, I have also considered the 'internal' features of the text. These include his selection and use of language, the general tone and style of his voice as a historian. Did he make assertions or suggestions? What emotional qualities (such as humour or sadness) do his texts evoke? I have also looked at the spatial qualities, the organisational structure, of his writing, attempting to discern the shape of his narratives and to consider their significance for his thought. Samuel typically rejected linear narratives in favour of a thematic approach. What does this suggest about his conception of time? He often approached an issue through deconstruction (the breakdown of concepts into component relationships), or through decentralisation (placing issues into wider contexts and frameworks). What were the underlying political implications of these techniques?

Finally, I have examined the genealogical relationships acknowledged in his texts; the extent to which the literature he referenced in making theoretical or historical arguments shared common or associational conceptual traits, or had roots in broadly defined philosophical traditions.

In attempting to discern the relationship between his thought and how it ultimately came to be expressed in his published texts or translated into his organisation of events, I have drawn on Samuel's archive, housed in the Bishopsgate Institute, near to his former residence in Spitalfields, East London. The archive is comprised of papers and oral recordings ranging across Samuel's life. *History Workshop: A Collectanea 1967–1991* (1991), a commemorative volume published by the HW to mark its 25th anniversary, was also a valuable collection of primary documents that charted the HW's development and various incarnations. These sources were accompanied by editorial commentaries from Samuel and other key participants providing some explanation and contextualisation for the material presented.

Whilst Samuel's archival collection was generous, not all of his more intimate personal correspondence was available for public access. Given that the focus of this study is on his public performance as a historian, this was not an insurmountable problem. Material relating to his teaching practices was ample and included course outlines, notes and oral recordings of HW meetings. I have emphasised the items that, within the outlines set out for this particular project, best illustrate the forms of intelligence in planning and organising that are not as readily apparent from reading his published writings.

Further critical insight was provided by a series of interviews given by Samuel to his friend and fellow historian Brian Harrison.[24] The first of these was held in 1979 to discuss methodology in oral history. The second and third were held in 1987, in conjunction with Harrison's research into left-wing politics at Oxford University.[25] Accordingly, they focused on his student years at Oxford and the origins of the first New Left. These interviews were crucial for illustrating some of the difficult periods in Samuel's life. Furthermore, they were conducted in conjunction with

---

24 Brian Harrison, 'Interview with Raphael Samuel', 23 October 1979; 'Interview with Raphael Samuel', 18 September 1987; 'Interview with Raphael Samuel', 20 October 1987, all held at 19 Elder Street, London, transcripts held in Raphael Samuel Archive (RSA), Bishopsgate Institute, London.
25 Brian Harrison, 'Oxford and the Labour Movement', *Twentieth Century British History*, 2, 3 (1991), 226–71.

research into separate topics, not as part of an intentional biographical study. They were conducted with someone familiar to him with whom he had worked closely in the past. Harrison, an experienced oral historian, noted on the transcripts that he:

> talked freely, and had no objection to very personal types of question, standing up for much of the time, and occasionally walking about, thinking deeply on how to answer some of the questions I asked. Although he was so deeply involved in these events at the time, he is remarkably distanced and objective in talking about them, though in no sense disengaging himself from the loyalties and affections that were so important to him at that time. A very fruitful discussion.[26]

In the interview context, Samuel was not able to control the questions posed to him (which was clear from the nature of his answers, which were not always fluent, occasionally stumbling on matters he found difficult to express). He did not have any responsibility for the final transcripts. Taken together, these factors suggest that the interviews took place in a relatively open and candid atmosphere in which Samuel spoke frankly and according to his true feelings as he experienced them at that particular time.

As personality is as much, if not more, to do with the 'impression' that it leaves upon other people, I have also drawn on autobiographies and memoirs written by his friends and colleagues. These were useful as they were not specifically about him as an individual, but refer to the ways in which people encountered him in the course of their own lives and activities. The best examples of this come from Hobsbawm's *Interesting Times* (2002), which provides a sense of how Samuel appeared to the 'older' generation of which Hobsbawm was a part. Equally, Rowbotham's *Promises of a Dream* (2000) gives an insight into how a figure like Samuel appeared to a younger generation within the giddying context of a 1960s radical culture.

I have also benefited from extensive discussions with Samuel's former colleagues and students, friends and family members. I carried out interviews with Alison Light, Anna Davin, Dave Douglass, Hilda Kean, Barbara Taylor, Sally Alexander, Gareth Stedman Jones, Stuart Hall, Alun Howkins and David Goodway. I also had a written correspondence with four former students: Paul Martin, Ian Manborde, Paul O'Connell

---

26 Brian Harrison, 'Interview with Raphael Samuel', 20 October 1987.

and Robert Micallef.[27] The purpose of these discussions was not to create a formal oral history of Samuel, but to guide my interpretation of his texts, to elucidate some of the more obscure references within them, and to gauge some sense of the atmosphere in which his activities took place. The oral discussions also went some way to addressing the lack of access to his more intimate personal correspondence. Above all, however, they were important in providing insight into him as a physical presence and intellectual persona.

The interviews, both written and oral forms, revealed a number of important methodological issues. One of these was a matter of proximity. Samuel died in 1996. There has been no previous in-depth, individual study of him. Furthermore, Samuel inhabited a world largely dominated by a framework of radical left-wing politics, the recent history of which was dominated by conflict and tension. Many contentious, difficult or even painful memories were, therefore, still relatively fresh and unprocessed.

Whilst the context of the interviews undoubtedly informed the nature of response, the accounts given of him, and the ways in which they were delivered, were nevertheless striking. This was true in particular in reference to the sheer number of 'folk legends' that have grown up around him, including a collection of anecdotes told about his supposed exploits, many of which were impossible to verify – not only told, but actively performed with his voice and mannerisms mimicked: 'Comrade, darling, could I just pick your brain…', followed by a reenactment of the subject's own mock exasperation: 'Oh Raphael!'

All this served to reinforce my view of the significance of performativity in Samuel's activities and self-deportment. Undoubtedly, he left behind a highly distinctive impression of himself. This, it should be stressed, is not to say that he was mendacious or manipulative in a cruel way, but that his political ideas, and ideals, were articulated through and imposed onto his physical being as much as they were on the page. Given his activist rather than scholarly background, these were most likely subject to a species of slight exaggeration. To foster interest and passion for historical research amongst those not necessarily predisposed to have either, he was, perhaps, compelled to be overly emphatic in the enthusiasm and exuberance that

---

27   All audio and written transcripts of communications are held in my private collection. They are available upon request and with the interviewee's consent. These will be deposited in the Raphael Samuel Archive at the Bishopsgate Institute.

he conveyed. So, rather than concern myself too deeply with the literal veracity of these stories, I approached them as authentic examples of the potency of his all-important personal charisma.

Whilst this intellectual persona and performance was crucial, there was still a need to gauge a sense of him in less guarded moments, such as his response to the breakdown of his earlier communist political convictions after the Khrushchev revelations of 1956. Here the interviews with long-term friends were critical. The account given to me by the late Stuart Hall was particularly helpful in providing a vital sense of Samuel's response to the events that caused him such acute emotional and mental discomfort.

The study takes the form of an analytical narrative that follows a loosely chronological order, which I found to be the most useful form for exploring the interaction between different factors that shaped the evolution of his thought. Whilst chapters 1 and 2 are quite clear in their periodisation, covering 1934–56 and 1956–62 respectively, chapters 3 to 6 take a more expansive approach, with overlapping features reflecting the dynamism and complexity of this period.

Chapters 1 and 2 concentrate on his formative years, experiences and encounters. They examine the nature of his early political convictions and how these were subject to dramatic change in young adulthood. Chapters 3 and 4 consider his early days as a Ruskin tutor, the impact of adult education on his historical thinking and how this contrasted with close contemporaries. Chapter 5 turns to his positioning within theoretical and political debates amongst the left, whilst Chapter 6 examines his responses to issues in public history and heritage.

Through his ideas and practices of history, he continually attempted to outline a democratic politics of practice that borrowed from many existing political ideas and traditions but cannot be easily conflated with any one alone. He never formally articulated this project. It was driven as much by his personal temperament and activist instincts as it was a fully formed conception. It was, however, guided by the notion of a dynamic common culture in which all people actively participated, a culture continually reflecting upon and renewing its own ideas of itself.

There are many places that Samuel's story could begin. For the sake of starting somewhere, this account of the life and work of this unique British historian begins deep in the Buckinghamshire countryside on a hot night in June 1944.

1
The Ingrained Activist: Communism as a Way of Life, the Communist Party Historians' Group and Oxford Student Politics

When Richard Lloyd Jones came to look back on his wartime school days at Long Dene, a progressive boarding school in Buckinghamshire, one particular incident stuck in his mind.[1] He remembered being kept awake during the hot summer of 1944. It was not the heat alone that was responsible for this. Nor was there any particular physical reason why he should have been so wakeful. Part of the school's ethos was a strenuous emphasis on the pupils participating in forms of outdoor and rural work such as harvesting. All that fresh air and exercise should have been quite sufficient to exhaust even the most active of small boys. What kept Richard Lloyd Jones awake was the incessant talking of a young, hyperactive 'Raf-Sam'. Lloyd Jones did not recall exactly what it was that so animated the juvenile Samuel, late into that sticky summer's night, but a reasonable assumption would be that it was politics, specifically communist politics, as the nine-year-old Samuel was already practising his skills as an aspiring communist propagandist and organiser.[2]

---
1   Lloyd Jones later became Permanent Secretary for Wales (1985–93) and Chairman for the Arts Council of Wales (1994–99).
2   Richard Lloyd Jones quoted in Sue Smithson, *Community Adventure: The Story of Long Dene School* (London: New European Publications, 1999), 21. See also: Raphael Samuel, 'Family Communism', in *The Lost World of British Communism* (London: Verso, 2006), 60; Raphael Samuel, 'Country Visiting: A Memoir', in *Island Stories: Unravelling Britain* (London: Verso, 1998), 135–36.

THE HISTORIES OF RAPHAEL SAMUEL

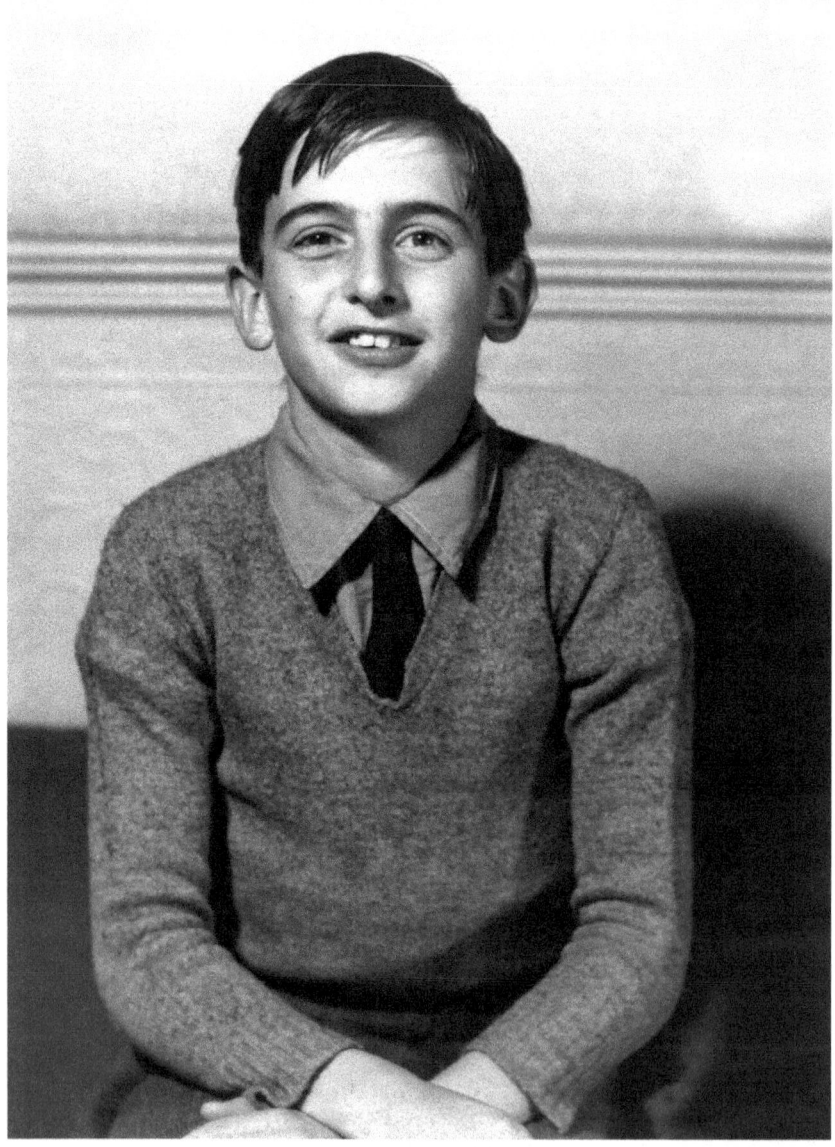

Raphael Samuel, Croftdown Road, London, c. 1945
Raphael Samuel Archive, Bishopsgate Institute, London, courtesy of Alison Light and the Raphael Samuel Estate.

1. THE INGRAINED ACTIVIST

As this anecdote suggests, Ralph or Raf, as he was then known, was already precociously political and steeped in Communist Party culture. This chapter explores the specific configurations of that youthful political commitment, arguing that it was multidimensional in nature, encompassing both conscious adherence to the party line but also an entire array of practices and values that were perceived less directly.

During this period of his youth (1934–52), the official party line changed several times. First founded in 1920, by end of the decade the Communist Party of Great Britain (CPGB) had adopted the uncompromising stance of 'class against class', which remained largely intact until the transition to Popular Frontism in 1935. Following the Nazi–Soviet pact in 1939, this was replaced by an Imperial War policy, compelling party members to reject the Allied war effort. After the collapse of the pact in 1941, Social Patriotism renewed the spirit of Popular Front and saw membership numbers increase substantially.[3] Following the war, the party entered a difficult period with the escalation of Cold War hostilities and tensions mounting amongst the national branches. In 1951, the CPGB announced its commitment to The British Road to Socialism through alliance with domestic progressive forces. The depth of this commitment, however, remains a matter for debate.[4]

As critical as these shifts were in sculpting the formal landscape of Samuel's communism, this chapter contends that for the child it was communism as direct experience, an entire way of life incorporating a set of values translated into behavioural norms and practices in day-to-day life that was important.[5]

---

3   See Kevin Morgan, 'The Communist Party and the Popular Front 1935–1938', in *Against Fascism and War* (Manchester: Manchester University Press, 1989), 33–55.
4   See Keith Laybourn, 'The Communist Party of Great Britain During the Emergence of the Cold War 1945–1956', in *Marxism in Britain: Dissent, Decline and Re-emergence 1945–c2000* (London: Taylor and Routledge, 2006), 11–56.
5   A point echoed by his uncle, Chimen Abramsky, in his tribute to his nephew following Samuel's death in 1996: 'As a result of the rise of fascism in Europe and the Second World War many Jews joined the communist movement. This had a major influence on the young Raphael. He absorbed many communist ideas on equality'. Abramsky reinforced this point later in the article, adding: 'There was more of William Godwin and Robert Owen in him, than of Marx and Engels'. 'Raphael Samuel', *The Jewish Chronicle*, 17 January 1997.

Communism as a way of life

Samuel was born on 26 December 1934, in North London, to Minna and Barnett Samuel, part of an extended Jewish family. Minna, born Minnie, was the daughter of Jacob and Fanny Nerenstein who had migrated to England from Grodno, Polish Russia, at the turn of century. Once in England, they had settled in the East End of London, where Minna was born in 1906 followed by two younger sisters, Miriam and Sarah. Here the family ran a bookshop and publishing house specialising in Jewish literature, Shapiro Valentine & Co. on Wentworth Street, East London. She married Barnett Samuel (1906–1971), a London solicitor from an orthodox Jewish family, in 1931 and moved to Hampstead Garden Suburb in North London. The marriage was short-lived, the couple separated in 1941 when Samuel was not quite seven years old, later divorcing in 1946. Minna raised Samuel, their only child. On returning to London following evacuation during the war, mother and son lived in Kentish Town, North London.[6]

The single most-defining feature of Samuel's early upbringing was communist politics, which dominated every aspect of his young life and burgeoning consciousness. His communist childhood was the subject of some of his most powerful pieces of historical writing, in particular his series of essays on 'The Lost World of British Communism' published in the *New Left Review* during the mid-1980s.[7] Historian and ex-communist John Saville criticised the essays, arguing that Samuel's communism was of a highly particular, even peculiar, kind, far from representative of a broader experience:

> I do not deny the validity of Raphael Samuel's own personal history, especially in his younger days ... The historian in him, however, might have acknowledged that it was a very unusual story, typical of some, perhaps many, Jewish comrades but not in any way relevant to the working-class militants who were joining the Communist Party at the time that Raphael was growing up in the 1940s.[8]

---

6   Gareth Stedman Jones, 'Samuel, Raphael Elkan (1934–1996)', *Oxford Dictionary of National Biography* (Oxford: Oxford University Press, 2004).
7   All references to *Lost World* are taken from the 2006 publication of these essays as a book: *The Lost World of British Communism* (London: Verso, 2006).
8   John Saville, *Memoirs from the Left* (London: Merlin, 2003), 9.

Saville may have intended this remark as a criticism, but in fact, this was the very point that Samuel was attempting to make in *Lost World*, a rejection of the idea that any sort of uniform experience of communist politics actually existed, that it always entailed a close and complex relationship with other factors, his own experience was not only that of a Jewish comrade, but also that of a child brought up by a single mother, of a Londoner during the war years. Above all, it must be understood as a communism shaped and mediated by the values implied by Popular Front politics.

In 1935, at the Seventh International Congress (a meeting of all national Communist Party branches), Georgi Dimitrov, the General Secretary of Comintern, announced the official transition towards a policy of Popular Front to be effective immediately amongst all the national branches. Suddenly, from strict adherence to a narrowly prescribed class politics, party members were compelled to seek alliance with a broad spectrum of progressive forces.[9] The switch to the Popular Front had been prompted in part by the catastrophic fate that had befallen the Communist Party of Germany that, too politically isolated to oppose Adolf Hitler's attacks, had been wiped off the German political spectrum and rendered powerless. Now Dimitrov urged the respective national branches of the Communist Party to collaborate, not just joining forces with other left-wing or centrist political groups such as the British Labour or Liberal parties, but also showing a willingness to cooperate with any social or cultural group who were opposed to fascism. He also stressed the importance of reclaiming national histories for the political left. The invocation of a lost national past was a recurrent feature in fascist rhetoric, a tactic that had proved gallingly effective as a form of psychological propaganda.[10]

Amongst the CPGB, there had always been some uneasiness with the implications of the 'class against class' policy, so the notion of a united or Popular Front was greeted with relative consensus amongst the party's

---

9   Matthew Worley, *Class against Class: The Communist Party in Britain between the* Wars (London: I.B. Taurus, 2002). See also Stuart McIntyre, *A Proletarian Science: Marxism in Britain 1917–1933* (London: Lawrence and Wishart, 1986).
10   Jim Fyrth, 'Introduction: In the Thirties', in Fyrth, ed., *Britain, Fascism and the Popular Front* (London: Lawrence and Wishart, 1985), 9–29; Morgan, 'The Communist Party and the Popular Front 1935–1938', in *Against Fascism and War*, 33–55.

membership.[11] The Popular Front, as it emerged in Britain, was also culturally familiar. As David Blaazer has argued, similar alliances amongst progressive forces, including the fledgling Labour Party, appeared in response to the Boer War (1899–1901) and again to the First World War (1914–18).[12] In 1935, many of these forces, in particular those amongst the Labour Party retained an attitude of deep suspicion, even hostility towards the communists. Mistrustful of the CPGB's loyalty and claim to desire working-class unity within the framework of the Labour Party, it rejected overtures towards a united front.[13]

The CPGB was more successful in its engagement with grassroots initiatives that emerged during this period, from which it would previously have remained aloof. One example of this was the Left Book Club (LBC), run by the charismatic editor Victor Gollancz, who whilst never a party member held communist sympathies. Intent upon revitalising an ailing popular left-wing movement, the LBC became one of the most effective methods of circulating left-orientated literature to a wide audience.[14] Similarly, communists were also able to collaborate in campaigns such as Aid in Spain (Samuel later recalled that it was her frustration with the Labour Party's position on the Spanish Civil War that first turned his mother further towards the radical end of the political spectrum).[15] Strategically, the CPGB's switch proved successful, resulting in a substantial increase in its membership, peaking during the war at 56,000.[16]

Popular Frontism had been a pragmatic policy change and was, broadly speaking, successful in its execution. Nevertheless, its implications raised significant problems not only within the alliances but amongst the CPGB itself. The critical issue here was on the extent to which the shift undermined the focus on *class* and even, as the threat of war turned to reality, obscured it altogether. One symptom of this unease could be

---

11   Matthew Worley, 'Comrade against Comrade: The CPGB in Crisis', in *Class against Class*, 116–54. James Eaden and David Renton argue that as early as 1931 the party line had been in transition. James Eaden and David Renton, *The Communist Party of Great Britain since 1920* (London: Palgrave Macmillan, 2002), 50.
12   David Blaazer, *The Popular Front and the Progressive Tradition: Socialists, Liberals and the Quest for Unity 1884–1939* (Cambridge: Cambridge University Press, 1992).
13   Morgan, *Against Fascism and War*, 35–36.
14   Paul Laity, 'Introduction', in Laity, ed., *Left Book Club Anthology* (London: Victor Gollancz, 2001), ix–xxxi.
15   Samuel, *The Lost World*, 66.
16   Noreen Branson, 'Appendix I Communist Party Membership', in *History of the Communist Party of Great Britain 1931–1951* (London: Lawrence and Wishart, 1997), 252.

discerned in the relationship with the intellectuals who joined the party following the transition charged with playing a key role in a battle of ideas. For many within the party's internal hierarchy, the intellectual represented a quintessentially bourgeois figure. In September 1932, Rajani Palme Dutt (the CPGB's chief ideologue) could still write expressing deep suspicion of intellectuals:

> [T]here is no special work and role for Communists from the bourgeois intellectual strata ... The intellectual who has joined the Communist Party ... *should forget that he is an intellectual* (except in moments of necessary self criticism) *and remember that he a Communist.*[17]

Whilst events might have forced a public revision of such a stance, the wariness, even hostility, expressed by Dutt (who remained a senior figure in the party throughout this time) remained.

One of the major informing factors for the increase in party membership following the transition was the perceived insufficiency of the official political response to the threat posed by the rise of the European fascist parties.[18] Throughout the 1930s, the British Government pursued an official policy stance of appeasement in its foreign relations with Germany, which many (including several members of the main political parties) found to be at best ineffectual or at worst wilfully blind in its underestimation of the threat of fascism. The uncompromising, anti-fascist stance taken by the CPGB, as a party, stood in stark contrast to the more ambiguous, or less equivocal, positions taken by other established political parties.

For a culturally Jewish family like Samuel's, a further consideration was that certain strands of fascism were anti-Semitic. Whilst Britain was never in the grip of state fascism, as Spain, Germany and Italy were, there were some smaller-scale domestic examples to provide a chilling insight. In 1934, former MP Oswald Mosley formed the British Union of Fascists (BUF) who adopted a hostile stance towards ethnic minority groups, including Anglo-Jewish communities. In September 1936,

---

17 Rajani Palme Dutt, 'Intellectuals and Communism', *Communist Review*, September (1932), 421–30.
18 Scott Hamilton and Peter Conradi both argue that this factor was critical for Frank Thompson and, to a lesser extent, E.P. Thompson's decision to join the party. Scott Hamilton, *The Crisis of Theory: E.P. Thompson, the New Left and Post War British Politics* (Manchester: Manchester University Press, 2012); Peter Conradi, *A Very English Hero: The Making of Frank Thompson* (London: Bloomsbury, 2012).

the BUF attempted to march through Cable Street in East London where a significant proportion of the population were Jewish. Angry protestors confronted the BUF, resulting in a pitched street battle and the abandonment of the planned march.[19]

The CPGB were active in organising the protest, offering those frustrated with what they perceived as indecisiveness on the part of community leaders (often divided amongst themselves on matters of both politics and religion) an assertive alternative form of leadership.[20] As Samuel's uncle, the scholar and historian Chimen Abramsky, said later, 'if you were for democracy Communism was the place to go'.[21]

There were obvious contradictions in this view of the party. It was, for example, complicit in the suppression of the Independent Worker's Party of Marxist Unification and of the Anarchist factions in the Spanish civil war. In Britain, the party's newspaper, *The Daily Worker,* made a robust public defence of the Moscow trials.[22] The Nazi–Soviet non-aggression pact (August 1939) prompted an official party line of imperialist war, compelling loyal CPGB members to sabotage war efforts, particularly in the factories. This was only altered following the Soviet Union's entry into the war in June 1941 and the restoration of 'Social Patriotism'.[23]

Most of this would have passed the young Samuel by. He was four and a half when the party line changed in 1939, six and a half when it changed again in 1941. These shifts, however, did have significance for the CPGB members amongst his immediate family who provided the critical means through which his early politics took shape. His mother, Minna, for example, was a pivotal figure in shaping his initial

---

19   Nigel Crosby, 'Opposition to British Fascism 1936–45', in *Anti Fascism in Britain* (London: Macmillan Press Ltd, 2000), 42–80.

20   David Cesarani, 'Who Speaks for British Jews?', *New Statesman*, 28 May 2012, 23–27. See also James Eaden and David Renton, 'The Zig Zag Left 1928–39', in *The Communist Party of Great Britain since 1920*, 58; Raphael Samuel, 'Jews and Socialism: The End of a Beautiful Friendship?', *The Jewish Quarterly*, 35, 2 (1988), 8–10.

21   Ada Rapaport-Albert, 'Chimen Abramsky Obituary', *The Guardian*, 19 March 2010. Samuel's mother Minna was also an 'implacable opponent of Oswald Mosley's Blackshirts'. Paul Conway, 'Minna Keal 1909–1999', April 2000, www.musicweb-international.com/keal/ (accessed 19 June 2014).

22   The Moscow trials took place between 1936 and 1938. Four prominent Bolshevik party figures were condemned for espionage, part of a wider process in which ordinary Russians were systematically imprisoned, tortured or murdered in unimaginable numbers all legally sanctioned by the state. Eaden and Renton, *The Communist Party of Great Britain since 1920*, 60–68.

23   The Soviet Union's entry into the war was prompted by Hitler's failed invasion attempt in June 1941. Branson, *History of the Communist Party of Great Britain 1941–1951*; Eaden and Renton, *The Communist Party of Great Britain since 1920*, 96–97.

sense of politics. Her enduring influence on him is most evident in his autobiographical writing in which she is a central figure, depicted in a tone that, whilst not uncritical, was always very affectionate. From the outset, Minna's communism was both an outlet for her natural energies and dynamism but also a means of escaping from what she regarded as her life's restrictions.

Minna had been raised in a deeply observant Jewish household, speaking Yiddish as her first language. She was a bright child, winning a scholarship to Clapton Country Secondary School run by Mrs Harris, a progressive Fabian Socialist. She quickly proved herself to be a talented musician strongly influenced by the Jewish folk music passed on to her through the Synagogue and by her uncle Leibel, a self-taught violinist. Her talent took her to study at the Royal Academy of Music, but she was forced to quit her music studies in order to help run the family business following the death of her father Jacob in 1926. In 1931 she married Barnett Samuel, a young solicitor from an orthodox Jewish family and moved to Hampstead Garden Suburb, North London, where she quickly found the genteel environs of the suburb claustrophobic after the bustle of the East End.[24]

Politics offered Minna activity and intellectual stimulation. She joined the Hampstead Garden Suburb Labour Party, becoming secretary of the women's group. Together with Barnett she formed a committee for refugee children from Germany, throwing herself wholeheartedly into the venture, seized and driven by the urgency of the situation. Barnett, a far less effusive personality, drew back at this whirlwind of activity, causing a rift to open up between them. Minna's radicalism increased through her work on Spanish Aid. Disappointed in the Labour Party's policy on Spain, she drifted further towards the radical left. In 1939 she followed her younger sisters in joining the CPGB, a move that precipitated the eventual breakdown of her marriage to Barnett in 1941.

Communism, with its levelling concept of comrade, allowed Minna to escape the confines of the ghetto, the suburb and married life. She threw herself into party life with gusto, becoming a progress chaser in an aircraft factory and later the key organiser of the large Slough branch of the CPGB. At different times she assumed the roles of literature secretary,

---

24 Hampstead Garden Suburb was the brainchild of the social reformer Henrietta Barnett who had envisaged a community of mixed social classes living together in pleasant green surroundings.

class tutor and engagements secretary for the Worker's Music Association. For a significant portion of Samuel's childhood, Minna was a one-woman dynamo of public activity, organising, teaching and public speaking.[25]

If his mother's influence was characterised by activism then that of his uncle, Chimen Abramsky, was defined by its deep intellectualism. Abramsky was born in Minsk, Russia, in 1916, the son of Yehezkel Abramsky, a rabbi and gifted Talmudic scholar. The young Abramsky received little formal schooling but had a procession of private tutors, later becoming a student at the Hebrew University of Jerusalem. During a visit to family in London, he became stranded by the outbreak of the Second World War. Taking a job in Shapiro Valentine & Co., Abramsky met and married Miriam Nerenstein, Minna's younger sister and Samuel's aunt. Abramsky joined the party in 1941, becoming the 'patriarch' of the family's communism.

Abramsky was a renowned bibliophile, extraordinarily widely read and learned. He was meticulous in his scholarship, an expert in socialist and Jewish history, a lively conversationalist and a compelling teacher. Samuel's aunt, Miriam Abramsky, was equally strong in her political convictions but preferred to express them through her warm and welcoming hospitality. The Abramsky's modest London household provided a second home for Samuel as he was growing up. It also provided an intellectual haven for a steady stream of scholars, intellectuals and leading political and religious figures, all of whom came to engage in intense political and philosophical debate that would often carry on late into the night. For all the gravity and passionate nature of the discussion, this was also a house of laughter, friendship and fun.[26]

---

25 Samuel, *The Lost World*, 63–68; Samuel, 'Country Visiting: A Memoir', in *Island Stories*; Alex May, 'Keal, Minna (1909–1999)', *Oxford Dictionary of National Biography* (Oxford: Oxford University Press, 2004); Conway, 'Minna Keal: 1909–1999'.

26 Rapaport-Albert, 'Chimen Abramsky Obituary'; Rapaport-Albert, 'Professor Chimen Abramsky: Historian', *The Times,* 19 March 2010; Samuel, *The Lost World*, 63; Peter Dreier, '*The House of Twenty Thousand Books* by Sasha Abramsky', Huffington Post, 8 June 2014, www.huffingtonpost.com/peter-dreier/the-house-of-twenty-thousand-books_b_5467086.html (accessed June 2014); Sasha Abramsky, *The House of Twenty Thousand Books* (London: Halden Publishers, 2014); Sasha Abramsky, 'The House of Twenty Thousand Books', 6 June 2014, www.youtube.com/watch?v=h37Gf-awf0E&feature=youtu.be (accessed June 2014).

In his later writing, Samuel respectfully acknowledged the intellectual and emotional debt owed to his uncle, but this acknowledgement did not carry the same warmth that animated the descriptions of his mother.[27] Equally, Abramsky's tribute to his nephew, following his death in 1996, was similarly reserved in some of its judgements, describing his nephew as a 'Narodnik' in his personal manners, implying the prevalence of a romantic utopianism in his political ideas and activities.[28] These subtleties in tone suggest his attraction to and admiration for activism. Abramsky's deep intellectualism could be, at times, a point of division between the two men. Nevertheless, the fact remains that the young Samuel was exposed early to complex subject matters and spoken to by adults with great frankness in an atmosphere that was also profoundly sociable.

So far, this chapter has discussed the significance of the Popular Front in relation to the political culture of 1930s Britain, the connection between the family's Jewish background and their political commitment, and the nature of the political commitment and activity exhibited by key individual members of his family. All of these were important and informing factors in shaping his youthful politics, but it is equally important to acknowledge the distinctive features of his individual experience.

Unlike the older members of his family, he was born into communism. Later, as a historian and left-wing intellectual, he would become aware of the broader political and conceptual contexts in which this was situated. It was first received, however, as a child, a highly distinctive physical and psychological developmental stage from that of an adult. Saville's critique of the *Lost World* essays as an 'incoherent personal sociology', might, in another light, be more rewardingly seen as communism from a 'child's eye view', encountered not as a theory of political economy that carried consequences for the daily lives of adherents but in terms of a series of direct, first-hand experiences and perceptions.[29]

In the first place, Samuel's communism was a real family affair. Not only Minna and Chimen but, in total, 13 members of his extended family, including aunts, uncles and cousins, were actively involved in the CPGB, or in the respective national equivalent in the country in which they lived.

---

27 Samuel, *The Lost World*, 63.
28 A Narodnik was a term used to describe a member of the nineteenth-century Russian populist movement. Abramsky, 'Raphael Samuel'.
29 Saville, *Memoirs from the Left*, 9.

If not actual members, many were supportive of radical political positions.³⁰ As a result, continuous political activity was normal, infused within his day-to-day life and domestic spaces. Political meetings were conducted in the living room, fellow comrades looked after him after school, political leaflets adorned the kitchen table, and his mother knitted white ribbed socks intended for use by the Red Army.³¹ It shaped his child's play through learning the names of Russian towns, marking out the military positions of the Red Army on a map and singing Russian songs, and it had all the qualities of an intriguing imaginary world with its own secret language, a pantheon of heroic figures and legends and even its own promised land (the Soviet Union).³² In all these ways, Samuel became attuned to politics as part of normal everyday life.³³

This youthful communism also furnished him with an early ethical framework for judging his behaviour and the behaviour of others. This hinged around an absolute antithesis to anything resembling individualism (the defining trait of bourgeois culture), the centrality of collectivism and the paramount importance of sustained political education and activity.³⁴ As an only child, surrounded by such an intense adult world, with no immediate siblings close to his own age to refer to, such a blueprint for social behaviour offered reassurance.³⁵ Communism, then, provided a 'complete social identity', even more important in the dark and confusing times of the war on the home front. Like many other city children, he was evacuated to the countryside (Buckinghamshire) and sent to a boarding school (Long Dene). Here, separated from his family and social network for the first time, his burgeoning sense of communist identity carried comforting connotations of the home he had left behind.³⁶

As he grew older, advancing towards more complex forms of abstract thinking, Marxism provided him with a conceptual framework and explanation of the world. In his own words:

---

30 Samuel, *The Lost World*, 63. Some members of Samuel's family lived in France, others in America.
31 Ibid.
32 Ibid., 59–62.
33 Ibid., 61, 66.
34 Ibid.
35 The second of Samuel's essays, 'Staying Power', focuses on the ways in which this ethical framework was constructed, transmitted and reproduced amongst the wider membership, *The Lost World*, 77–156.
36 Samuel, *The Lost World*, 67–68.

> Marxism, or what we called Marxism, reinforced this cosmic sense. It dealt in absolutes and totalities, ultimates and finalities, universals and organic wholes ... As a political economy, it showed us that capitalism was a unified essence ... As a science of society, if offered itself as an all-embracing determinism, in which accidents were revealed as necessities, and causes inexorably followed by effects. As a mode of reasoning, it provided us with a priori understandings and universal rules – laws of thought which were both a guide to action and a source of prophetical authority.[37]

But the important point here is that initially his communism had been non-theoretical. It had been primarily social and behavioural.[38]

Whilst communism was the dominant force in the development of his consciousness, the key means by which he encountered the world and protected himself from things he found threatening or uncomfortable, it was not an unadulterated force. It was inextricably entwined with the English political and social culture in which he lived. The notion of a Popular Front in the late 1930s and war years was given greater plausibility by its correspondence to coexisting notions and principles of unity active within the British culture of the times.[39] This principle had, for example, long roots in the traditionally conceived British class system, finding its most demonstrable expression in the idea of working-class solidarity, the animating principle behind the organised labour movement as a political force. In socialist thought, the capacity to act together was deemed the most critical weapon in the struggle against capitalist oppression.

In a distinctive variation of the unity principle, the appeal to collectiveness was given a revised definition and renewed urgency during the war years. Rather than class unity, it was *national* unity that infused the political rhetoric, propaganda and media representation of wartime Britain. The country was hastily recast from a nation riven by class divisions and discontent into one united in a people's war, a collective stand in the face of a common enemy.[40] The invocation of a nation pulling together in extreme circumstances both reinforced and justified the unprecedented

---

37 Ibid., 49.
38 On communism as providing a 'total identity' see: Thomas Linehan, *Communism in Great Britain: From Cradle to Grave 1920–1939* (Manchester: Manchester University Press, 2007).
39 Ibid., 9.
40 For critical analysis of the 'myth' of the 'people's war', its construction, imposition and the enduring potency of its appeal see: Angus Calder, *The Myth of the Blitz* (London: Pimlico, 1992); Lucy Noakes, *War and the British: Gender, Memory and National Identity* (London: I.B. Tauris, 1998).

levels of state economic and social control that came to define not only the war but also the postwar period. As historian Peter Hennessey put it: '[N]ever before and never since has a British Government taken so great and so intrusive a range of powers over the lives of its citizens'.[41] So intense was this appeal that it even prompted some, from both ends of the political spectrum, to speculate that, as a result of the war, Britain had drifted towards becoming a 'classless' society.[42] Others would not go so far, but believed that the experiences fostered by the war and the ideas that informed plans for postwar reconstruction would contribute in bringing such a society about.

Such was the extent of interplay between communism and British culture that even the austere figure of Stalin was subtly adapted to the English climate:

> The English Stalin ... was an altogether more down-to-earth figure, corresponding in some way to our idealized conceptions of ourselves. He was a man of few words and simple tastes, personally modest, and of an essentially practical intelligence. We admired him, as a kind of Russian Churchill, for his combination of indomitable courage and earth commonsense.[43]

Whilst the adaptation of Stalin was not necessarily done consciously, Samuel's personal experience of anglicisation *was* deliberate. Following his return to London after the war, he joined the St Pancras branch of the Young Communist League where his fellow junior comrades struggled to pronounce Raphael. Determined to be a good communist and to subjugate his individuality for the sake of the group, he changed his name to Ralph.[44]

---

41 Peter Hennessey, *Never Again: Britain 1945–51* (London: Cape, 1992), 40.
42 For example, Winston Churchill told the boys of Harrow school in December 1940: 'There is no change which is more marked in our country than the continual and rapid effacement of class difference'. Quoted in Paul Addison, *Churchill on the Home Front: 1900–1955* (London: Jonathan Cape, 1992), 327. It should be noted, however, that this was never the view taken by the CPGB.
43 Samuel, *The Lost World*, 134.
44 Ibid., 87. 'Ralph' appears to have been intimately bound to an explicitly political persona. Following the breakdown of the first New Left (1956–62) and his appointment at Ruskin College (1962), he no longer referred to himself in this way in personal or professional correspondence, reverting back to 'Raphael'. Furthermore, whilst all of his political writing was published under 'Ralph', this was not the case for any of his history work.

These were some of the most striking ways in which the communism of Samuel's youth merged with existing English culture and traditions. There were other factors that also intimately informed his intellectual development. A direct form of exposure to existing English radical traditions came through his experiences of an English progressive education. He attended two progressive schools: Long Dene, a boarding school in the Buckinghamshire countryside, and later King Alfred School (KAS), in Hampstead North London, as a day pupil.

In Britain, forms of progressive education were often attached to left-libertarian politics drawing equally upon both scientific and moral rationales for their critique of conventional forms of education. Common features of this radical-libertarian educational philosophy included an emphatic sense of the child as an individual and active participant in the learning process. Progressive schools were also more expansive in their approach to subject matter, not necessarily privileging academic subject matter in their teaching. This was the case at both of his schools. Long Dene strongly emphasised rural and agricultural traditions. Similarly, KAS taught an eclectic curriculum including a significant amount of arts and crafts.[45]

In one sense, he used his political identity to differentiate himself from the politics of the schools he attended. As a communist, he saw himself as being on the side of collectivism, science, progress and modernisation, and was, therefore, disapproving of the indulgently liberal concern for individualism and the backward-looking enthusiasm for traditional crafts that were taught at his various progressive schools. Nevertheless, the unusual ethos and nature of this form of education was significant. For a bright and precocious youth, the greater respect and tolerance given to the student was quite unlike what he might have encountered in a more conventional institution. Ironically, as a self-professed communist during a time of general suspicion towards communism, he would have been amongst the most strikingly individualistic of all the students at the school.[46]

---

45 Samuel, 'Country Visiting: A Memoir', in *Island Stories*; Ron Brooks, *King Alfred School and the Progressive Movement 1889–1998* (Cardiff: University of Wales Press, 1998); Smithson, *Community Adventure: The Story of Long Dene School*.
46 To be a communist was considered a 'cachet'. Ron Jones quoted in Smithson, *Community Adventure: The Story of Long Dene School*, 21.

In progressive schools like the ones he attended, it was not uncommon for the teaching staff to be intellectually and personally sympathetic to the more radical forms of politics. Violet Hyett, his tutor in junior classes at KAS, emphasised historical method and global perspectives over narrowly British political and constitutional history. She was even known to teach some principles of Marxist economics in her classes.[47] Another influential history tutor was John Handford, a fellow communist (given the Cold War politics of the period, he allegedly denied this when applying for the job) who was instrumental in introducing him to the eminent Marxist historians of the day and in encouraging him to apply for Oxford University.[48]

It was not, however, only *English* society and traditions that shaped his youthful communism. There was also the important nuance provided by his family's Jewish origins. This relationship was complex. In his mother's case, Judaism was one of the factors that she viewed as an encumbrance on her activities. The rejection of her Jewish upbringing and her desire to escape from it had fuelled her attraction to communism.[49] Accordingly, she guided the young Samuel in his first political act, telling God that he did not exist.[50] His relationship with Judaism was not fraught in the same way as his mother's (although he bitterly resented being forced to have a Jewish education, which was part of the terms of the divorce between his parents, and defiantly smuggled Thomas Paine into his Hebrew lessons). Several members of his family, including his uncle and grandmother, retained their faith, speaking Yiddish and Hebrew, recognising Jewish traditions and marking Jewish holidays.[51] For all that he rejected the explicit religious connotations of Judaism as a faith, it was still present in his life as a cultural identity.

One conscious effect of the influence that his Jewish identity had on him was an early assumption that Jewish people were more likely to be progressively minded and attracted to socialism.[52] Another was the access and exposure to intellectual, linguistic and literary traditions of cultures that

---

47 Brooks, *King Alfred School*, 119–20, 127. Samuel remembered arguing with Hyett in history lessons. Samuel, *The Lost World*, 88.
48 Brian Harrison, 'Interview with Raphael Samuel', 18 September 1987, 19 Elder Street, London, transcripts held in Raphael Samuel Archive (RSA), Bishopsgate Institute, London.
49 Samuel, *The Lost World*, 67.
50 Samuel, 'Jews and Socialism: The End of a Beautiful Friendship?', 8.
51 Ibid.; Samuel, *The Lost World*, 63.
52 Samuel, 'Jews and Socialism: The End of a Beautiful Friendship?', 8.

lay outside of Englishness. Arguably, he picked up on the Jewish tradition of 'sociable argument' with alacrity![53] On a more subconscious level, a Jewish cultural identity might have played some part in reinforcing the sense of living amongst a wider society whilst simultaneously being apart from it, able to view it from a distanced, de-familiarised perspective. Moreover, learning Jewish history, with its recurrent themes of persecution and exile embedded deeply within Jewish customs and stories, further underlined the paramount importance of justice and the value of democracy.

Samuel's early communism must be understood as informed by multiple contending factors, referencing both the wider historical context of the times but also the more personal histories implicit within his background. This, in effect, was one of the key arguments in his reflections, sketched out in the *Lost World* essays. Less explicitly stated but nevertheless a discernible current throughout those essays was an underpinning ethos of collectivism that drew the eclectic components together. The core value underpinning the particularities of his Anglo-Jewish, child's-eye-view communism was the paramount importance of popular participatory democracy, achieved by forging alliances and mobilising social movements from below. It was this that, from his youthful perspective, lay at heart of the Marxist science of society. It was what the entire Communist Party was geared towards, the rationale behind the demands it placed on its membership and what it sought to achieve in its practices. It was what the Soviet Union and Stalin were supposed to embody. This sense of justice was what underpinned both his conviction and his ardent commitment to communism.[54]

As a teenager, growing up in the more conflicted years of the Cold War, he came to identify a more specific political role for himself, desiring to become a CPGB organiser.[55] In this ambition he followed his mother (the key organiser for the Slough branch of the party), indicating once again the significance of her influence upon him. In terms of the overall CPGB organisational structure, the 'organiser' was drawn from amongst the rank-and-file membership. They were distinguished from their comrades by their self-taught intellectual prowess, forming a sort of 'proletarian clerisy'. The role of the organiser forged a bridge between the wider body of party members and the party's hierarchy.[56] Samuel's aspiration to this role

---

53 Deborah Schiffrin, 'Jewish Argument as Sociability', *Language and Society*, 13, 3 (1984), 311–35.
54 Samuel recalls an early school report noting that at the age of six he already had an obsession with 'justice and fairness'. Samuel, *The Lost World*, 59.
55 Samuel, *The Lost World*, 88.
56 Ibid., 201.

provides an intriguing insight into his youthful character. As a precocious and intelligent child from a family who had become well established within the party structure (Abramsky also held key party positions serving as the secretary of the party's Jewish committee, the editor of *The Jewish Clarion* and chairman of the party's Middle East committee), he might well have aspired to a more high-profile position.[57] And yet he remained attracted to this particular role that placed him in much closer relation to the rank-and-file membership.

In the *Lost World*, he supplied some descriptions of the nature and the implications of these sorts of more practical activist-leadership roles in the party drawing on both his personal experiences and official party documentation to do so. They make revealing reading (italics are my own):

> In the localities, too, authority was expected to be self-effacing. Branch secretaries were expected to *comport themselves as co-workers*, taking on a good deal of the dogsbody work, as the price of the trust which reposed in them. At branch meetings he/she was to *exercise a pastoral care, drawing the members in by allocating tasks to them, 'involving' them in the processes of decision making ... encouraging new comers to 'express' themselves ...*[58]

and:

> One started at the 'level' of the sympathiser, emphasising common ground, 'building' on particular issues, while at the same time investing them with Party-mindedness. Plied with Party literature, invited to Party meetings, above all 'involved' in some species of Party work ... the sympathiser was drawn into the comradeship of the Party by a hundred subtle threats ...[59]

And again:

> Recruiting – the only Party activity I was any good at – involved, I now realize, *a tutor-pupil relationship*, not least in its elaborate pretence of equality between the teacher and the taught; it was a *learning process* which *demonstrated the power of knowledge*.[60]

The role, as he described it, has some notable features. Firstly, it was an acutely social role dealing directly with people. Secondly, it required the individuals in question to have a clear consciousness of their own performance in relation to the people they were dealing with, coming

---
57 Rapaport-Albert, 'Chimen Abramsky Obituary'.
58 Samuel, *The Lost World*, 125.
59 Ibid., 125–26.
60 Ibid., 195.

across as a co-worker, being welcoming and inclusive, and so on. Thirdly, much depended upon the individual's ability to synthesise different areas of expertise into a collective endeavour and identify areas of common ground between their interests and the person(s) they were engaging with. Finally, it called upon skills in using that common ground as the basis to infuse the subject with 'party mindedness', to provoke an internal transformation, all the more plausible and effective because the subject was complicit in the process. To summarise, this role utilised forms of intelligence and skill both pragmatic and profoundly psychological in character.

As the anecdote provided at the beginning of the chapter suggests, Samuel showed an early prowess and zeal for organisation. Later he would continue his efforts to convert his school mates over to communism, even setting up his own branch of the Young Communists League at KAS.[61] What is important to note is that as extraordinary as his upbringing was – heavily political, set against the backdrop of the looming threat of fascism, the experiences of war on the British home front and, as shall be discussed in the next section, the Cold War in the years that followed – his childhood was fundamentally a happy one, with plenty of mental stimulus and a tight knit, supportive social network, much of which was provided by the party. This was never a time that he would come to think badly of.

The Communist Party Historians' Group

The Communist Party Historians' Group (CPHG) (1946–56) provided a first-hand example of the ways in which connections could be forged between the popular, the political and the intellectual. Initially formed to discuss a second edition of A.L. Morton's *A People's History of England* (1938), part of the effort to 'reclaim the national past' and consequently a popular Left Book Club choice, the group's project consequently evolved through regular meetings held at either the Garibaldi restaurant or Marx House in London over the course of a decade. Membership was a mix of academic and non-academic historians, older and younger generations of communists.[62] Samuel was the youngest member of the group, joining at the age of 16 in 1951. He was introduced to it by John Handford,

---

61 Brian Harrison, 'Interview with Raphael Samuel', 18 September 1987; Samuel, *The Lost World*, 87.
62 Eric Hobsbawm, 'The Historians' Group of the Communist Party', in Maurice Cornforth, ed., *Rebels and Their Causes: Essays in Honour of A.L. Morton* (London: Lawrence and Wishart, 1978).

and eagerly seized the opportunity to see at close quarters figures that he had glimpsed at his uncle's gatherings or read about in communist literature – well-established warriors in the communist battle of ideas.

The CPHG is credited with making a substantial contribution to British historiography, both in propelling social history to prominence and for containing the seeds of 'history from below' through the work of members such as Christopher Hill, Eric Hobsbawm and E.P. Thompson (although he was not as closely affiliated with the group as is commonly assumed).[63] Other commentators, however, whilst acknowledging the group's significance, have drawn greater attention to the tensions and complexities that both surrounded and underpinned the group's endeavours.[64]

Whilst the CPHG's work was a very deliberate continuation of the Popular Front people's history, part of a wider battle of ideas (or, more accurately, battle of beliefs), at the same time it was first formed within a very different political atmosphere to that of the late 1930s when the party enjoyed a growth in its popularity. The late 1940s, by contrast, was dominated by the early years of the Cold War in which suspicion and hostility towards the CPGB and its membership intensified considerably.[65] Even former socialists, such as the writer George Orwell, were already advancing strong critiques of state socialism, advocating instead the merits and virtues of a distinctively domesticated socialism characterised by civil liberties.[66]

The tensions between the internationalism of its aspirations as a political movement and the contending claims and realities presented by its national manifestations also remained unresolved. The 1948 Yugoslav Crisis provided a vivid illustration of this. In Moscow, the break between General Tito, the Yugoslavian leader, and Stalin was depicted as a betrayal of the communist movement. In Yugoslavia, and sections of the western

---

63 Jim Obelkevich, 'New Developments in History in the 1950s and 1960s', *Contemporary British History*, 14, 4 (2000), 125–26; Harvey Kaye, *The British Marxist Historians* (Cambridge: Polity Press, 1984).
64 Bill Schwarz, '"The People" in History: The Communist Party Historians Group 1946–1956', in Richard Johnson, Gregor McLennan, Bill Schwarz and David Sutton, eds, *Making Histories: Studies in History-Writing and Politics* (Minneapolis: University of Minnesota, 1982); Alastair MacLachlan, *The Rise and Fall of Revolutionary England: An Essay on the Fabrication of Seventeenth Century History* (London: Macmillan, 1996); Dennis Dworkin, *Cultural Marxism in Postwar Britain: History, the New Left, and the Origins of Cultural Studies* (Durham and London: Duke University Press, 1997).
65 Harriet Jones, 'The Impact of the Cold War', in Paul Addison and Harriet Jones, eds, *A Companion to Contemporary Britain 1939–2000* (Oxford: Blackwell, 2005), 24–26.
66 See, for example, George Orwell, *The Lion and the Unicorn* (1941), *Animal Farm* (1945), *1984* (1948).

media, it was framed as a triumph of national pride over Soviet oppression.[67] In 1951, the CPGB formally announced its intention of pursuing The British Road to Socialism. This was a ground-breaking move in which the party *appeared* to break from its unquestioning loyalty to Soviet-style communism. As party leader Harry Pollitt phrased it, 'The progress of democratic and Socialist forces throughout the world has opened out the new possibilities of transition to Socialism by other paths than those followed by the Russian Revolution'.[68] Despite what seemed to suggest a radical departure, this remained a profoundly sensitive and divisive issue amongst the CPGB membership.

There was also a continuing unease with the role of intellectuals amongst the party's membership.[69] The firm assertion of a party line was, inevitably, restrictive for those whose vocations across all the various disciplines, perhaps particularly in the humanities and creative arts, demanded the freedom to experiment, dissent and pursue their inquiries freely. The pressure to conform led a number of brilliant party intellectuals, such as scientists J.D. Bernal, J.B.S. Haldane and the writer Arnold Kettle, to become increasingly isolated, the importance of their work marginalised due to their slavish accord with Moscow. Others, finding the situation untenable (including literary scholar Raymond Williams and writer Doris Lessing), retreated or withdrew altogether from the party during this time.[70] Hobsbawm, in a highly selective memoir of the group, argued that the historians enjoyed a better relationship with the party than others, but he was forced to acknowledge that the CPGB took a far more interventionist stance when it came to writing the history of the British labour movement or the party itself. Given this context, as Bill Schwarz has suggested, the group's project might best be described as providing a more substantial theorisation of the Popular Front political project.[71]

---

67 The 14-year-old Samuel had conformed with the Moscow line on this issue, instructing wavering relatives in the correct interpretation. Samuel, *The Lost World*, 87.
68 Harry Pollitt, 'The Road to British Socialism', in *Looking Ahead* (London: Communist Party of Great Britain, 1947).
69 On the Communist Party and intellectuals see: Andy Croft, 'Authors Take Sides: Writers in the Communist Party 1920–1956', in Kevin Morgan, Nina Fishman and Geoff Andrews, eds, *Opening the Books: New Perspectives in the History of British Communism* (London: Pluto, 1995); Andy Croft, 'The Boys around the Corner: The Story of Fore Publications', in Croft, ed., *A Weapon in the Struggle: The Cultural History of the Communist Party in Britain* (London: Pluto Press, 1998), 142–62. For a source more contemporaneous to the times: Neal Wood, *Communism and British Intellectuals* (London: Gollancz, 1959).
70 David Childs, *Britain since 1945: A Political History* (London: Routledge, 2001), 49; Robert Hewison, *Culture and Consensus: England, Art and Politics since 1940* (London: Methuen, 1995), 58.
71 Schwarz, '"The People" in History'.

Samuel was already familiar with many of the group's membership, having followed their work in the party's press outlets.[72] Many were well-known figures across the movement. Christopher Hill's essay on the English revolution, for example, had inspired a young E.P. Thompson to study history at university.[73] Born in 1912 into a committed Methodist family in York, Hill had gone on to read modern history under Vivian Galbraith (1889–1976) at Balliol College, Oxford.[74] He had conceived an early interest in seventeenth-century literature, later recalling how Galbraith had encouraged him to explore the ways in which it illuminated the period.[75] Having graduated from Oxford in 1934, he joined the CPGB, which, in addition to a 10-month research trip to the Soviet Union, brought his literary and historical interests into dialogue with Marxist political-economy. The first major fruits of this had been *The English Revolution, 1640* (1940), a heavy-handed attempt to recast the English civil war as bourgeois revolution. He later described the book as that of a young man full of anger in the midst of the Second World War.[76]

Hill's essay 'The Norman Yoke', which, as Schwarz argued, came to be emblematic of the group's activities, saw him break from his usual terrain of seventeenth-century high politics and turn his attention towards popular ideology.[77] He opened with a sketch of the *story* of the 'Norman Yoke' as it was commonly known: before the Norman invasion of 1066, the Anglo-Saxon inhabitants of Britain has lived as free and equal citizens, governing themselves through representative institutions. The Norman Conquest had destroyed this, replacing it with a hierarchical feudal system of political organisation. The struggle to regain those lost rights had been continuous, occasionally punctuated by concessions, such as the signing of the Magna Carta treaty, this notwithstanding, that harmonious world remained lost.

---

72   Samuel followed Hill's work in *The Daily Worker*. Brian Harrison, 'Interview with Raphael Samuel', 18 September 1987.
73   'E. P. Thompson [interview by Mike Merrill]', in Henry Abelove, Betsy Blackmar, Peter Dimock and Jonathan Schneer, eds, *Visions of History* (Manchester: Manchester University Press, 1983).
74   Robin Briggs, 'Hill (John Edward) Christopher (1912–2003)', *Oxford Dictionary of National Biography* (Oxford: Oxford University Press, 2007).
75   Christopher Hill, 'A First Class Performer', *History Workshop Journal* (*HWJ*), 42 (1996), 207–9.
76   Ibid. Christopher Hill, *The English Revolution, 1640* (London: Lawrence and Wishart, 1940).
77   Christopher Hill, 'The Norman Yoke', in John Saville, ed., *Democracy and the Labour Movement: Essays in Honour of Dona Torr* (London: Lawrence and Wishart, 1954), 11–67.

Moving first to his home territory, the English seventeenth century, Hill retraced the story's fractured lines of historiographic (re)interpretation. For jurist Edward Coke (espousing the 'bourgeois' position), the treaty signified an important restoration of lost rights and provided the historical basis for the rule of law. The Levellers, however, (advancing a 'bourgeois-democratic' position) argued that the Magna Carta had not gone far enough in redressing the damages wrought by the Normans. The Diggers (advocating the most radical and revolutionary position) fixed their view firmly on the restoration of that lost world and demanded a complete abolition of property rights.

The historiographer's tale continued. Hill then considered the account as it had been contested by arch-Whig Edmund Burke (the Magna Carta as an opening chapter in the evolutionary development of British civil liberties as embodied, enacted and protected within its legal and political institutions) and the radical Thomas Paine (that the Magna Carta had been little more than a means of abating the worst excesses of tyranny) in the late eighteenth century. In the imaginative hands of nineteenth-century artist, poet and socialist thinker William Morris, his views already tempered by exposure to the work of Marx, it was not, as for the Diggers, a literal restoration of Anglo-Saxon England (already tainted by the seeds of feudal organisation) that captivated him, but the importance of the *ideal* represented by reference to a pre-feudal society: the organic, egalitarian, self-determining community.

The 'Norman Yoke' was not just history as political propaganda between contending groups. It had been the prompt for substantial historical research, later benefiting from the insights afforded by developments in scientific anthropology. Only in Marxism, argued Hill reaching the crux of his 'reconciliatory operation', was the story's real significance fully subsumed and clarified as being, at core, about 'the recognition of class struggle as the basis of politics, the deep sense of *Englishness* of the common people'.[78] This Englishness, he warned in his closing lines, was not peripheral but essential. Whilst Marxism offered the best, most scientific explanation of the story, which the Marxist intellectual was compelled to extrapolate and explain, what had given it imaginative vitality and emotional resonance down the ages was just such an appeal to nation and 'true' patriotism as love of that nation.[79]

---

78   Ibid., 66.
79   Ibid.

The work of Hill and others with the group offered a bold and compelling attempt at uniting national history with Marxist theory. Despite this, there were some obvious problems and contradictions that arose from this project. The attempt to discern an immanent socialism from within the English past could feel contrived. At times it could fail to fully account for important historical facts.[80] Moreover, it raised critical questions about the nature of human agency and its relationship to social and economic structures. Equally, the relationship between history as a discipline and critical theory remained largely unresolved. These issues prefigured many of the debates that would come to dominate radical historiography in later years.[81]

Nevertheless, such a dramatic interpretive intervention in the making of the English past and the innovative engagement with popular ideologies had a lasting impact on the landscape of British historiography, not least because it also provided the crucible for the journal *Past and Present: A Journal of Scientific History* (*P&P*; 1952–) founded by several members of the group in conjunction with non-Marxist academic historians. Whilst a means of continuing and communicating the groups' work, the journal was never a CPGB mouthpiece or propagandist tool. It set out with a far more ambitious agenda – to champion and advance a whole new way of thinking about and practising history. In an academic teaching and research culture still largely preoccupied with the high politics and legislative fine print, *P&P* historians like Hill, Hobsbawm and medievalist Rodney Hilton posed a dramatic revision to notions of causation in change over time. Rather than take the acts and actions of individuals, politicians, military leaders or legislators as the critical site of action, the contributors of *P&P* transferred their attention to charting the development of socioeconomic forces and tracing their effects on political decision-making and social organisation.

To return to this experience from Samuel's perspective, it must be remembered that on joining the group he was still a schoolboy, not a trained historian. His interest in history was, at this time, entirely ideological, supplemented by the guidance of his uncle and later politically

---

80   See, for example, the critique of Hill advanced by fellow group member Victor Kiernan. MacLachlan, *The Rise and Fall of Revolutionary England*, 117–18; Dworkin, *Cultural Marxism in Postwar Britain*, 35–37.
81   Richard Johnson, 'Edward Thompson, Eugene Genovese and Socialist-Humanist History', *HWJ*, 6 (1978), 79–100; Schwarz, '"The People" in History', 70–71; Dworkin, *Cultural Marxism in Postwar Britain*, 44.

sympathetic teachers like Hyett and Handford.[82] The 'monuments' of his historical reading had included Max Weber's *The Protestant Ethic and the Spirit of Capitalism* (1905) and R.H. Tawney's *Religion and Rise of Capitalism* (1926), both of which had made a critical examination into the relationship between religious belief and the development of capitalism.[83] Another youthful favourite was the French historian George Lefebvre's *The Coming of the French Revolution* (1939), the first to commemorate the 150th anniversary of the revolution. Lefebvre, the first to coin the term 'history from below', had approached his study of the revolution and the experience of class struggle from the eyes of the French peasantry.[84]

In joining the CPHG, his excitement was piqued by the prospect of political battle rather than the musk of ancient documents. He was, at this time, far less invested, intellectually or emotionally, in the literal substance of the more specific historical debates that took place amongst the group (which is not to say that he was entirely ignorant of or oblivious to them). Furthermore, for a committed activist, it was natural that he would be just as inspired by the group's other main *raison d'etre*, its educational activities. This manifested not only in the dissemination of its work but in the organisation of large conferences and the facilitating of publications, such as *Our History* or the *Local History Bulletin* to encourage a wide cross-section of popular participation in history-making.

One of the most critical figures in orchestrating these initiatives was Dona Torr, a CPGB member since its inception in 1920. She had taken on a range of responsibilities as a party worker including editorial work and translation.[85] In Torr there was a model for the exemplary party worker, indefatigable and entirely committed to encouraging others in their work for the sake of the wider cause. Her importance for members such as John Saville and Christopher Hill was expressed in the introduction to *Democracy and Labour Movement* (1954):

---

82 Brian Harrison, 'Interview with Raphael Samuel', 18 September 1987; Rapaport-Albert, 'Chimen Abramsky Obituary'.
83 Max Weber with T. Parsons, tr., and R.H. Tawney, *The Protestant Ethic and the Spirit of Capitalism* (London: Allen and Unwin, 1930); R.H. Tawney, *Religion and Rise of Capitalism* (London: J. Murray, 1936).
84 Georges Lefebvre with R.R. Palmer, tr., *The Coming of French Revolution, 1789* (Princeton: Princeton University Press, 1947).
85 V.G. Kiernan, 'Torr, Dona Ruth Anne (1883–1957)', *Oxford Dictionary of National Biography* (Oxford: Oxford University Press, 2004).

> Always [Torr] claims to be learning from the humblest student, to see new lines of thought opening from the tritest remark: though it is she who discovers them. She has taught us historical *passion*. For her the understanding of the historical process is an intense emotional experience … History was the sweat, blood, tears and triumphs of the common people, our people.[86]

Torr's passion for history had led her to chair the party committee advising on scripts for 'People's History' projects organised in the late 1930s. These had included 'March of History' summer pageants featuring figures like Oliver Cromwell and commemorating democratic milestones like the thirteenth-century founding of parliament by Simon de Monfort.[87] In the CPHG she was a dedicated mentor to the younger, emerging scholars and the general editor for the documentary book series *History in the Making*, supposedly comprised of 'the very words and thoughts' of ordinary people as they made their own history.[88] Whilst Torr was, in many ways, the embodiment of a good communist intellectual, in other respects, as for many party workers, the democracy of her practices often clashed with the dogmatism entailed by her deep political commitment. Her loyalty to the party and the party line was unquestioning and, in her desire to uphold it at all times, she could be as severe and authoritarian as she was generous and supportive.[89]

The schoolboy Samuel drew important lessons from the group. Firstly, that history showed (or could be written to show) the critical role played by the popular movement in social and political change. Secondly, that the act of history-making was in itself deeply political and that historians should be as conscious and aware of the present as they were of the past.

---

86 John Saville, 'Introduction', in Saville, ed., *Democracy and the Labour Movement: Essays in Honour of Dona Torr* (London: Lawrence and Wishart, 1954), 8. See also an acknowledgment of Torr's intellectual support and assistance in E.P. Thompson, 'Introduction', in *William Morris, Romantic to Revolutionary* (London: Lawrence and Wishart, 1955). This description of Torr bears some striking parallels with those that would later be written about Samuel as a historian-educator, reinforcing the extent to which communism was as much a mode of behavioural practice and ethical conduct amongst its adherents as it was an identification with a specific Marxist political-economic theory.
87 Raphael Samuel, *Theatres of Memory: Past and Present in Contemporary Culture* (London: Verso, 1994), 207; Anthony Howe, 'The Past is Ours: The Political Usage of English History by the British Communist Party and the Role of Dona Torr in the Creation of its Historians' Group 1930–56', PhD thesis, University of Sydney, 2004; David Renton, 'The History Woman', *Socialist Review*, 224 (1998).
88 Dona Torr, ed., *History in the Making* (London: Lawrence and Wishart, 1948). These words and thoughts were often remarkably 'Marxist' in their nature, suggesting the work of skilful editing. MacLachlan, *The Rise and Fall of Revolutionary England*, 83. The extent of admiration for Torr is evident by the effusive acknowledgement of her work in Saville, *Democracy and the Labour Movement*. See also Thompson, 'Foreword', in *William Morris, Romantic to Revolutionary* (1955 ed.).
89 MacLaclan, *The Rise and Fall of Revolutionary England*, 83.

Thirdly, that history-making ought to be a popular thing, not merely the preserve of scholars. Finally, there was the working atmosphere of the group itself. A figure like Torr set another strong example of a communist historian-educator in the comradeship and collaboration demonstrated in many (although not all) of her practices. In this sense, the group served, on several levels, as a prime example of what political scholarship and history-making 'should' be about.

Oxford student politics

Raphael Samuel, Balliol College, 1956
Raphael Samuel Archive, Bishopsgate Institute, London, courtesy of Alison Light and the Raphael Samuel Estate.

In 1952, aged 17, Samuel went up to Oxford to read modern history. Whilst he had long been practising the skills of the aspiring organiser, it was during his student days that he really honed them. Encouraged by Handford to apply for an exhibition at Balliol College, he did so purely for the chance to work closely with Hill (then a senior tutor at Balliol), later claiming to have been unmoved by the university's prestige and 'extremely disappointed by the coldness … of the history course'.[90] He could not, however, have been insensitive to the practical opportunities it afforded him.

---

90   Brian Harrison, 'Interview with Raphael Samuel', 18 September 1987.

As a communist, he was under pressure to be a 'good student' lest he discredit the party's reputation for engendering a culture of moral seriousness and intellectual studiousness.[91] Although Hill was the primary draw for him, the relationship with him during this time seems to have been cooler than might have been expected. There were several reasons for this. The Cold War meant that whilst Hill was politically active, he was under pressure to keep his political convictions and academic responsibilities distinct from one another. He was also a reserved personality notoriously favouring a tutorial approach of 'question and answer', posing a question to his students and waiting with unrelenting patience for the answer. If unprepared, the student would be left to flounder terribly whilst Hill watched on in unremitting silence.[92]

He was, of course, exposed to different tutors and, consequently, to forms of history and political perspectives that were sceptical if not overtly critical of Marxism. This did not prevent him from forming good relationships with them, in particular A.B. Rodger, whom he described as a 'Tory Radical' in his politics. He found Rodgers' animated and discursive approach to tutorials more stimulating than the austere silence of Hill.[93]

In his undergraduate studies, he was, naturally, an enthusiastic early member of the *Past and Present* society, developing a strong passion for economic history. He attended the lectures of economic historian John Habakkuk, which he thought of as being the most subversive form of history available given its focus on large social forces and processes, rather than the internal wrangling of political leaders.[94] His work from the time reflects this, including lecture notes on 'The Trade Cycle: 1780–1850' or 'Iron and Steel in the Industrial Revolution' and essays written on 'The Significance of the Banking and Company Legislation on the Peel Administration'.[95] Collectively, this work focused on industrialisation in nineteenth-century Britain, a compelling subject for a young Marxist. Despite this, the Oxford undergraduate modern history syllabus that he followed from 1952 to 1956 remained firmly wedded to traditional forms

---

91   Ibid. See also a speech made by Communist MP Willie Thompson to Cambridge students in 1934 expressing the party's need for intellectuals as quoted in Jonathan Clark and Margot Heinemann, eds, *Culture and Crisis in Britain in the Thirties* (London: Lawrence and Wishart, 1979), 32.
92   Brian Harrison, 'Interview with Raphael Samuel', 18 September 1987. This was a style of teaching that Hill was renowned for. Briggs, 'Hill (John Edward) Christopher (1912–2003)'.
93   Brian Harrison, 'Interview with Raphael Samuel', 18 September 1987.
94   Brian Harrison, 'Interview with Raphael Samuel', 20 October 1987.
95   Ralph Samuel, 'Undergraduate Notes and Essays', Samuel 080/ University Notes, Raphael Samuel Archive (RSA), Bishopsgate, London.

of constitutional and political history, which it was not only necessary but imperative to study in order to pass the final examinations (there was no opportunity for independent research work) and gain a degree.[96]

Samuel's student years were conducted after the CPGB's adoption of The British Road to Socialism (1951) and were, therefore, dominated by a sustained and continuous effort to forge alliances with a broad spectrum of left-wing political positions. Some picture of the intense and eager student can be discerned from accounts written of him by his contemporaries from this time. In a reflective memoir-come-tribute to his long-term friend and Oxford contemporary, Stuart Hall remarked that he was both 'the pariah and the heart and soul of the Oxford political scene' and that 'nothing of significance happened in Oxford without Raphael being in some way involved in it'.[97] Jean McCrindle, a Scottish-born fellow communist, Oxford student and his partner during this time, described him as a dedicated and tireless recruiting officer for the party, whose utter political commitment and seriousness could verge on the 'tyrannical'.[98]

His political output during this time was tremendous. He was actively involved in the university's Communist group throughout his student years, becoming its secretary in the second year of his degree. He engaged with a range of other left-wing groups and initiatives including the Socialist Club. He was the key moving force behind numerous political petitions and campaigns, always remaining alert to potential recruitment opportunities for the party. Towards the end of his Oxford years, he set his sights increasingly towards working with the Oxford Labour Club. In the midst of all this overwhelming activity, it is remarkable that he managed to fit in any academic work whatsoever!

Student and college life, as he experienced it in the Balliol College of the mid-1950s, encouraged this intensive round of clubs, groups and discussion parties. In his eyes, Balliol was inherently subversive of the prevailing English 'ancient regime' under which the university as a whole was still in thrall. This perception was not purely a form of tribal loyalty to his college. Balliol boasted an impressive alumnus of prominent socialist

---

96 Jose Harris, 'The Arts and Social Sciences 1939–1970', in Brian Harrison, ed., *A History of Oxford University*, Vol. VIII: *The Twentieth Century* (Oxford: Oxford University Press, 1995), 236.
97 Stuart Hall, 'Raphael Samuel: 1934–1996', *New Left Review* (*NLR*), I/221, Jan–Feb (1997), 119–27.
98 Jean McCrindle, 'The Hungarian Uprising and a Young British Communist', *HWJ*, 62 (2006), 196.

thinkers such as Tawney, and social reformers such as Tawney's brother-in-law, William Beveridge, author of the Beveridge report upon which much of the postwar social welfare reforms were based. Then, of course, there was Hill who, despite his communism, had retained a prominent position at a time when others, such as Hobsbawm, were often overlooked or passed over.[99]

The college took in high numbers of international students and those who might be called 'internal emigres', people of Scottish, Welsh, Irish or, like Samuel and his fellow communist and New Left co-founder, Gabriel Pearson, Jewish social and cultural backgrounds. In short, it collected people who had complex relationships to 'English' society, which suited him.[100] These were people often predisposed towards dissenting or radical political positions. All these factors had helped to give a sense that Balliol represented, if not exactly meritocracy, then certainly scholarly prowess over hereditary birth and privilege, placing it in 'opposition' to the university at large.[101]

This subversiveness needs contextualisation. In the Oxford of the 1950s, student life was still relatively regulated. Student life had not quite the degree of freedom then that would later be associated with it. Students were subject to curfews, the gates to the Balliol were locked at midnight, forcing anyone inclined towards more nocturnal activities to either scale the walls or confine their social activities to within the grounds. Colleges were still mostly single-sex environments, often fuelling the development of intense friendships amongst members. Moreover, the university bore the heavy impress and consciousness of tradition and prestige. In the eyes of some, at Oxford on scholarships achieved through hard work, a significant proportion of the main student body still retained the aura of self-confidence typical of a life of privilege and elitism.[102]

Samuel's activities were not confined to Balliol College, but involved sustained attempts at engaging with left-wing groups across the university. Navigating the intricate and pseudo-tribal world of the left in Oxford required that he be highly conscious of the sociological, psychological and

---

99 Neil Ascherson, 'Profile: The Age of Hobsbawm', *The Independent on Sunday*, 2 October 1994.
100 One might take 'English' to mean predominantly white, middle-class and Protestant Christian. Stuart Hall, 'The Life and Times of the First New Left', *NLR*, 61, Jan–Feb (2010), 177–95; Brian Harrison, 'Interview with Raphael Samuel', 20 October 1987.
101 Hall, 'The Life and Times of the First New Left', 178.
102 Ibid., 182.

emotional structures of political allegiance.[103] Oxford's Labour politics was made up of a significant proportion of middle-class Fabian reformists, with a fair smattering of political careerists in their midst. It also contained a significant proportion of working-class scholarship or mature-aged students for whom supporting Labour was an act of loyalty and solidarity, but who would often find themselves uncomfortable amongst the other strands. Then there were 'independent' socialists unaffiliated, many coming from a position outside of mainstream English society and commonly from liberal middle-class family backgrounds. Finally, of course, there were a very small number of communists, a striking number of which had come through public schools and were, definitively, *not* working class in their social origins.[104]

Samuel, committed to a minority political party viewed by many with hostility and suspicion, had to work extremely hard in order to gain a voice in Oxford student political debate. Reinforcing this was the fact that he was now encountering a greater number of people who were adept at 'playing politics'. One strategy he adopted for dealing with these issues was simply to cultivate a charming and agreeable public persona.[105] He later described this situation:

> the great fear of Communism was of being an outcast. The whole effort was simply to accept our legitimacy. And that meant quite a lot of bending, in effect, to, as it were, present a political position in a palatable way, as it were in liberal terms. So a lot of my Communism by force of necessity became a re-presentation of belief in terms that could be sympathised with, and ideally, supported by liberals. So a lot of my work was on colonialism in Oxford. And that was sort of finding a common language with people who were anti-colonial for other reasons.[106]

Whilst he typically attributed the imperative to be 'palatable' to his communist training, it was more unique to his own personality and preoccupations. On Samuel's arrival at Balliol, the incumbent secretary of the Oxford student communist club (from whom he took over in 1954) felt no such compulsion to promote the party in the same way and would not be drawn into political argument in public, keeping his communism

---

103 For a detailed history of Oxford and the Labour movement see Brian Harrison, 'Oxford and the Labour Movement', *Twentieth Century British History*, 2, 3 (1991), 226–71.
104 Hall, 'The Life and Times of the First New Left', 181–82; Brian Harrison, 'Interview with Raphael Samuel', 20 October 1987.
105 One might view his earlier decision to anglicise his name to Ralph as part of this desire.
106 Brian Harrison, 'Interview with Raphael Samuel', 18 September 1987.

as a form of private faith and personal counsel.¹⁰⁷ Samuel, by contrast, was 'evangelical', selling party literature around the colleges and pursuing all opportunities for public debate.

So intently did he attempt to seek out the common ground through discussion that he would take great pains to find the most acceptable phrasing for a petition. He was even willing to adopt the less esoteric language of liberalism, resplendent with references to that comforting cover-all concept of 'tolerance'. In the course of this process, he could not help becoming 'a bit liberal himself', reinforcing the extent to which he immersed himself into other people's political languages.¹⁰⁸

Another tactic he adopted was organising campaigns on issues that cut across party-political lines. One revealing instance of this was his efforts to forge an alliance with existentialist philosophers against the prevailing dominance of Oxford analytical philosophy. The motivation behind this was that whilst both the analytical and the Marxist approach to philosophy gave a privileged position to materialist explanation, analytical philosophy was characterised by the stress that it placed on the pursuit of 'objectivity' in knowledge and in its emphasis on words rather than things. Marxism rejected both the notion that language could be detached from the material conditions and the productive relationships in which it was embedded or that knowledge *could* ever be entirely 'objective' or value free. Samuel, as a communist, found common ground with those attracted to existentialist philosophy and its austere insistence on existence over essence. It was during this venture that he encountered Charles Taylor, a French-Canadian philosophy student (and future co-founder of the first New Left).¹⁰⁹

There were further examples of his attempts to find issues or campaigns that brought together a number of disparate strands of the left-wing student body. He worked intently on a campaign against the hydrogen bomb (in response to early H-bomb tests carried out in November 1953), his work here taking him outside of the official party policy of this time.¹¹⁰ He also dedicated a considerable amount of energy to issues relating to anti-colonialism, becoming active in the campaign against the British Government's deposition of the Guyanese Government in 1954.

---

107 Ibid.
108 Brian Harrison, 'Interview with Raphael Samuel', 20 October 1987.
109 Ibid.
110 Brian Harrison, 'Interview with Raphael Samuel', 18 September 1987.

During his various campaigning activities, he encountered other figures who would go on to play key roles in the first New Left, including Stuart Hall, a Jamaican Rhodes Scholar graduate student and Peter Sedgwick, a grammar school boy from a Christian family in Liverpool.[111]

Apart from these specific campaigns, a more structured example of his attempts to liaise across political lines can be seen in his involvement, at the behest of the party, with the Oxford Socialist Club. The club, a 1930s breakaway group that had formed out of what had been the Oxford Labour Club, had been dormant for some years. The CPGB, committed to The British Road to Socialism, viewed the club as an opportunity to create a broad front organisation, and so he, along with several of his friends, set about reviving it. In part it acted as space that allowed for those outside of the official party to interact with communist ideas and politics. Hall later described debate in the club as wide ranging, preempting many of the issues that would later come to preoccupy the first New Left.[112] He also recalled Samuel's remarkable ability to bring even the most expansive and apparently abstract of questions in socialist political philosophy back into some kind of direct connection with worker unrest at the local Cowley car plant, an early glimpse of his prowess for connective and highly imaginative thinking.[113]

Samuel became closely involved with the club's journal *The Oxford Left*, initially taking charge of publicity (Trinity 1953), advancing to the editorial board (Hillary 1954) and eventually becoming the sole named editor (Michaelmas 1954).[114] The journal gives some sense of his interests and political approach during this time. Pieces on 'Socialism and the Middle Classes' and 'The Mind of British Imperialism' demonstrate his concern about and sensitivity towards the internal dynamics of political mentalities and the ways in which these were reformulated over time.[115]

---

111 Brian Harrison, 'Interview with Raphael Samuel', 20 October 1987.
112 Hall, 'The Life and Times of the First New Left', 182.
113 Stuart Hall, oral communication with author, May 2012, Hampstead, London.
114 Both the Socialist Club and the club's journal, *The Oxford Left*, anticipated many of the themes and issues that preoccupied the first New Left and dominated the contents of *Universities and Left Review*, addressing issues such as the role of intellectuals, colonial issues, questions of contemporary socialism and the politics of popular culture.
115 Raphael Samuel, 'Socialism and the Middle Classes', *The Oxford Left*, Hillary Term (1954); Raphael Samuel, 'The Mind of British Imperialism', *The Oxford Left*, Michaelmas Term (1954).

After 1954 he began to harbour some scepticism about the party's strategic use of the club, feeling that it 'stopped people being faced with the hard question of whether or not they would become Communists'.[116] This discomfort could be construed as an example of his unease with the stance of the CPGB and his absorption of the Cold War Cominform concern to demarcate and clarify political positions. Equally, for a 20-year-old man, still making the journey from youth to adulthood, such sectarianism might also be connected to the psychological and emotional processes of late adolescence, and the desire for sharply defined lines between those who were 'one of us' and those who were 'fellow travellers', to be approached with caution.

From another perspective, this can be seen as evidence of his genuine belief in alliance between openly *different* factions amongst the left. Rather than claiming communism to be the superior political model, the inevitable inheritor of the various branches of political left-wing thought, as members of the CPHG had done, Samuel's discomfort suggests willingness to acknowledge and debate difference openly rather than to integrate them artificially.

Although deeply immersed in student politics he was equally involved in communist activity in Oxford city. This was not consciously undertaken as a form of university condescension or patronage towards the city. In theory, working-class people constituted a more natural milieu for the party to be targeting. He had a particularly close relationship with the local party organiser, Ernie Keeling, whom he deeply admired. Keeling, an Oxfordshire man and long-serving communist activist, provided another exemplar of the self-taught party worker and a mentor who he later described as a fatherly figure towards younger comrades.[117] This period also planted some of the early seeds of what would become a long-term relationship with Ruskin College. Ruskin's ties with the trade unions and its student base of working-class adults constituted an attractive potential crucible for communism and the party would canvass Ruskin continuously.

---

116 Brian Harrison, 'Interview with Raphael Samuel', 18 September 1987. Whilst the CPGB had committed to The British Road to Socialism in 1951, it was only after the death of Stalin in 1953 that a greater sense of the party 'opening up' was experienced.

117 Keeling had led the pressed steel strike in Cowley, Oxford, 1934. Brian Harrison, 'Interview with Raphael Samuel', 20 October 1987.

1. THE INGRAINED ACTIVIST

His growing interest in the Oxford Labour Club was in keeping with his doubts concerning the use of the Socialist Club in party strategy. It was also compatible with his desire to forge connections beyond the confines of student life and his efforts to expand the grounds for intellectual debate. Following the CPGB's 1951 policy transition and after the death of Stalin in 1953, there was a slight thaw in the intensity of the Cold War hostility that mellowed, marginally, the general feeling towards communists. On becoming the branch secretary of the university's communist group in 1954, Samuel became even more concerned to take the Labour Party seriously as a political force. This drew him into a closer relationship with the Labour Club which, again, brought him perilously close to being in direct violation of his instructions from the CPGB whose relationship with Labour remained uneasy.[118]

The intellectual and emotional constitution of the Labour Club students was distinctive from those who identified with the harder line of communism. Communists, Samuel would later suggest, formed a sort of 'literati', typically harbouring interests in literature, poetry or philosophy and often knowing very little about the practicalities of political life.[119] Despite articulating a formal (theoretical) appreciation for the natural sciences, the student communists that he engaged with were more likely to approach politics on the basis of larger metaphysical or moral terms. The Labour Club, by contrast, had a more pragmatic character in its understanding of politics. More importantly it had a greater appreciation for the mechanics and apparatus of political power.

This growing interest was further compounded by his close relationship with Denis Butt. Butt was a mature-aged student and former wool sorter who had come to Oxford University from Ruskin College. A long-standing Labour man he went on to become a 'prize recruit' for the CPGB and one of Samuel's closest friends.[120] In the process of attempting to recruit Butt, he immersed himself in the cultural, psychological and emotional values involved in Labour politics saying later that: 'my effort, which lasted

---

118 Brian Harrison, 'Interview with Raphael Samuel', 18 September 1987. Whilst the CPGB initially sought a close working relationship with the Attlee-led Labour Government, by 1947, after repeated rejections, the party began to criticise Labour Party policy. Following the defeat of Labour in 1951 the relationship remained hostile. See Laybourn, 'The Communist Party of Great Britain During the Emergence of the Cold War 1945–1956', in *Marxism in Britain*, 21–22.
119 A sample of Samuel's immediate friendship group reflects this: Pearson and Hall were English literature students, Taylor a philosophy student. Sedgwick initially read classics, later changing to psychology.
120 Brian Harrison, 'Interview with Raphael Samuel', 18 September 1987.

about a year, to recruit him, as it were, on Labour ground. And I actually, without knowing it, made myself into a kind of labour person', further illustration of the intensive personal investment and impact on his own mindset that recruitment entailed.[121]

Whilst this dedication, consciousness and continual political activity were serious pursuits in both subject matter and general character, they were also crucial sources of social life for Samuel and his friends. As secretary of the Oxford communists, he would also organise concerts alongside the more explicitly political meetings, convincing prominent communist folk singers such as Ewan MacColl and A.L. Lloyd to come and perform. The act of political debate itself had profoundly social qualities, conducted over drinks and meals in college common rooms or in student bedrooms late into the night. Nor was the act of debating entirely austere. It involved a fair amount of posturing, jostling, teasing and sparring, all of which had entertaining, even comedic elements about them. He later recalled that he had:

> actually liked arguing with Tories, and we used to get quite a lot of fun – in a way, almost as court jesters. It was such an improbable thing for anybody to be a Communist – and they were very tolerant of us, and we were delighted to be tolerated.[122]

Protests attended by only a handful of people (promptly dispersed by the college rugby club) provided a sense of camaraderie and solidarity amongst the motley few who had turned out. In this sense, politics was the source of deep-rooted long-lasting friendships, amplified and intensified in their intimacy by the single sex college environments in which so much of this discussion and organising took place.[123]

Politics was even the basis for his early romantic relationships. At the age of 21, with great flair and romance, he proposed to his partner, fellow communist Jean McCrindle, at the summit of Arthur's Seat in Edinburgh. In his eyes, McCrindle's credentials lay in her skills at collecting 'good' people for the party. Given his own enthusiasm for political recruitment and organisation, it struck him that she would make an 'ideal comrade'

---

121 Brian Harrison, 'Interview with Raphael Samuel', 20 October 1987.
122 Brian Harrison, 'Interview with Raphael Samuel', 18 September 1987.
123 Samuel later commented that these were 'extremely intense male friendships', sharing similarities with 'heterosexual relationships and jealousies'. Brian Harrison, 'Interview with Raphael Samuel', 20 October 1987.

in his imagined life of political activity.[124] Initially, McCrindle accepted his proposal, but the engagement would later become a casualty of the upheavals caused by the events of 1956.

Up until the age of 21, Samuel's communism was an all-encompassing world.[125] It was a happy one of close relationships, intellectual stimulus and activity, experienced first and foremost as an entire way of living and mode of behaving. As a child communisim had provided an anchor point for Samuel's sense of identity, his social relationships and intellectual development. As a young adult in the early 1950s the heart of his communist activism was based on seeking out opportunities for strategic alliances and potential conversions.

Whilst the CPGB's explicit policy provided his conscious political framework, the behavioural implications fostered by communism were of equal importance. His attraction to the roles of the activist and organiser provided him with clear values about intellectual work and the need to form a bridge between political activity on the ground and larger political ideas. This required that he work closely and collaboratively with a range of people, seeking out common ground and languages. For this he had already begun to develop a sophisticated public persona, drawing on strong interpersonal and communicative skills designed to make palatable and appealing a politics widely regarded as suspicious and alien. Such a project had also been reflected in the endeavours of the CPHG, who also sought to connect the familiar coordinates of the national past to the critical framework of Marxist analysis in a manner that was both accessible and popular.

Samuel's time at Oxford University gave him an opportunity to further rehearse these skills of argument, persuasion and performance in the intimate arena of student politics. His student years also challenged some of his thinking, forcing him into closer contact with people outside of communist or radical left-wing cultures. The necessity of confronting these challenges made *some* inroads into his self-conscious communist sectarianism but did not amount to a threat to it. At the time of his

---

124 Samuel, *The Lost World*, 88.
125 Ibid.

graduation from Oxford in 1956, with the first-class degree in modern history desired by the party, he fully expected to take a full-time position in the party.[126]

The events that unfolded across the course of that year were to irrevocably disrupt this intense and intimate world. Immediately following his graduation, and still acting on party orders to be an exemplary student, he began a PhD at the London School of Economics which he soon abandoned as political activity began to dominate his life more dramatically than ever.[127]

---

126 Brian Harrison, 'Interview with Raphael Samuel', 20 October 1987.
127 Ibid.

2
Reinventing the Organiser: Anti-authoritarianism, Activist Politics and the First New Left

Raphael Samuel and Jean McCrindle, Trafalgar Square, London, 1956
Raphael Samuel Archive, Bishopsgate Institute, London, courtesy of Alison Light and the Raphael Samuel Estate.

On a wintry evening in November 1956, Raphael Samuel and Jean McCrindle, a picture-perfect communist couple, engaged to be married, went to see a performance of John Osborne's play *Look Back in Anger* at the Lyric Theatre in Hammersmith, London. The production starred

Richard Pasco as the central protagonist Jimmy Porter who, finding himself increasingly alienated from English society, grows steadily more and more consumed with a destructive anger that brings tragic results for those around him.[1]

Following the production, Samuel and McCrindle found themselves in disagreement over the play. As he recalled it, she thought Jimmy Porter's anger a form of middle-class self-indulgence. Samuel had found himself moved by it, responsive to Porter's sad lament for the want of any brave causes. They broke off their engagement.[2] Their separation was, of course, about more than just a difference of opinion on a play. It was just another example of the way in which the extraordinary events of that year had plunged so many British communists, like Samuel and McCrindle, into an emotional maelstrom that dramatically altered the way they understood the world. For Samuel this was a turbulent time of transition, but also a critical crucible for consolidating what would become the political, intellectual and moral cornerstones of his historical work.

As discussed in Chapter 1, at the beginning of 1956 Samuel was a committed communist and student activist destined, so he thought, for a career within the Communist Party of Great Britain (CPGB). By the end of that year, following the fallout from the Khrushchev revelations and the Soviet invasion of Hungary he had, reluctantly, left the party and become a critical driving force in the creation of the New Left movement, first as an organising force behind the journal *Universities and Left Review* (*ULR*) (1957–59), then as a member of its editorial collective and chairman of the New Left clubs, later as member of the editorial collective for the *New Left Review* (*NLR*) (1960–).[3]

---

1   Philip Barnes, *A Companion to Post War British Theatre* (Totowa, NJ: Barnes and Noble, 1986), 179.
2   Brian Harrison, 'Interview with Raphael Samuel', 18 September 1987, 19 Elder Street, London, transcripts held in Raphael Samuel Archive (RSA), Bishopsgate Institute, London.
3   The New Left was an extremely diffuse movement encompassing many related but distinctive strands. Here it is used specifically to refer to the figures and activities clustered around the two journals *The New Reasoner* (1957–59), edited by E.P. Thompson and John Saville, and *Universities and Left Review* (1957–59), edited by Oxford graduates Stuart Hall, Gabriel Pearson, Raphael Samuel and Charles Taylor. In 1960 these journals merged together to form *New Left Review*, initially edited by Hall (1960–61), then, for one edition, by an editorial collective led by Samuel in 1962 before being taken over by Perry Anderson in 1962. For memoirs of the New Left see: Stuart Hall, 'The Life and Times of the First New Left', *NLR*, 61, Jan–Feb (2010), 177–96; Robin Archer, Diemut Bubeck, Hanjo Glock, Lesley Jacobs, Seth Moglen, Adam Stenhouse and Daniel Weinstock, eds, *Out of Apathy: Voices of the New Left 30 Years On* (London: Verso, 1989).

2. REINVENTING THE ORGANISER

This chapter focuses on Samuel's role in the New Left. It argues that whilst the changes that he underwent during this time, in particular leaving the CPGB, were dramatic and that many of his endeavours were consequently couched in terms of 'newness', there were strong strands of continuity with his earlier communist values, activist experience and organisational skills. At the same time, this was also a period during which his Marxist 'faith' was challenged and subject to processes of rethinking.

Despite assuming a significant role in the New Left, his contribution has gone relatively unacknowledged. Early commentaries and assessments were first offered by Perry Anderson, the 'heir apparent' following his takeover as editor of *NLR*, the New Left's flagship journal, in 1962.[4] Concerned to distinguish his own political project from those of his predecessors, Anderson stressed the ambiguities and conceptual limitations of what he perceived as its unexamined appeals to humanist morality.[5] Subsequent studies have adopted a more contextualising approach but deviate little from Anderson's main conclusions, offering little in-depth analysis of the complex personalities and relationships involved.[6]

More recently, Madeleine Davis has argued the need for a revised perspective on the New Left, stressing the significance of what she terms an 'activist politics' which she identified with the *ULR* contingency.[7] Davis singled out the extensive infrastructure of the New Left Club network and the Partisan Café as two critical examples of this activist politics in application. Despite this, she made little acknowledgement of Samuel, their primary initiator. This chapter shall demonstrate that it was Samuel who most personified Davis' 'activist politics', which he expressed through the implicit politics of his actions rather than his writing.

---

4   Wade Matthews provides an extensive discussion of changing interpretive patterns in New Left historiography in *The New Left, National Identity, and the Break-up of Britain* (Leiden and Boston: BRILL, 2013).
5   Perry Anderson, 'The Left in the Fifties', *NLR*, I/29, Jan–Feb (1965), 3–18. For a later, more considered account see: Perry Anderson, *Arguments within English Marxism* (London: Verso Editions, 1980).
6   For an overview of the first New Left see: Lin Chun, *The First British New Left* (Edinburgh, Edinburgh University Press, 1993); Michael Kenny, *The First New Left: British Intellectuals After Stalin* (London: Lawrence and Wishart, 1995); Dennis Dworkin, 'Socialism at Full Stretch', 'Culture is Ordinary', in *Cultural Marxism in Postwar Britain: History, the New Left, and the Origins of Cultural Studies* (Durham and London: Duke University Press, 1997), 45–124. For a critique of New Left literature see: Dorothy Thompson, 'On the Trail of the First New Left', *NLR*, I/215, Jan–Feb (1996), 93–100.
7   Madeleine Davis, 'Reappraising Socialist Humanism', *Journal of Political Ideologies*, 18, 1 (2013), 57–81.

The first New Left and 1950s Britain

The New Left was a product of, and a response to, the rapid social and cultural changes which seemed to define life in 1950s Britain.[8] These were strange times, both turbulent and jubilant in nature. The British empire was unravelling, America was rising and Cold War tensions simmering. On the home front, the Conservatives were 'modernising' whilst the Labour Party was revising (or attempting to).[9] The welfare state was a decade old and generally proclaimed a success, unemployment was low and wages were rising. Formerly luxury items became more widely accessible, not only washing machines and cars but record players and televisions conveying a ready-made stream of news and entertainment directly into people's homes.[10]

Young people, ever hungry for novelty, asserted their presence as a distinctive social group with spending power, distinguishing themselves from their parents' generation through their receptivity to American music, food, clothes and film.[11] Consciousness of different cultures gained impetus from rising migration levels (initially from Eastern Europe, later from Africa, South Asia and the Caribbean), which provided a strikingly visual sense of change and, at the same time, introduced new foods, languages and customs into everyday British life.[12]

By the end of the decade, Britain *appeared* to be a prosperous, forward-facing society, but was all as it seemed? For some, prosperity was an illusion, encouraging a dangerous complacency. In the artistic and literary culture of the time a cynical mode prevailed, characterised by the work

---

8   For general overviews of this period see: Peter Hennessy, *Having It So Good: Britain in the Fifties* (London: Penguin, 2007); David Kynaston, *Family Britain 1951–1957* (London: Bloomsbury, 2009).
9   See Lawrence Black, 'Must Labour Lose? Revisionism and the Affluent Worker', in *The Political Culture of the Left in Affluent Britain 1951–64: Old Labour, New Britain?* (London: Palgrave Macmillan, 2003).
10   On consumption and mid-twentieth-century British social and cultural life see: Alan Sinfield, *Literature, Politics and Culture in Postwar Britain* (Los Angeles and Berkeley: University of California Press, 1989); John Benson, *The Rise of Consumer Society in Britain 1880–1980* (London: Longman, 1994); A.H. Halsey and Josephine Webb, eds, *Twentieth-Century British Social Trends* (Basingstoke: Macmillan, 2000), 342–43; Miriam Akhtar and Steve Humphries, *The Fifties and Sixties: A Lifestyle Revolution* (London: Boxtree, 2001); Andrew Rosen, *The Transformation of British Life 1950–2000: A Social History* (Manchester: Manchester University Press, 2003).
11   Bill Osgerby, 'Youth Culture', in Paul Addison and Harriet Jones, eds, *A Companion to Contemporary Britain* (Oxford: Blackwell, 2005), 128–31.
12   Wendy Webster, *Imagining Home: Gender, 'Race' and National Identity 1945–64* (London: Routledge, 1998).

of 'movement' writers such as the novelist Kingsley Amis whose hapless antiheroes, such as Jim Dixon in *Lucky Jim* (1954), made a satire of the petty jealousies and rivalries of smug suburban middle-class life. But aside from mockery, there was little offered by way of an alternative.[13] Elsewhere anger, frustration and alienation were the dominant motifs. John Osborne's protagonist, Porter, seemed to speak for a generation when he bewailed the lack of brave causes.[14]

The lack of brave causes formed the central New Left problematic. What did affluence, and all its attendant implications, mean for class politics? What impact did increasing levels of social mobility and changes to community composition have for concepts such as 'equality' and 'fraternity'? How was a flourishing mass media, conveyed through accessible technologies, able to influence popular consciousness in unprecedented ways? These were the longer-term issues informing the cohort. In the short term, however, it was the events of 1956 that provided the catalyst for its formal creation.

Events of 1956

On 25 February 1956, the closing day of the Twentieth Congress of the Communist Party of the Soviet Union, close to midnight, Nikita Khrushchev delivered a four-hour speech denouncing Stalin, unveiling, as he did so, a devastating catalogue of brutalities ranging from Stalin's petty and vindictive vanities as a leader to full-scale, systematic atrocities under his leadership. As news of the speech travelled, shock reverberated around both the communist and the wider world. In Russia only a fragment of the speech was published but it was enough to generate a response 'like the explosion of a neutron bomb'.[15] The revelations sparked a backlash against communist governments in Eastern Europe, with popular uprisings in Poznan, Poland, in June and a later one in Hungary in November.

For British communists, word of the speech filtered out slowly in a disjointed manner. An account of the speech was published in the London *Observer* newspaper in March 1956. *The Daily Worker*, the CPGB's official paper, began to receive a steady stream of letters from readers horrified at the contents and implications of the speech. At first,

---

13 Dominic Sandbrook, *Never Had It So Good* (London: Abacas, 2006), 158.
14 Ibid., 177.
15 Zhores A. Medvedev and Roy A. Medvedev, *The Unknown Stalin* (London: I.B. Tauris, 2006), 98.

some of these appeared in print but on 12 March 1956 J.R. Campbell, the newspaper's editor, ceased to publish them. Pressure for a more open discussion continued to mount in the following months but still the party's leaders made no acknowledgement or concession, suggesting their meek acceptance of the official party line from Moscow. As Samuel later recalled, the party of his youth had been singularly free of 'rows':

> Political differences, so far from being envenomed by personal rivalries – the normal condition of the Labour Party – were suppressed for the sake of comradeship. If there were political divisions on the Executive Committee, the members did not know about them, nor would it have been conceivable for confidential reports to be leaked to the capitalist press – something which passes without comment today. Party proceedings, by comparison with those in the Labour Party, were exceedingly decorous.[16]

As such, the CPGB was unaccustomed and, therefore, ill-equipped to respond effectively to the members' need to express and discuss what had taken place. Arguably, it was this failure that prompted many to leave. Some, like Christopher Hill, stayed on in the party for a further year attempting to negotiate democratic changes to its internal structures but eventually conceded that this was not a possibility.[17]

The revelations of 1956 had not come out of nowhere. Almost from the beginning of the great socialist experiment in the Soviet Union, there had been rumblings and ominous signs.[18] More recently, the party's line on Spain, the Moscow show trials (1936–38) and the Nazi-Soviet pact (1939–41) had caused a vexing situation for Anglo-Communists. The Cold War had further compounded these tensions as the Soviet Union had tightened the party line, attempting to bring the various branches of national communism into a more rigid unity. This had led to clashes between individual members and party officials.[19]

To some extent, the revelations of 1956 were the final straw in an accumulative process of doubts, frustrations and misgivings confirmed once and for all by Khrushchev's ghastly admissions. In another sense,

---

16 Raphael Samuel, *The Lost World of British Communism* (London: Verso, 2006), 79.
17 Robin Briggs, 'Hill, (John Edward) Christopher, (1912–2003)', *Oxford Dictionary of National Biography* (Oxford: Oxford University Press, 2004).
18 For example, anarchist thinkers and activists Emma Goldman and Alexander Berkman wrote a letter warning workers about the atrocities they witnessed following a visit to the Soviet Union. The letter was first published by Freedom Press in 1922.
19 See Doris Lessing, *Walking in the Shade: Volume Two of My Autobiography 1949–1962* (New York: Harper Collins, 1997).

these revelations were also distinctive from anything that had gone before. The full extent of the Stalinist purges was now laid bare, as Khrushchev had intended, in the public arena, leaving no possible means of dismissing the information as a distortion at the hands of capitalist forces.[20]

The Khrushchev revelations and subsequent response to the Hungarian uprising provided one major impetus; the Suez Crisis, which ran almost concurrently, provided another. The crisis, which saw the British Government embroiled in an unedifying military operation with Israel and France to wrest control of the Suez Canal back from the Egyptian Government, demonstrated the prevalence of a mendacious and imperialist cast of mind within the Conservative Government led, at this time, by Anthony Eden. The invasion was met with popular outcry and within 24 hours of it being announced a large crowd marched on Whitehall in protest. Ultimately, Britain was forced into a humiliating retreat from the action after it met with strong international condemnation, in particular from America.

Naturally, communists like Samuel were an active presence amongst the outraged protesters who descended upon Trafalgar Square. But the Soviet suppression of Hungary, just days before, undermined the capacity of any communist to talk convincingly about peace, justice or anti-imperialism. The deeply traumatic effect of this year for many of the party's members cannot be underestimated. McCrindle would later say:

> We stayed up all night, or it seemed that way, for the whole of 1956–7, constantly reeling from unbearable revelations, eye-witness accounts, and new tragic stories of wrongful persecution inside the Soviet Union, including, horrifyingly, loyal Party members.[21]

Memoirs by those involved at the time provide further insight into the extent of shock and betrayal many party members felt as the revelations emerged.[22] Accompanying these emotions was also a strong sense of humiliation, particularly acute for intellectuals, whose confident, even

---

20   John Rettie, 'How Khrushchev Leaked His Secret Speech to the World', *History Workshop Journal* (*HWJ*), 62 (2006), 182–93.
21   Jean McCrindle, 'The Hungarian Uprising and a Young British Communist', *HWJ*, 62 (2006), 198.
22   Ibid.; John Saville, *Memoirs from the Left* (London: Merlin, 2003); John Saville, 'The Twentieth Congress and the British Communist Party', *The Socialist Register*, 13 (1976); Malcolm McEwan, 'The Day the Party Had to Stop', *The Socialist Register*, 13 (1976); Margot Heinemann, '1956 and the Communist Party', *The Socialist Register*, 13 (1976).

arrogant, claims made for communism had been exposed as fraudulent. They were left looking naive and foolish, or, worse still, like liars. Perhaps above all else was sheer frustration at the CPGB's failure to respond.

Disenchanted and outraged, party members John Saville and E.P. Thompson began to publish *The Reasoner*, a critical journal from within the party, which included on its editorial board prominent party intellectuals such as Doris Lessing, along with the anthropologist Peter Worsley and the economist Ronald Meek. *The Reasoner* was intended to act as the forum for discussion that the party had failed to provide.[23] Saville and Thompson produced two editions before being ordered to cease publishing or face 'excommunication' from the party. The two men agreed to produce one further edition in which they planned to state that future publication would henceforth cease: an example of how, despite the revelations, there was not an immediate move to leave the party.[24] The concern for many British communists, like Thompson and Saville, was more about forcing the CPGB into some position of reflection and critical response.

The June uprising in Poznan, Poland, had been neutralised through a compromise achieved between the Soviet Union and the Polish government, the Hungarian one was a different matter. The Soviet Union responded to this with force, sending in armed forces to crush it, dashing any hopes that Khrushchev's speech might mean a renewal of the core values of the communist political project. With the British party still flailing in response, Saville and Thompson left the CPGB, urging others to follow them. Around 7,000 CPGB members did so. *The Reasoner* was transformed into *The New Reasoner* (*NR*), which declared its intention of formulating a 'new' form of socialist politics, independent from the party structure and apparatus, expressed in Thompson's concept of socialist humanism.[25] This was socialism reconstituted from the purely economic implications of Stalinism and restored to a more holistic view of the individual human being as a creative agent; and of socialism as a moral force which, argued Thompson, could be discerned in the early work of Marx and had been even better expressed by the nineteenth-century artist, entrepreneur and socialist, William Morris.

---

23 John Saville and E.P. Thompson, 'Why We Are Publishing', *The Reasoner*, 1 (1956), 1–3.
24 Saville, 'Edward Thompson, the Communist Party and 1956'.
25 John Saville and E.P. Thompson, 'Editorial', *The New Reasoner* (*NR*), 1, Summer (1957), 1; E.P. Thompson, 'Socialist Humanism: An Epistle to the Philistines Part I/II', *NR*, 1, Summer (1957), 105–43.

Thompson's appeal to socialist humanism, far from a knee-jerk reaction to recent events, was an articulation of views long in gestation. During the 1950s Thompson, at this time a tutor in English literature and history for the Workers' Educational Association (WEA) in Halifax, Yorkshire, had been in search of a means of convincing his worker students of the relevance of literature to their everyday lives. He became 'seized' by the figure of Morris,[26] finding in him a striking example of the ways in which Marxist political-economic rationalism could be reconciled with the best qualities of individual human creativity and agency. In 1955, Thompson (with considerable help from Dona Torr) published a biographical study of Morris, arguing for his enduring relevance to contemporary left-wing political thought.[27]

The publication of the biography had, of course, preceded the events of 1956 and was, as Thompson later acknowledged, studded with 'Stalinist pieties', but within it could be discerned the seeds of his socialist humanism.[28] Now detached from the party, he set out his case for socialist humanism and its application to the postwar world in an imposing polemical article, 38 pages in length, bristling with outrage and rich in literary allusion. It concluded with an urgent call to arms: mankind must realise its own creative agency, turn upon the barbarians pressing at the gate and confront its most deadly enemies.[29] This was rousing stuff, but despite the assertion of a new political vision, the *NR*, not least in terms of the personnel on its editorial board, still bore a sense of being a journal of ex-communists.

As Michael Kenny argues, Thompsonian 'socialist humanism' was an important and defining coordinate in New Left discourse, further reinforced by a renewal of interest in Marx's early work such as the *Economic and Philosophic Manuscripts of 1844* (first released by Soviet researchers in 1927), which showed a greater sensitivity for individuality and social alienation.[30] This was not to say that there was a consensus surrounding its definition. Even amongst the inner circle of the New

---

26 'E. P. Thompson [interview by Mike Merrill]', in Henry Abelove et al., eds, *Visions of History* (Manchester: Manchester University Press, 1976), 13.
27 Thompson acknowledges this in his preface. E.P. Thompson, *William Morris, Romantic to Revolutionary* (London: Lawrence and Wishart, 1955).
28 E.P. Thompson, 'Foreword', in *William Morris: Romantic to Revolutionary* (New York: Pantheon Books, 1977).
29 Thompson, 'Socialist Humanism: An Epistle to the Philistines', 105–143.
30 Kenny, *The First New Left*, 69.

Left milieu, Thompson's invocation of an early Marx and an 'authentic' communism was questioned. For example, Charles Taylor (responsible for translating the 1844 manuscripts from French into English) argued that Stalinism could not be so easily dismissed as an aberrant mutation of the true spirit of Marxism; there was a serious need to scrutinise the inherent authoritarianism discernible within even the earliest work of Marx.[31]

What of Samuel's reactions to the events of 1956? Samuel later described his initial response to these events as one of 'total disbelief', followed by a reluctance to leave the CPGB. He did leave, but was motivated more by loyalty to his friends than from a deeper personal inclination.[32] All this might seem astonishing, especially given that the revelations made by Khrushchev inevitably carried an extra dimension of significance for his family. The anti-Semitism of events such as the 'Doctor's Plot' in 1952 combined with the fate of the Jewish anti-fascist committees and of Jews in Russia more broadly, was something that his family, particularly through Chimen Abramsky, the secretary of the CPGB's Jewish committee, was able to gain a lot of information about.[33]

The idea that an anti-Jewish sentiment had been so prevalent in the Soviet Union was shocking, especially when considered in light of the horrifying acts of anti-Semitism perpetuated by the Nazis.[34] The claim that state communism stood in polar opposition to the authoritarian politics of fascism was no longer credible. Further to this, Samuel's maternal family's Polish roots made the subsequent popular uprising in Poznan *against* the Communist government all the more poignant.[35]

It could not be argued that Samuel, despite his youth, had been blissfully ignorant of the wider context of international communist politics. He had been no soft Marxist or fellow traveller. On the contrary, he had been an extremely zealous one, thoroughly well versed in party strategy and well informed of all the developments within the movement. He had had close contact with figures who commanded significant roles in the party (such as his uncle); he himself had been the Secretary of the Oxford

---

31   Charles Taylor, 'Marxism and Humanism', *NR*, 2 (1957), 92–98.
32   Brian Harrison, 'Interview with Raphael Samuel', 18 September 1987.
33   The 'Doctor's Plot': in 1952, an ageing, unwell, and increasingly paranoid Stalin came to believe that Jewish doctors were planning to assassinate him. Scores of Soviet Jews were dismissed from their jobs, arrested, sent to the Gulag or executed. This persecution was accompanied by anti-Semitic propaganda in the state-run mass media.
34   Brian Harrison, 'Interview with Raphael Samuel', 18 September 1987.
35   Ibid.

University branch of the party, even having his own minor struggles with the party line over matters such as his campaign against the H-bomb and his collaboration with the Labour Party.

Why had Samuel been reluctant to give up the Communist Party? His primary political role and intellectual energies were first and foremost in grassroots activism rather than political theory or strategy. (As Hobsbawm would later put it, he was 'an ingrained activist'.[36]) His political energies and intellectual creativity had therefore been trained upon the pragmatic implications of enacting or facilitating political campaigns and activities rather than focused on the manoeuvres of high politics. There was also the sheer totality of his immersion in communist politics to be reckoned with. His relationship with communism was different from that of Thompson, who had come to it independently in his late teens, or from his friend Stuart Hall who had been sympathetic but never an official party member. It had been almost lifelong in duration, with 13 members of his family, not to mention his wider community, all embedded within a communist network. Like many others, his family had first joined the CPGB because they believed that it stood for social equality, tolerance and democracy. Once inside the party structure, this belief had been entwined into an elaborate code of language, behaviour and values that adherents had understood as the cultural expression and enactment of these beliefs. All this had effectively woven the party and class politics deep into their sense of self-identity. As his mother, Minna, would later say, the experience of breaking with the party was 'shattering … far worse than giving up Judaism'.[37]

So, more in a spirit of solidarity than personal choice, Samuel followed his friends and family members in resigning from the party.[38] His response to the situation was not one of a straightforward rejection of communism or of the party. It was complex, entwined with a sense of divided loyalties and confusion. His unwillingness to openly criticise the party caused tension between him and his friends like Hall and Taylor. Unlike some, he found himself incapable of having any bad memories of his communist childhood.[39] Nevertheless, he would later acknowledge that a 'break' of sorts did occur in thinking as a result of the events of 1956, saying:

---

36 Eric Hobsbawm, *Interesting Times: A Twentieth Century Life* (London: Abacus, 2002), 212.
37 'Obituary: Minna Keal', *The Daily Telegraph*, 1 December 1999.
38 Brian Harrison, 'Interview with Raphael Samuel', 18 September 1987.
39 Brian Harrison, 'Interview with Raphael Samuel', 20 October 1987, 19 Elder Street, London, transcripts held in Raphael Samuel Archive (RSA), Bishopsgate Institute, London.

> I've never been able to recreate a trust in any political leadership … I would like to, but I've never been able to give my trust or faith to any political leadership of whatever kind since then. So to that extent … there actually was a break in '56.[40]

Over the summer of 1956, Saville, a family friend of his uncle's, guided him in his first 'faltering steps in opposition' but this process was not a straightforward one.[41] Following the catastrophic events of November, Saville and Thompson's publication of the *NR*, and his eventual official break from the party, his major concern was to avoid the danger of becoming trapped in the negative identity of an 'ex-communist'. The *NR* with its origins as a critical journal *within* the CPGB was, he felt, too closely associated with this identity. He became increasingly concerned to create an opportunity for a new politics to be developed, a 'positive' with which to move on from the rubble left behind by shattered illusions.[42]

He resumed the elements of political activity that he knew best, had done the most of, and was most proficient at: organisation. As he later put it. 'I really was an organizer and believed in organization and believed really in discipline, I suppose, and it was a belief in unity and above all … I … believed in being positive'.[43]

Whilst the revelations of 1956 had begun what would be a slow process of detaching this organisational role from the specific framework of the party, the skills, instincts and values of the role lent themselves to the creation of a 'new' political project.

Universities and Left Review

Of course, as Samuel would later concede, this project was far from being entirely new.[44] Its roots were varied but undoubtedly it owed a debt to his interpretation of the 1930s Popular Front, albeit one painted in the thick primary colours of childhood memory. More directly, it was informed by his student days at Oxford, through ventures like the revival of the Oxford

---

40 Ibid.
41 Brian Harrison, 'Interview with Raphael Samuel', 18 September 1987.
42 Ibid.
43 Ibid.
44 Raphael Samuel, 'Born Again Socialism', in Robin Archer et al., eds, *Out of Apathy: Voices of the New Left Thirty Years On* (London: Verso, 1989), 39–58.

Socialist Club and the whole lifestyle engendered by student politics: the close friendships across the political spectrum, the late night debates and collaborative political campaigns.

As for Thompson, this new politics borrowed from the older traditions of left-wing libertarianism with its stress on the creative individual, the self-organising community and the workers' control of industry.[45] But whilst William Morris provided Thompson with inspiration, for Samuel these ideas were more directly conveyed through the work of the historian G.D.H. Cole. During the mid-1950s Cole had presided over a weekly political discussion group, held at All Souls College, Oxford, of which Samuel, always eager to represent a Marxist perspective on any political question going, had been a regular participant. In the spring of 1956, Cole was involved in organising a conference in Paris, attended by Hall, to discuss the formation of an international socialist society based around similar principles of worker autonomy and self-direction.[46] Another contemporary source of inspiration was provided by the Geneva Group set up by John Berger and Peter de Francia early in 1956, which sought to reunite artists and intellectuals, separated by the ideological divisions of the Cold War, in a shared political debate.[47]

It was out of this blend of old and new that Samuel, Hall, and two other of their close friends, Charles Taylor and Gabriel Pearson, went on to set up the *Universities and Left Review* (*ULR*). Its birth had homespun beginnings. The idea started as a private joke between Samuel and Hall about an imaginary journal in which all the small group of friends, with their quirks and concerns caricatured, wrote about their particular political bugbears.[48] This in-joke moved rapidly into reality as the political events around them intensified.

A letter from Samuel to Hall written on 15 November 1956, shortly after the events in Hungary and literally days after leaving the party, outlined his entire rationale and vision for the journal in extraordinary detail.

---

45   Often referred to as 'guild socialism', whereby industry is controlled by a number of trade-specific 'guilds' who negotiate amongst each other.
46   Brian Harrison, 'Interview with Raphael Samuel', 18 September 1987; Hall, 'The Life and Times of the First New Left', 178.
47   Brian Harrison, 'Interview with Raphael Samuel', 18 September 1987.
48   Ibid.

This letter demonstrates the extent to which Samuel, typically neglected in accounts of the first New Left, truly was the initial 'moving engine' behind the *ULR*.[49]

He opened the letter by clearly indicating the purpose of the magazine (this term is generally preferred to journal in the letters):

> [T]he magazine should be designed to appeal to left wing dons especially younger dons – and the more active left wing students. In addition if we can give it a fair amount of ideological content it should appeal to ex University Lefts, to Ex Communists (recent) and liberal Communists still fighting inside the CP (people like Hill and Hobsbawm) and to left intellectuals generally.[50]

It went on to advise that a close working relationship be formed with the Labour Party, not necessarily out of any ideological alignment, but out of a pragmatic acknowledgement that it constituted the political arm of socialism in parliament. He then discussed strategies for achieving a wide readership and for using the *ULR* as a platform for generating networks of associations and affiliations:

> It seems to me that the only way to provide for the interests of such diverse groups of readers as those listed above is by printing a large number of readers' letters in each issue. I think we should aim at printing a minimum of fifteen readers' letters in each issue. A great advantage of printing so many letters is that people who have had letters printed tend to buy and sell the magazine. By printing a large number of letters we could build up a large network in every University and technical college. If we could have fifteen letters on say ten different topics we could show the range of interest offered by the magazine.[51]

He continued allocating roles: 'yourself and myself as editors. Gary as literary editor. Chuck as ideological editor', and discussed layout, printing costs and issues regarding distribution.[52] He also set out proposals for the contents of the first edition. Whilst permitting 'Gary' editorial determination over the literary section (no more than three or four pages here), he intervened rather more comprehensively on the ideological

---

49   Stuart Hall, 'Raphael Samuel: 1934–1996', *NLR*, I/221, Jan–Feb (1997), 121.
50   Raphael Samuel to Stuart Hall, 15 November 1956, RS.1: New Left/001, '1956', Raphael Samuel Archive (RSA), Bishopsgate Institute, London.
51   Ibid.
52   Ibid. 'Gary' is an anglicised version of Gabriel (Pearson). Chuck refers to Charles Taylor. Elsewhere, Stuart Hall is referred to as Stewart.

section (supposedly to be overseen by 'Chuck'), listing what he thought would be appropriate. In total, he made 22 'possible' suggestions for topics and authors including:

> The Future of Marxism: An intermediate statement, Eric Hobsbawm; Labour Re-think Economics, Joan Robinson; French Intellectuals and the French Working Class, J.P Sartre; The Class Structure of Britain Today, Stewart Hall; Oxford Philosophy and Socialism, Chuck Taylor; The Marxist view of History: Can it be modified, Ralph Samuel; [this suggestion was accompanied by a note warning that this could cause controversy] and Labour Careerism, Thomas Balogh.[53]

There were further suggestions, unassigned to authors, on town planning (on which he advised a series of articles) and the British education system.

Having communicated his thoughts to the other editors, a further letter, dated two weeks later (1 December 1956), saw him reiterate what he saw as the key objectives of the journal:

> one of our most important tasks will be to create a new mass basis in the Universities for socialist ideas – to greatly enlarge the numbers of those keenly interested in problems of re-thinking, to take the discussion out of the relatively narrow circle of LP, CP and Fabian activists in which the discussion is at present confined. I think that if we are to do this we shall have to present in agit-prop form in each issue the fundamental ethical and political ideals of socialism. Obviously we shall have to do this in ways relevant to contemporary Britain. Obviously we shall have to do this in ways that will have particular appeal to post war intellectuals.[54]

It is striking how the former CPGB organiser showed an acute awareness of the journal's role as a bridge between specific issues and the broader conceptual frameworks they referred to.

For the first edition, the fledgling student editors sought out and persuaded (cajoled) 'senior' figures amongst the intellectual left, including Cole and Thompson, into contributing articles. Samuel worked with particular energy here, applying his personal charm through writing letters and arranging meetings, even travelling the country in order to canvass support amongst some of the best-known figures on the political left. These included several former party members such as Victor Kiernan, Rodney Hilton and Thompson, who, in a polite, rather formal letter

---

53 Ibid.
54 Ralph Samuel to Stuart Hall, 1 December 1956, RS.1: New Left/001, '1956', RSA.

promised a polemical essay (rather than a study) on intellectuals and the class struggle.[55] He even tried his luck with R.H. Tawney, the 'grand old man' of English socialism, who replied with a handwritten note kindly refusing the request but sending 'all best wishes for the success of the Review'.[56]

Having gathered together the contributions, the articles were painstakingly cut and pasted together, late into the night, on Hall's kitchen table in his student digs on Richmond Road, Oxford. (They returned the following morning to find, portentously or otherwise, that Hall's cat had given birth to her kittens on the mock up.[57]) Samuel was responsible for persuading a publisher to print thousands of copies of the first issue (and to reprint the issue before the first debt had been repaid), which the determined group hauled to and from Oxford railway station on trolleys.[58]

The first edition of the *ULR*, which appeared in early 1957, clearly shows the potency of his persuasive capacity. It deviates very little from the outline he had proposed to 'Stewart' in November. The opening editorial announced the need for socialist intellectuals to address the damage done by both Stalinism and the 'miraculous renewal of capitalism'. It made a call for the regeneration of the whole tradition of free, open and critical debate; emphatically refusing to attach itself to a political 'line' but positioning itself instead as a forum where the different traditions of socialist discussion were 'free to meet in open controversy'.[59]

In terms of *ULR*'s content, his original vision was largely realised.[60] What did not appear in the first issue (the focus on town planning for example) appeared in a later one. One significant omission was his own proposed article on 'The Marxist View of History' (another article by him, 'The Liquidation of the Thirties', apparently thrown over to the second edition for reasons of space, also failed to materialise). Why these did not appear is inevitably speculative. Perhaps he was pragmatic enough

---

55　E.P. Thompson to Ralph Samuel, 18 December 1956, RS.1: New Left/001, '1956', RSA.
56　R.H. Tawney to Ralph Samuel, 24 December 1956, RS.1: New Left/001, '1956', RSA.
57　Stuart Hall, oral communication with author, May 2012, Hampstead, London, recording in author's possession.
58　Hall, 'Raphael Samuel: 1934–1996', 121; Stuart Hall, oral communication with author, May 2012.
59　Stuart Hall, Gabriel Pearson, Charles Taylor and Raphael Samuel, eds, 'Editorial', *ULR*, 1, 1 (1957), 1.
60　See: 'Editorial and Contents', *ULR*, 1, 1 (1957), 1.

to avoid stirring up the controversy that he had warned against. Perhaps he was unable to thoroughly formulate his ideas on these questions yet. Perhaps he was simply too busy organising everything. As it was, he was the only one of the four young editors not to publish a piece, aligned with his personal interests, in the first edition. Whilst offering no explicit statement of his political ideas at this time, he nevertheless retained a silent but omnipresent organisational influence, even providing his personal (home) address for all editorial communications.

Aside from the journal, Samuel was also the primary architect behind the first New Left Club, conceived in the first place as a venue for journal readers to hear the Marxist historian Isaac Deutscher speak. Having hired a room in a Bloomsbury hotel for the event, the *ULR* editors returned from a leisurely Indian meal to find a queue of 700 people impatiently waiting for the event. This was the catalyst for creating a more permanent infrastructure. Relentlessly canvassing the full range of his political network for funds, he managed to procure 7 Carlisle Street, in London's Soho district, as a permanent headquarters for the *ULR* and the New Left Club. Many other New Left readers' clubs followed, with branches materialising up and down the length of the country (clubs opened in Manchester, Sheffield, Cardiff, Fife and Edinburgh amongst others).[61]

The clubs came to act by way of 'resource centres', appropriated by various groups pursuing particular campaigns. These were often local and community-based in character. The Notting Hill branch, for example, emerged as a direct community response to the 1958 race riots and concentrated its efforts on promoting local community organisation. In Croydon, one of the afflicted birthplaces of the Teddy Boy, the branch undertook research into youth culture.[62] One campaign with more nationwide ramifications was the Campaign for Nuclear Disarmament (CND) which, in the early days of its organisation, made use of the Soho club as a makeshift headquarters.[63]

Popular concern about the threat posed by nuclear weapons had heightened since the use of the atomic bomb by the Americans against the Japanese in 1945. Following the bombing of the Japanese cities of Hiroshima and Nagasaki in the final stages of the war, the shocking

---

61 Hobsbawm, *Interesting Times*, 212.
62 Kenny, *The First New Left*, 39.
63 Mike Berlin, 'The Partisan Café', BBC Radio 4, First broadcast 4 December 2008.

image of the mushroom cloud and reports of the horrendous death tolls and devastating after effects of the bomb had prompted widespread consternation over the force of these weapons, compounded by the subsequent testing of hydrogen bombs (H-bombs) in the early 1950s.[64]

In November 1957, when the first British H-bomb was tested on Christmas Island, the sinister threat of nuclear power was brought uncomfortably close to home. The first public meeting of the CND in February 1958, held in Central Hall, Westminster, attracted over 5,000 participants and included an impressive line-up of supporters from respected 'elders' such as the philosopher Bertrand Russell to a more glamorous array of left-wing intellectuals and celebrities: Peggy Ashcroft, Doris Lessing, Lindsay Anderson, Kenneth Tynan, Iris Murdoch and of course, E.P. Thompson. The highlight of this movement became the annual Aldermaston marches, the first of which was orchestrated in the library of the Soho club.

Aside from political campaigns, the clubs also played host to a number of study and research groups, meeting for regular discussions or holding courses and summer schools. The intellectual seriousness of these pursuits and endeavours was, on occasion, leavened as the clubs doubled as venues for evening socials such as skiffle or jazz nights.

In order to provide an independent source of finance for the journal and the club's activities, Samuel hit upon the idea of the Partisan Café. The 1950s had seen the massive growth of milk bars and coffee shops in Britain, particularly in London with the first milk bar opening in 1952.[65] Spying an opportunity to engage and make use of the popularity of this trend (whilst simultaneously reappropriating a capitalist symbol for socialism) the café was envisaged as a space in which all manner of people, from all walks of life, could gather and discuss politics over coffee and food. Samuel's vision was initially rejected by the rest of the editorial board at a late night meeting in Taylor's rooms at All Soul's College. Undeterred, however, he ploughed ahead regardless, eventually persuading his friends through the sheer force of his enthusiasm.[66]

---

64 Whilst a student at Oxford, Samuel had been a key figure in spearheading a campaign against nuclear testing in 1953. See the 'Peace Issue' of the *Oxford Left*, 16 June (Trinity Term) 1954.
65 Sandbrook, *Never Had It So Good*, 140–42.
66 Hall, 'Raphael Samuel: 1934–1996', 122.

The café was established in the basement of 7 Carlisle Street, with the New Left Club and a library on the upper floors. It had large communal tables and an eclectic (or eccentric) menu designed by Samuel himself, which drew inspiration from continental European, Jewish and English cuisines.[67] The café and the club were successful in attracting people. Hundreds gathered at a time to hear speakers, to play chess (whilst nursing a single coffee) in one of the Partisan's alcoves, or to attend one of the many activities that were based there, which included art exhibitions and film screenings.[68]

Ultimately, it was not a successful business venture. Samuel, an inspired ideas man, was no shrewd business manager, nor, perhaps, did he have much intention of trying to be one. Nevertheless, the café can be seen as symbolic of the driving ethos and motivation underpinning the New Left, particularly as the younger cohort of the *ULR* conceived it. What they were trying to do was to make politics a part of everyday social and cultural life, much like it had been for them as students.

The New Left was a time of feverish activity during which he continually drew upon the organiser's persuasive skills in order to convince people to contribute or participate in his schemes. In this sense, his experience of the New Left was less about a theoretical reformulation of socialist edicts and more of an initiative to galvanise a dynamic and diverse popular movement. A further example of this can be seen in his 'response' to one of the early *ULR* debates on 'Socialism and the Intellectuals' (prompted by the polemical essay promised by Thompson for the *ULR*'s first edition).

One of Thompson's main diagnoses of the crisis that had befallen the international socialist movement was his view that it had drifted too far away from addressing large moral questions, an absence he also discerned more generally in 1950s British public debate. British intellectuals, far from rallying against this, were, in some cases, responsible for perpetuating this apathy. Amongst the guilty was the author Kingsley Amis whose pamphlet 'Socialism and the Intellectuals' (Fabian Society, 1957) disparaged the 'political' intellectual as an irrational romantic inclined towards the causes of others for want of one of their own.[69]

---

67 Ibid.; Hall, 'The Life and Times of the First New Left', 178; Hobsbawm, *Interesting Times*, 213–14.
68 Mike Berlin, 'The Partisan Café', BBC Radio 4; Stuart Hall, oral communication with author, May 2012.
69 Kingsley Amis, *Socialism and the Intellectuals* (London: Fabian Tracts 304, 1957).

Thompson's 'Socialism and the Intellectuals' responded directly to Amis and criticised those who had retreated from the front line, and urged intellectuals to reenter the fray:

> Goodness knows that human reason and conscience are imperfect instruments enough; they glow fitfully amongst the bric-a-brac piled all around, which threaten at any moment to topple over and extinguish their light – self-interest and self-esteem, indigestion, guilt, class conditioning, memories of the woodshed, old superstition, the lot. But we continue our intellectual work because we believe that, in the last analysis, *ideas matter*.[70]

Thompson's intellectual appeared as a moral guardian, rising above the 'bric-a-brac' of everyday life, refocusing attention on life's most pressing and important questions.

The article gave rise to a lively debate.[71] Unsurprisingly, there was a general consensus about the need for intellectuals to reengage with popular and public debate, but the nature of this engagement was not unproblematic. How should the relationship between the intellectual and the people be configured? The intellectual depended upon on a capacity to retain a sense of distance from the day-to-day concerns that, as Thompson had argued, could overwhelm a sense of the larger picture.

On the other hand, too much distance left the intellectual an isolated figure whose words of warning and wisdom gained no popular audience. Furthermore, where were these intellectuals going to come from? The figure of the working-class autodidact, self-schooled in politics, seemed to belong to a different age.[72] How was an intelligentsia that evolved from the working classes to be encouraged? What values should the public intellectual espouse? On close scrutiny, how universal was Thompson's conception of socialist humanism and how was it to be integrated with Marxist principles of political analysis?[73]

---

70 Thompson also revisited this issue in his essay 'Outside of the Whale' a pointed inversion of George Orwell's earlier essay 'Inside the Whale'. E.P. Thompson, 'Socialism and the Intellectuals', *ULR*, 1, 1 (1957), 33.
71 Mervyn Jones, 'Socialism and the Intellectuals – One', Harold Silver, 'Socialism and the Intellectuals – Two', Charles Taylor, 'Socialism and the Intellectuals – Three', Rodney Hilton, 'Socialism and the Intellectuals – Four', and E.P. Thompson, 'Socialism and the Intellectuals – A Reply', *ULR*, 1, 2 (1957), 15–22.
72 Silver, 'Socialism and the Intellectuals – Two', 17–18; Taylor, 'Socialism and the Intellectuals – Three', 18–19.
73 Ibid. See also Charles Taylor, 'Marxism and Humanism', *NR*, 2 (1957), 92–98.

Samuel's voice was not amongst those who joined the direct debate. He did, however, pass comment on the matter in the 'A Left Notebook' entry published in the same edition, where he suggested that the crucial test for British Marxist intellectual creativity should be how socialist thinkers responded to contemporary issues like consumer capitalism and cultural change. Pointing to the New Left clubs, he claimed them as a living example of socialist thinking revitalised and put into action. Although brief, the entry was studded with loaded meaning: a socialist theory that was sent down, ready-made, by intellectuals or party officials from above was not just undesirable, but 'a libel on the Socialist tradition'. Conjecture about the theoretical 'role of the Socialist intellectual' on behalf of 'ex-communists' was tantamount to a form of 'moral cleansing', a direct response to the turmoil caused by the break from the party.[74]

Whilst his comments only referred to the debate indirectly, the notebook entry can be viewed as enacting the alternative role that Samuel saw for the intellectual. Firstly, there was its form as a *notebook* entry rather than a polemical essay or serious study. As a mode of communication it was informal; informative rather than instructive in nature. It summarised and disseminated information about what had taken place, the key points to be extracted from these actions and what was intended in the future. For example, 'The Town Planning study group aims to synthesise of town planners, architects, sociologists, economists and councillors in an attempt to recapture and carry forward the work of the early post-war period' or 'We hope that our Labour Movement History group can provide the nucleus for a Society of Labour Movement History'.[75]

---

74   Ralph Samuel and Charles Taylor, 'A Left Notebook', *ULR*, 1, 2 (1957), 79–80.
75   Ibid.

Raphael Samuel (far left) and others at the Partisan Café, Carlisle Street, London, c. 1959
Raphael Samuel Archive, Bishopsgate Institute, London, courtesy of Alison Light and the Raphael Samuel Estate.

Secondly, the entry was written in his personal capacity as *chairman* (rather than president) of the New Left clubs and working groups. A *chairing* role is not explicitly authoritative; its primary function involves the organisation and facilitation of meetings. Within those meetings, the chair acts to provide guidance or advice. For example, to a group studying contemporary capitalism: 'it will not be very helpful if members of the Left continue to counter [C.A.R.] Crosland's arguments with the charge that they are "not socialist"'; or to the Marxist group:

> With many Marxists now agreeing ... that their arguments must be developed 'in such a way that their validity does not depend on any specifically Marxist assumptions' the way is now perhaps open for a fruitful dialogue on the subject.[76]

There are clear parallels between the club chair and the party organiser. Contrast Samuel's actions here with his own description of the role of the organiser: 'at congresses and aggregates [district organisers] would make the opening report and "sum up" at the end ... "little Gods",

---

76 Ibid.

descending on the branches from time to time to "galvanise" the members into activity'.[77] Ironically, whilst he sought to distance himself from the authoritarianism of the party or the exercises in 'moral cleansing' that other ex-communist intellectuals indulged in, he also re-enacted both the communist attitude and role that he had grown up with, aspired to and practised in his youth.

Cultural questions

Samuel's reaction to the events of 1956 had been to draw upon the form of politics most familiar to him: grassroots activism and organisation. Nevertheless, this was not a seamless shift but involved a considerable challenge to his existing political ideas. This section explores how he responded to this, with particular reference to his contribution to debates on culture and class consciousness.

In contrast to its counterpart the *NR* (which also launched in 1957), the *ULR* adopted a lighter, more exuberant tone. Its articles were typically shorter, the writing less dense and it contained much more visual imagery.[78] In its general presentation it bore more resemblance to a magazine format than the traditional, scholarly format of the *NR*.[79] Thompson was quick to assert the differences that he saw between the two journals. In a letter to Samuel written shortly after the first edition had appeared, he said:

> You see we cut different characters: *ULR* is mercurial, sensational, rides loose to theory & principle, goes for gimmicks and so on: all this is excellent, and the right way to break the crust especially with the younger people. The *NR* is middle aged & paunchy and strikes a note of political responsibility, and dogged deaf endurance.[80]

Whilst Thompson's comment implied the dangers of such eclecticism, the wide-ranging liveliness was indeed calculated to attract the broader, younger readership that Samuel coveted. One of the key differences between the two journals was the extent to which the *ULR* engaged with

---

77 Samuel, *The Lost World*, 122.
78 The second edition, for example, carried two photographic supplements: John Smith and Gordon Redfern, 'The Crisis in Town Planning'; Lindsay Armstrong, 'Free Cinema', *ULR*, 1, 2 (1957).
79 This would be reinforced in later editions when the *ULR* was printed on glossy paper.
80 E.P. Thompson to Ralph Samuel and Michael Barrett Brown, 6 February 1957, RS.1: New Left/002, '1957', RSA.

questions concerning the politics of culture and cultural change, an issue addressed through a close engagement with the work of Richard Hoggart and Raymond Williams.[81]

In his iconic book *The Uses of Literacy* (1957), Hoggart examined working-class consciousness and the impact of the mass media. Drawing on his own upbringing, he re-created a vivid portrayal of working-class life, presenting a largely pessimistic picture of a narrow, inward-looking world populated by a beleaguered people with a restrictive and intellectually limited cultural life. This depiction was not itself unique but distinctive in the link it made between sociolinguistic ability and conceptual capacity. Working-class culture did not simply reflect working-class sensibility, it also created it.[82]

The book went on to reflect on how this world had narrowed further as a result of exposure to forms of mass culture that exacerbated its worst aspects, such as shallowness and sensationalism. Assuming the mantle of the cultural critic, he decried mass culture's appeal to the basest of human instincts, typically sex and violence, and lamented the passivity of its consumption, used for short-term pleasure rather than intellectual stimulation. As he said in his concluding comments:

> Most mass-entertainments are in the end what DH Lawrence described as 'anti-life.' They are full of a corrupt brightness, of improper appeals and moral evasions … These productions belong to a vicarious spectator's world; they offer nothing which could really grip the brain or heart.[83]

Williams was also interested in contemporary cultural change but expressed a more optimistic view than Hoggart.[84] His book, *Culture and Society* (1958), was a literary history of the idea of culture as expressed by writers and critics from Edmund Burke and the eighteenth-century Romantic poets, through the rapidly industrialising society of the

---

81 *ULR* 2 carried a substantial engagement with *The Uses of Literacy* shortly after its publication in 1957. Raymond Williams became a frequent contributor to the journal, with five articles appearing across the seven editions that were published. See also Stefan Collini, 'Critical Minds: Raymond Williams and Richard Hoggart', in *English Pasts: Essays in History and Culture* (Oxford: Oxford University Press, 1999), 210–32.
82 See Stuart Hall, 'Richard Hoggart, *The Uses of Literacy* and the Cultural Turn', in Sue Owen, ed., *Richard Hoggart and Cultural Studies* (London: Palgrave Macmillan, 2008), 20–32.
83 Richard Hoggart, *The Uses of Literacy: Aspects of Working-class Life, with Special References to Publications and Entertainments* (London: Chatto and Windus, 1957), 277.
84 Whilst critical of his colleague on several points, Williams was also concerned to point out the parallels in their work and thought: 'The Uses of Literacy: Working Class Culture', *ULR*, 1, 2 (1957), 29–32.

nineteenth century, and concluding with the first half of the twentieth century, overshadowed by the threat and experiences of war. Williams teased out the tectonic shifts that had occurred in the general meaning of the word 'culture', from referring to the possession of a social elite, to identification with intellectuals or artists and, finally, moving towards a term denoting a 'whole way of life'. Like Hoggart, he acknowledged that culture did not merely reflect the world but was complicit in creating it.[85]

In the final section of the book, he too expressed concern about the mass-entertainment industry. Williams also felt intellectuals had an important educational contribution to make, not by exhorting one standard of cultural excellence over others but in fostering the development of a more diverse common culture. Only through 'conceding the practice of democracy', Williams reasoned, could the theory truly be substantiated.[86]

Williams and Hoggart both addressed the impact of cultural change on working-class consciousness. Their books raised strong concerns about the implications of mass culture in impoverishing popular intelligence, moral sensibility and political commitment. The extent to which the ideas of the two men were metabolised amongst the *ULR* contingent can be seen in the 'Sense of Classlessness' exchange that went straight to the core of some of the most critical issues confronting the New Left.

Hall prompted the debate, adapting the topic originally allocated to him by Samuel (on the contemporary British class structure). Taking the insights of Hoggart and Williams as his point of departure, Hall argued that changes to *ideas* of class as a distinctive social and political identity were informing far deeper structural transformations in modern British social and cultural life than either of the two men's analyses had fully appreciated.[87]

Work, he argued, had become an ever more fragmented process, whilst authority in the workplace concealed its claws more insidiously in the forms and language of 'scientific' management styles. The relationship

---

85 Raymond Williams, *Culture and Society 1780–1950* (London: Chatto and Windus, 1958). Williams resumed his study, situating it more deeply in the sociopolitical context of nineteenth-century industrialisation in *The Long Revolution* (London: Chatto and Windus, 1961). Both *Culture and Society* and *The Long Revolution* were criticised by Thompson for failing to take fuller account of the significance of *class* struggle in cultural change. E.P. Thompson, 'The Long Revolution I', *NLR*, I/9, May–Jun (1961), 24–33; 'The Long Revolution II', *NLR*, I/10, Jul–Aug (1961), 34–39.
86 Williams, *Culture and Society*, 341.
87 Stuart Hall, 'A Sense of Classlessness', *ULR*, 5 (1958), 26–31.

between workers and the objects produced had also changed as increased consumer power enabled the worker to consume the objects they had made. Whilst Hall acknowledged that owning bourgeois products did not in-itself translate directly into espousing bourgeois values, such patterns of acquisition took on and produced their own distinctive set of values. The objects transformed from their own intrinsic worth into so many potent symbols of social status; a proliferation of lifestyle choices.

This process was reinforced and perpetuated by powerful forces such as mass marketing and a media industry that worked on deep psychological levels to encourage individual expression through consumption, to manufacture desire as much as the objects of desire themselves:

> Every form of communication which is concerned with altering attitudes, which changes or confirms opinions, which instils new images of the self, is playing its part. They are not peripheral to the 'economic base', they are part of it.[88]

All these factors, Hall concluded, were acting to sever any sense of common working-class experience, vital to forging a common identity, and to make the worker complicit in their own permanent alienation.

The implications of Hall's argument were that working-class consciousness was shaped not only by physical labour processes but by the images and languages through which value and meaning were inscribed by the skilful manipulations of the mass media. What he suggested was that there were severe limitations in appealing towards 'traditional' forms of working-class solidarity as the critical site of political action. New (or at least thoroughly revised) analytical models and practical strategies for dealing with a highly distinctive form of capitalism were urgently required.

The following edition of the *ULR* (6) carried replies from Thompson and Samuel. Thompson, drawing on his favoured polemical mode, criticised what he saw as a lack of historical context in the making of such an argument. The working class was not, he asserted, a single, homogenous entity moving through time, space and place. The core of class identity was not defined by one particular set of social arrangements or material conditions but in terms of 'a whole way of struggle' which was multifarious and dynamic in nature.

---

88 Ibid., 31.

Thompson continued, upbraiding the 'young turks of the *ULR*' for treating the working class as a manipulated mass and for assuming the position of distant intellectuals peering down at the working class through so many mediating sociological theories. He urged that they rekindle their political commitment and 'bring to [the working class] hope, a sense of their own strength, and potential life'.[89] In short, Thompson proposed, it was solidarity and commitment, rather than explanation, which was really needed.

In his reply, 'Class and Classlessness', Samuel (clearly, according to Thompson's formula, an errant 'young turk') advanced a similar line to his former comrade. He questioned the sociological modelling that underpinned Hall's argument, arguing that it showed a selective, restrictive, view of working-class history.[90] The working classes, he argued, had always been subject to forces of persuasion, manipulation and the promise of mobility and affluence (where once religion had occupied the main pervasive and instructive role in working-class life, now the mass media assumed a similar one). Furthermore, for all the changes in the nature of work and industry, a brief survey of the personnel in upper echelons of company management (the majority of whom, at this time, still came from wealthy families, were educated at public schools and were graduates from Oxford or Cambridge universities) revealed the continuation of a clear class bias.[91] He concluded his article with the assertion that:

> Socialism must start from the existing strengths of working people, from their power to assimilate what is valuable and reject what is false in post-war society ... Socialism is not only ... a society for people – it is also a society that they will create.[92]

Underpinning this exchange were two different readings of history informing divergent views of what socialism, as a political position, really meant and what the role of the socialist intellectual should be. For Hall, the changes wrought by postwar capitalism implied a break with older forms of economic, political and social life. Such a break meant that the nature of class consciousness was fundamentally different to what it

---

89   E.P. Thompson, 'Commitment in Politics', *ULR*, 6 (1959), 55.
90   Ralph Samuel, 'Class and Classlessness', *ULR*, 6 (1959), 44–51.
91   He did, however, acknowledge an alarming trend towards viewing the boss as hero, an idea further developed in Samuel, 'The Boss as Hero', *ULR*, 7 (1959), 26–31.
92   Samuel, 'Class and Classlessness', 51.

had once been. The role of the contemporary socialist intellectual was, therefore, to identify and analyse these new forms and understand their internal dynamics.

In the eyes of the two former communists, aligned despite the generational divide, the new capitalism was not so distinct from the old.[93] Nor had it fundamentally transfigured the deeper structures of working-class culture which had never been a single or homogenous entity. At its core, the two men shared a view of class politics as primarily defined by struggle against oppression and domination. This struggle was not only concerned with acquiring equal conditions of material well-being but with the capacity to realise full emotional and intellectual potential through active participation in social life and decision-making. Both men drew upon history to show both the distinctiveness of this struggle as it manifested at different times in different conditions, but also, simultaneously, to demonstrate the continuity of its nature.

Whilst united in this view, on the role of the socialist intellectual the two men once again differed. In Thompson's vision, the intellectual should offer sustained critique, enduring solidarity and inspiration. For Samuel, this role was rooted even more directly amongst the people, working with them to create their society. In this sense at least, Samuel, whilst not necessarily sharing Williams' larger political or historical vision, *did* follow his call for intellectuals to 'concede the practice of democracy' in the learning process.

The Institute of Community Studies

Samuel's ideas were also reshaped outside of the immediate milieu of the first New Left. In 1958 he took a job as a researcher for the London-based Institute of Community Studies (ICS). The direct experience of 'on the ground' research work, in particular oral interviewing, was valuable in planting the seeds for his future work. At the same time, the institute's use of sociological modelling in service of social policy reinforced his scepticism towards sociology which he saw as reductive, giving an undue authority to the intellectual in determining its shape and meaning.

---

93   Samuel explored this idea more directly in: 'Bastard Capitalism', in E.P. Thompson, ed., *Out of Apathy* (London: New Left Books, 1960), arguing here for the parallels with what Rodney Hilton, fellow CPHG member and medieval historian, had once termed 'bastard feudalism'.

The ICS was officially established by Michael Young in 1953 as an independent, not-for-profit organisation.[94] During the Second World War and the immediate postwar years, Young had worked closely with government agencies and the Labour Party on social planning, an experience which left him disillusioned with party politics and in search of a more independent means of combining policy development with relevant research.[95]

Young combined forces with fellow researchers Peter Willmott, sociologist Peter Townsend and former psychology student Peter Marris.[96] An advisory board was formed, boasting an impressive array of figures from sociology including Richard Titmuss (Young's former doctoral supervisor at the London School of Economics), English sociologist-cum-anthropologist Geoffrey Gorer, American sociologist Edward Shils, and Charles Madge, formerly one of the architects behind the Mass Observation movement.[97]

The ICS set out to undertake original research into postwar social change and to chart the impact of social policies, with particular reference to the effect of these on working-class communities. One of the major features of postwar social planning was the clearance and redevelopment of inner-city slums and the relocation of families to newly built suburban settlements. One such area to be targeted was Bethnal Green in London's East End, a place of enduring fascination to social researchers including Beatrice and Sidney Webb. It was here that Young and Willmott focused the institute's first major study resulting in the publication of *Family and Kinship in East London* (1957).

The study was split into two, the first half concentrating on Bethnal Green, the second on Greenleigh, one of the new suburbs. The bulk of it drew on standard quantitative research methods; teams of researchers carrying out surveys covering a range of issues from family background, occupation and

---

94 A.H. Halsey, 'Young, Michael Dunlop, Baron Young of Dartington (1915–2002)', *Oxford Dictionary of National Biography* (Oxford: Oxford University Press, 2006).
95 Asa Briggs, *Michael Young: Social Entrepreneur* (London: Palgrave Macmillan Ltd, 2001), 110–54.
96 Michael Young, 'Willmott, Peter (1923–2000)', *Oxford Dictionary of National Biography* (Oxford: Oxford University Press, 2004); Howard Glennerster, 'Townsend, Peter Brereton (1928–2009)', *Oxford Dictionary of National Biography* (Oxford: Oxford University Press, 2004); Peter Townsend, 'Peter Marris', *The Guardian*, 5 July 2007.
97 See James Hinton, *The Mass Observers: A History 1937–1949* (Oxford: Oxford University Press, 2013).

household income to voting behaviour. What made *Family and Kinship in East London* more distinctive was its use of qualitative data including unstructured, open-ended interviews, which were carried out in person.[98]

As others before them, the two researchers were captivated by Bethnal Green, describing it as: 'encasing the history of three hundred years', with its 'gaunt buildings riding above narrow streets of narrow houses' where the 'cottages built for the descendants of Huguenot refugees stand next to Victorian red brick on one side and massive blocks of Edwardian charity on the other'. Streets cluttered with 'funny fading little pubs', 'street barrows piled high with fruit, fish and dresses' and 'tiny workshops squeezed into a thousand backyards'.[99] In this enchanting space of intersecting histories, what struck the researchers was the strength of familial and kinship connections which acted as a crucial means of survival. The book acknowledged the sense of emotional loss experienced by some on leaving for life in the new suburb.[100]

Family and Kinship in East London enjoyed a good public reception, even winning critical praise from Amis.[101] As a text it stood at a point of juncture. In part, it resumed an older English tradition of empirically informed social observation, as practised by figures like the Webbs.[102] At the same time, it reflected the growing popularity of social science writing and of sociology as the intellectual *mode de la jour*.[103] Either way, it introduced the institute as a dynamic force in British social research.[104] Further projects and books followed, including the ones that Samuel was employed as a researcher to work on.

---

98 Michael Young and Peter Willmott, 'Introduction', in *Family and Kinship in East London* (London: Routledge and Kegan Paul, 1957), 4. See also Peter Marris, 'Knowledge and Persuasion: Research at the ICS', in Geoff Dench, Tony Flower and Kate Gavron, eds, *Young at Eighty: The Prolific Public Life of Michael Young* (Manchester: Carcanet Press, 1995), 75.
99 Ibid., 97–98.
100 Whilst *Family and Kinship in East London* is often criticised for presenting a 'romantic' view of working-class community life and an overly negative view of the new suburbs, passages in the book did recognise the positive qualities offered by life in the new suburbs. Young and Willmott, *Family and Kinship*, 148.
101 Kingsley Amis, 'I Don't Like to be Old', *The Spectator*, 28 March 1958, 22.
102 This interpretation is posed in: Asa Briggs, 'Michael Young: The Last Victorian', in Briggs, *Michael Young*, 329–31.
103 Also suggested by the spread of sociology departments and research centres across British universities.
104 Sandbrook, *Never Had It So Good*, 182.

Samuel joined the institute following a talk by Willmott on 'The New London', given at the Soho branch of the New Left Club in late 1958. At first he responded to the research ethos and practices of the institute with enthusiasm (after this point he ceased to be listed as the New Left Club chairman, demonstrating the extent to which his energies were occupied with this new project).[105] It brought him back to the home of his maternal family, a place whose many histories were inscribed upon its streets.[106] In the early 1960s, Samuel, along with Marris, his colleague and close friend, acquired 19 Elder Street, Spitalfields, a modest terrace house in what had once been an eighteenth-century slum. This remained his home for the rest of his life.[107]

Along with his natural affinity with East London, the ICS's emphasis on oral interviews was attractive as they brought him into close contact with people whose lives were far removed from Oxford student life, or radical left-wing intellectualism. This work was mentally and emotionally tough but also exciting. Initially his role at the institute was as an interviewer working on the 'New Towns', another postwar initiative intended to relieve pressure on the inner cities and improve quality of life by creating purpose-built, self-contained settlements.

He first worked on Stevenage, which, despite opposition from the residents, became Britain's first New Town (under the *New Towns Act, 1946*). Six new neighbourhoods had been planned, four of which had been completed by 1953.[108] It was in these neighbourhoods that interviewers like Samuel were despatched, armed with in-depth questionnaires covering a range of issues such as household composition, distribution of roles within the household, occupations, political views and voting behaviours.[109]

---

105 Brian Harrison, 'Interview with Raphael Samuel', 23 October 1979, 19 Elder Street, London, transcripts held in Raphael Samuel Archive (RSA), Bishopsgate Institute, London; Brian Harrison, 'Interview with Raphael Samuel', 18 September 1987.
106 Alex May, 'Keal, Minna (1909–1999)', *Oxford Dictionary of National Biography* (Oxford: Oxford University Press, 2004).
107 Douglas Blain, 'Raphael Samuel', *The Spitalfields Trust Newsletter,* December 1996.
108 David Kynaston, *Modernity Britain: Opening the Box 1957–59* (London: Bloomsbury, 2013), 129.
109 Ralph Samuel, 'Stevenage Surveys and Notes', RS 1: New Left/ Institute of Community Studies, 301, 304, 306, RSA.

For the social researchers at the institute, the New Towns were a fascinating barometer of social change. They provided a unique insight into so-called working-class affluence. They also constituted rich case studies in community formation as individual family units began to inhabit the new purpose-built neighbourhoods and forge relationships amongst themselves, comparatively freer of the ties of necessity and tradition. What the researchers set out to discern was the impact of these changes on social identities. Samuel showed particular zeal for this project, conducting up to nine of these intensive questionnaire-interviews in one week.[110]

Another ICS project that he was involved with looked at adolescent boys in Bethnal Green. This project responded directly to a 1950s discourse on youth culture that, as argued by Dick Hebdige, oscillated between a celebration of teenage consumption as an economic driving force and concern for the paucity and violence of youth culture.[111] The project, officially headed by Willmott, started in 1959 and the research initially took the form of open-ended interviews; the fruit of cultivating close relationships with the study's subjects and the development of networks of connections. Later the boys were encouraged to keep personal diaries documenting their experiences and feelings.[112]

He carried out a huge quantity of research on this project, forging relationships with the interview subjects over a protracted period of time, coming to know the boys in question, winning their confidence and trust in order to encourage them to reveal more about the nature of their lives. Questions and topics ranged widely – from the boys' experiences of education and the workplace, to the intimate topographies of their social worlds, hopes, fears and dreams.[113]

---

110 Ibid., 301.
111 See Dick Hebdige, 'Hiding in the Light: Youth Surveillance and Display' and 'Towards a Cartography of Taste, 1935–1962', in *Hiding in the Light: On Images and Things* (Routledge: London 1988), 17–36, 45–76; Geoffrey Pearson, 'Falling Standards: A Short, Sharp History of Moral Decline', in Martin Barker, ed., *The Video Nasties: Freedom and Censorship in the Media* (London: The Works, 1984), 88–103.
112 Peter Willmott, 'Introduction', in *Adolescent Boys of East London* (London: Routledge & K. Paul, 1966), 6.
113 Ralph Samuel, 'Bethnal Green Youth Survey Interviews 1957–1962', RS 1: New Left/ Institute of Community Studies, 308, RSA.

His research notes from the project show the extent to which he utilised this form of close observation, immersion and empathy in attempting to understand both the personal dimensions of male adolescence, but also the ways in which those experiences were mediated by wider social contexts such as class, family and community relationships. A typical comment from his observations noted sympathetically 'wildness not roughness'.[114] He would later say that the research into juvenile delinquency had not been a good thing for him to be doing, perhaps referring to the turbulence of his own feelings at this time.[115]

The enthusiasm that he had initially felt at the institute's working methods and techniques soon gave way to some scepticism and critique. Some hint of this can be seen from the final published study, *Adolescent Boys of East London* (1966). Willmott's introduction to the study explained that whilst the project had begun heavily based in qualitative research, after five years (1964) it had become apparent that more quantitative data was required: 'at this stage, therefore, we had a good deal of impressionistic and illustrative material, but almost nothing in the way of statistical information', which had been conducted via formal questionnaire surveys carried out on a sample of 246 young men.[116]

The appendices at the back of the book give further insight into the nature of this second research phase. Appendix Four, for example, revealed how the responses of subjects to the questions posed were used to 'classify' them into social types. When asked their opinion concerning 'the reasonableness of rules' (no further context provided for the term rules), a 'middle class or working class' boy was expected to reply in the affirmative; that all, most or about half of rules were reasonable. A 'rebel', on the other hand, was expected to reply in the negative, feeling all or most rules to be unreasonable.[117] Subsequent pages detailed further the scales of social class or rebelliousness used by the researchers, revealing how factors including schooling, exams, work location, occupational class, friendship group, marital expectations and financial habits were used to determine a more precise definition of social class and attitudes.[118]

---

114 Ralph Samuel, 'Notes towards draft report', RS 1: New Left/ Institute of Community Studies, 309, RSA.
115 Brian Harrison, 'Interview with Raphael Samuel', 23 October 1979.
116 Willmott, 'Introduction', in *Adolescent Boys*, 14–20.
117 Willmott, 'Appendix Four', in *Adolescent Boys*, 212.
118 Ibid., 216.

The schematic nature of this approach stood at sharp variance with the unstructured, explorative and deeply personal nature of the interviews and relationships first cultivated by Samuel who, as Willmott acknowledged, had 'carried the main burden of the research' in its initial stages but had not been involved in the later stages, due to his taking up a teaching position at Ruskin College in 1962.[119] As the institute became more established as a research centre, the subjective, at times anecdotal, approach which had animated the pages of *Family and Kinship* came increasingly under pressure to become more 'rigorous' and scientific in order to be 'of use' in policy decisions.[120]

This was something that Samuel found unsatisfying, feeling that it lacked a wider sense of history or deeper understanding of human life.[121] He prepared a substantial collection of notes for Willmott, urging against too simplistic a view of working-class history:

> The image of the new 'open' society of the post-war world gains a deceptive strength from the comparison with the nineteenth century. Nineteenth century W.class – it is suggested – was depressed and immobile. The w.class way of life – from its formal institutions such as the Trades Unions to the informal solidarity of the streets, the Pub and the Club – was built up as a protection against the barbarism of the I.Revolution and the production system which treated men as things. I think this is partly true but there were other pressures too, in the society, which militated against the formation of W.C. community but which were overcome.[122]

Not only was he critical of the assumptions implied by sociological models, he was also uncomfortable about the uses of social research for policy decisions. Treating people by aggregates, as social entities to be arranged and positioned, gave to the sociologist a distance and authority over the subjects that he was uneasy with. In a draft report on the adolescent boys research, he put the case as follows:

> My conclusion is concerned not to make recommendation, but rather to underline the extreme limits of this kind of study. If it has any use it is rather to correct, to suggest how little we know … It seems to me

---

119 Willmott, 'Introduction', in *Adolescent Boys*, 6.
120 An internal 'philosophical debate' on the aim of the institute and nature of its research was prompted by Townsend, whose sociological training had been more formal than that of Young or even Willmott, as early as 1956. See Briggs, *Michael Young*, 146.
121 Brian Harrison, 'Interview with Raphael Samuel', 23 October 1979.
122 Ralph Samuel to Peter Willmott, 'Notes on Nineteenth Century Working Class', RS 1: New Left/Institute of Community Studies, correspondence 1957–1962, 308, RSA.

> the sociologist's role should be altogether more modest, and should be confined in the main to social enquiry, to finding out the facts that are readily available and without much change. Once you begin to quantify you assume a comparable weight and importance to opinions; and this you cannot do.[123]

In the same way that he had rejected a privileged role for the 'socialist intellectual', he also rejected the idea of the sociologist's authority to determine social policy based on their research.

Characteristically proactive, he set about undertaking his own research project into issues relating to working-class life and class consciousness. Recruiting youthful members of the London branch of the New Left Club to help him, he undertook his own studies of class and political consciousness in Bethnal Green.[124] His questionnaires relied upon qualitative interviewing techniques in which the interviewee was given free rein.[125]

The ICS was an important influence for Samuel. Firstly, the emphasis placed on the researcher being 'in the field', engaging with people as they found them, can certainly be seen translated into his later oral histories. Secondly, it reinforced in him a wariness of sociological modelling and the dangers of presenting an overly homogenised view of the working class, drawing on restrictive assumptions of history and leading to an overly emphatic assertion of the changes brought about by increased working-class affluence.

It also underlined his dislike of the authority that the sociologist assumed when constructing data for political purposes. A new society, he insisted, could not be imposed from above, built on the findings of selective sociological research, insensitive to difference and nuance. It had to be one that working-class people were active participants in the making of.

---

123 Ralph Samuel, 'Notes towards Bethnal Green Youth Survey', RS 1: New Left/Institute of Community Studies, Bethnal Green Youth Survey draft report, 309, RSA. He expanded on his critique of sociology in a draft article: Ralph Samuel, 'The Vanity of Measurements (c.1961)', RS 1: New Left/Institute of Community Studies, 1959–1960, 302, RSA. For further discussion on these issues see: Jon Lawrence, 'Social-Science Encounters and the Negotiation of Difference in 1960s England', *HWJ*, 77 (2014), 215–39. Lawrence discusses the social research interview in terms of 'performance'. He examines how the researchers' cultural backgrounds and the assumptions made about working class and affluence influenced their role of the 'performance', in turn impacting upon that of the interview subjects.
124 Robin Blackburn, 'Raphael Samuel: The Politics of Thick Description', *NLR*, I/221, Jan–Feb (1997), 133–38. Robin Blackburn would later become the editor of the *NLR* (1981–99).
125 Ibid.

Socialism: A way of thinking about people?

In 1959, troubled by financial pressures, the *ULR* and the *NR* combined to form the *New Left Review* (*NLR*) which was intended to consolidate and continue on with the New Left project. Far from allaying the tensions, the merge exacerbated them. From the outset there was conflict over the choice of editor. Thompson seemed the obvious choice, but he was unwilling.[126] In the end, Hall took on the role, despite his relative youth and inexperience with the complexities of the English labour movement. He quickly found himself in an impossible position, under pressure from all sides. Some called for him to use the journal as the basis to develop a more concerted political infrastructure of the New Left movement whilst others were equally passionate in their opposition to this proposition.[127]

Despite the pressures attendant on its young editor, the journal made its debut appearance early in 1960. The first edition, appearing in the wake of the Labour Party's third successive electoral defeat in the 1959 election, addressed itself largely to the questions posed by the party's unpopularity. Whilst several of the contributors concentrated on the official institutions of the labour movement and the party itself, Samuel considered the question from the ground, confronting directly that perplexing phenomenon of the working-class Tory voter and asking why a substantial proportion of the working class voted Conservative.[128] The Labour Party's own review of the election had offered one answer: 'we were defeated by prosperity: this was without doubt the prominent factor'.[129] Samuel, however, proposed another.

Drawing on material garnered through his interviewing work in Stevenage, he based his investigation on a close reading of direct quotations from his subjects. From these he gleaned two key insights. Firstly, that the working-class Tory voter was not necessarily a middle-class aspirant. Many (the majority in his findings) voted as self-identified members of the working class, expressing this through comments such as: 'The Conservative Party is the gentleman's party. They're the people who have

---

126 Samuel was also considered to be a good choice but the chaos that generally accompanied his endeavours placed him out of contention. Stuart Hall, oral communication with author, May 2012.
127 Ibid.
128 Ralph Miliband, 'The Sickness of Labourism', *NLR*, I/1, Jan–Feb (1960), 5–9; Mervyn Jones, 'The Man from Labour', *NLR*, I/1, Jan–Feb (1960), 14–17.
129 Quoted in Kevin Jeffreys, *Retreat from New Jerusalem: British Politics 1951–64* (New York: St Martin's Press, 1997), 82.

got the money. I always vote for them. I am only a working man and they're my guv'nors'; or 'They have done a lot for the working people. A few years ago I would have said that they stood for themselves – making money and getting rich. But now they're certainly looking out for us'.[130]

Secondly, and related to the first insight, he suggested that far from a sense of contemporary affluence, the crucial factor was a sense *of the past*: 'The Conservatives have had more experience over the centuries. It's in the blood for them, running the country'.[131]

He concluded his article by appealing to Labour, and to socialists in general, to take more seriously this prevailing view of British history, and (much as Dimitrov had done 25 years earlier) pressed the need for 'an equally imposing alternative presence to that of the governing class, with an equally compelling, but socialist view of the way this country can live'.[132]

A second article, appearing later that year, reiterated his critique of sociological methodology. In this instance, his target was market researcher and sociologist Mark Abrams, the author of a series of articles, 'Why Labour Has Lost Elections?'[133] Based on the results of his 'comprehensive' surveying, Abrams argued that just as working-class homes were being transformed by material goods, so even manual workers were turning into middle-class conservatives. Young people in particular, he contended, were likely to identify with the Conservatives who they felt represented 'skilled craftsmen, middle-class people, forward-looking people, ambitious people, office workers and scientists'.[134] Since prosperity was expected to last well into the sixties, Labour, it seemed, had no choice but to reinvent itself for the age of affluence or be condemned to political oblivion.

---

130 Ralph Samuel, 'The Deference Voter', *NLR*, I/1, Jan–Feb (1960), 9–13.
131 Ibid., 13
132 Ibid.
133 The articles were initially run across four editions of *Socialist Commentary*. They later appeared as a book: Mark Abrams and Richard Rose, *Must Labour Lose?* (Harmondsworth: Penguin, 1961). The book is the source reference used here.
134 Abrams and Rose, *Must Labour Lose?*, 42–43.

His reply, 'Dr Abrams and the End of Politics', took pride of place as the lead article (it was his longest piece of published political writing). It differed from the style of his previous contributions in its open anger.[135] Abrams's survey, he fumed:

> does not tell us anything new about the reasons for Labour's defeat, nor does a close reading support its claim to offer a 'reliable understanding of contemporary British political loyalties.' Its importance lies rather in the underlying approach to man and politics it reveals and which, in turn, it supports.[136]

He proceeded to unveil the sociologist's 'box of tricks' (drawing here on his first-hand experiences with the institute), exposing the unseen processes behind the selection of samples and the framing of questions:

> Dr Abrams is probably right to suggest that had he used a much larger sample his results would not have been very different. It is not only his remarkable dexterity in handling statistics which makes one suspect that, whatever they had shown his conclusions would hardly have altered. It is also that many of the 'answers' were plainly determined by the questions themselves.[137]

Not only this, he contended, but the application of sociological formula and models to those answers also reconfigured their original meanings:

> Ted and Mods, Beatniks and Ravers, Aldermaston Marchers and Nuclear Campaigns, they all disappear amidst the whirrings of his Hollerith Machines, to reemerge, on his Punch Cards, an almost undifferentiated mass whose principal 'identification' is with 'middle class progressive optimists.'(!)[138]

What Abrams claimed to be a general trend or pattern was, Samuel proposed, little more than a carefully constructed *appearance* of one.

---

135 Ralph Samuel, 'Dr Abrams and the End of Politics', *NLR*, I/5, Sep–Oct (1960), 1–8. So striking is the difference from the general tone of his earlier pieces, I have found it worth quoting at some length.
136 Ibid., 1.
137 Ibid., 5.
138 Ibid., 4.

His concluding remarks set out his own perspective with clarity:

> If the Labour Movement were finally to abandon its traditional way of thinking about people – and that alone is truly fundamental – to lose its faith in the power of the word to move people, and of the idea to change them, if it were to let go its conviction in the capacity of human beings rationally to choose between the alternatives which face them, and purposefully to re-shape the society in which they live, then it would be finished and would find itself trapped in that limbo of the political imagination whose features Dr Abrams has so meticulously outlined.[139]

Whether or not labour history could fully bear out the claim of a 'traditional way of thinking about people' (his later investigations in this area would suggest it could not), the sentiment reveals the nature of Samuel's socialism as an ethical position animated by a faith in people as creative actors and ideas as active agents of change (Abrams might have smiled at this, and promptly filed its author under 'middle-class progressive optimist').

Quite likely the spirited anger of the 'End of Politics' article was provoked by more than just Abrams's dismal view of human nature. Even as the fledgling *NLR* proclaimed a continuation and revitalisation of New Left discussion, the New Left, as a movement, was losing momentum. Membership of the clubs dwindled; the impetus provided by the relationship with the Campaign for Nuclear Disarmament began to subside as fears of the immediate threat of nuclear warfare were abated.

In 1961 internal tensions grew too great for Hall and he resigned as editor. Samuel took control of editing the journal for one edition. This arrived very late, far too big but extremely impressive, covering a range of issues including: a thorough examination of social housing; discussions on film and literature; and, of course, a reprinting of an old classic, 'On the Puritan Character', an excerpt from Tawney's *Religion and the Rise of Capitalism* (1926).[140] It was, however, to be the last journal produced by those ostensibly from the first New Left group. In 1963 the young

---

139 Ibid., 8.
140 *NLR*, Jan–Apr (1962). The *NLR* is usually published bimonthly, *not* quarterly. R.H. Tawney was a personal hero and Tawney's *Religion and the Rise of Capitalism* an old favourite from his youthful history reading. Brian Harrison, 'Interview with Raphael Samuel', 18 September 1987.

historian and Marxist political theorist Perry Anderson assumed full editorship (in circumstances that Thompson would later describe darkly in terms of a hostile take-over), quickly asserting his intention to take the journal in a more explicitly theoretical direction.[141]

Samuel, weary of the interminable disputes that preoccupied the New Left and appalled by the Labour Party's pursuit of modernisation, removed himself to Ireland (which he considered to be the least afflicted by modernisation), where he attempted to write history and poetry but mostly, due to an inability to find work, starved.[142] During this time, worn down by frustration, disenchantment and hunger, he suffered from a severe depressive episode.

For Samuel the period of the first New Left was a bewildering time in his life, but this trauma had not been entirely inhibitive. It provided him with a critical and creative basis upon which to lay the foundation stones for his later ideas and practices of history. His reaction to the breakdown of his commitment to the CPGB was complex. It did not constitute a complete break from the values of communism, but at the same time he came to recognise and reject the authoritarianism inherent in Stalinist versions of Marxist thought. This hostility towards political authoritarianism, in all its guises, was reflected in the force of his reaction against quantitative sociology and his increasing insistence on human agency.

It was also during this time that the real core of his political project was given a more conscious form of expression: a form of direct democracy, realised via a common participatory culture, created by people, guided and assisted, but not *instructed*, by intellectuals. For Samuel, such a role for the socialist intellectual did not generally involve dense pages of philosophical or moral debate in a journal; it was always focused around practical enterprises or initiatives to create spaces in which to extend and expand political conversation. The *ULR*, the Partisan Café and the New Left clubs were some examples of his attempts to create this sort of space. The HW would be another.

---

141 E.P. Thompson, 'The Peculiarities of the English', *The Socialist Register*, 2 (1965); Perry Anderson, 'Components of the National Culture', *NLR*, I/50, Jul–Aug (1968), 3–57.
142 Hall, 'Raphael Samuel: 1934–1996'; Brian Harrison, 'Interview with Raphael Samuel', 23 October 1979.

3

The Workshop Historian: Ruskin College and the Early Years of the History Workshop

It is rare to hear of a history conference being described as a 'festival of history' or a 'carnival of scholarship', but these are exactly the phrases used to convey a sense of the atmosphere of a History Workshop (HW) meeting.[1] By the late 1960s these Workshops were attracting all the tribes of socialism, along with various of their kin or 'fellow travellers': young and old, students, activists, amateur enthusiasts, all descending upon and crowding into Ruskin College's Buxton Hall.[2] The HW's makeshift, make-do and do-it-yourself charm were made all the more potent against the stern gothic grandeur of its Oxford surroundings.

Established historians and graduate students stood side by side with Ruskin students delivering papers that delved into the suffering and struggling, the dismay and defiance of working-class lives. These papers drew not only from archival research but also from oral testimonies. Sometimes they even broke out of the comfort of the hall and meeting room to take living history walks around the ancient city they found themselves in. They celebrated the pasts inscribed onto human minds, bodies and environments. Beyond the papers themselves, the Workshops were opportunities for animated debate, socialising, films and folk music,

---

1   Raphael Samuel, 'Editorial Introduction', in Samuel, ed., *History Workshop: A Collectanea 1967–1991* (Oxford: HW 25, 1991), iii; Colin Ward, 'Fringe Benefits', *New Society*, 17 November 1989.
2   Workshops were held at Ruskin College's Walton Street, Oxford, location during this time.

reunions and new encounters.³ What was lacking in elegant catering arrangements was made up for in passion, of which there was no shortage, both in its political and personal guises.⁴ Acts of unity and solidarity abounded in all possible forms.⁵

Central to this action was the lean figure of Raphael Samuel dashing about, seemingly everywhere, his trademark dark hair in a state of perpetual disarray as he seamlessly switched from supportive tutor to event organiser to coparticipant, talking avidly all the while. This was Samuel in his element and at the height of his powers, revelling in the dynamic atmosphere, the intense discussions, the converging of politics with history and personal conviction. The liveliness and dynamism of these events gave him purpose and energy, quite different from the forlorn and half-starved figure that arrived at Ruskin in late 1962.

Like the New Left, the HW is also subject to various interpretive incarnations. Alongside Samuel's own accounts of its genesis and development, discussion has ranged in the assessments offered: from those who view it as a key crucible for the development of cultural history or as a model of emancipatory pedagogic practice to those critics who perceived in its political-intellectual orientation limitations which were both fostered and exacerbated by its militant populism.⁶

---

3   Raphael Samuel, 'Afterword', in Samuel, ed., *People's History and Socialist Theory* (London: Routledge and Kegan Paul, 1981), 411.
4   Anna Davin, 'The Only Problem Was Time', *History Workshop Journal (HWJ)*, 50 (2000), 239–45.
5   Sheila Rowbotham, 'Remembering 1967', in Samuel, ed., *History Workshop: A Collectanea 1967–1991*, 3.
6   See Raphael Samuel, 'Afterword: History Workshop 1966–1980', in Samuel, ed., *People's History and Socialist Theory*, 410–17; Samuel, *History Workshop: A Collectanea 1967–1991*. For a discussion of the HW in conjunction with the development of cultural history see: Gareth Stedman Jones, 'Obituary: Raphael Samuel', *The Independent*, 11 December 1996; David Feldman and Jon Lawrence, 'Introduction: Structures and Transformations in British Historiography', in Feldman and Lawrence, eds, *Structures and Transformations in Modern British History: Essays for Gareth Stedman Jones* (Cambridge: Cambridge University Press, 2011), 11. For discussions of the HW in relation to radical pedagogical practice and traditions of workers' education see: Hilda Kean, 'Public History and Raphael Samuel: A Forgotten Radical Pedagogy?', *Public History Review*, 11 (2004), 51–62; Hilda Kean, 'People, Historians and Public History; De-mystifying the Process of History Making', *Public Historian*, 32, 3 (2010), 25–38; Kynan Gentry, 'Ruskin, Radicalism and Raphael Samuel: Politics, Pedagogy and the Origins of the History Workshop', *HWJ*, 76 (2013), 187–211. For critical reviews of the HW see: David Selbourne, 'On the Methods of the History Workshop', *HWJ*, 9 (1980), 150–61; Harvey Kaye, *The Education of Desire: Marxists and the Writing of History* (London: Routledge, 1992), 122; Dennis Dworkin, *Cultural Marxism in Postwar Britain: History, the New Left, and the Origins of Cultural Studies* (Durham and London: Duke University Press, 1997). These are discussed in more detail above, 'Introduction', 1–3. For other personal memoirs of the HW see: Rowbotham, 'Remembering 1967', 1–6; James R. Green,

3. THE WORKSHOP HISTORIAN

Looking back in later years, Bill Schwarz, a former workshopper, explained this profusion of opinion by arguing that the early Workshop had encompassed three distinctive historical-political 'moments' which he characterised as 1935 (Popular Front), 1956 (New Left) and 1968 (Countercultural Revolution). He defined these 'moments' in reference to their positioning of class as the critical political category of focus. The first, 1935, viewed an alternative or popular history as one firmly embedded within a framework of the labour movement and workers' history. The second, 1956, adapted this by offering a more expansive view of class, sensitive to questions concerning working-class consciousness and its expression through cultural form. The third, 1968, signalled a move towards the decentralisation of class in favour of a more diffuse range of political-cultural identities (such as gender, race or sexuality). Whilst compatible on many points, Schwarz argued that these 'moments' contained fundamental differences in their respective political and intellectual agendas generating conflict in later years.[7]

Whilst Schwarz is right to identify distinctive political and conceptual strands active within the HW, these were far from being clearly defined. The boundaries between them were porous and fluid, reflective of the eclecticism characteristic of the times more generally. For the political left, the late 1960s contained a curious mixture of confidence and confusion.[8] A resurgence of enthusiasm for Marxism coexisted with renewed interest in anarchist and libertarian traditions in which the creative individual and the 'organic community' were extolled over the planned society.[9]

Taking History to Heart: The Power of the Past in Building Social Movements (Boston: University of Massachusetts Press, 2000), 53; John R. Gillis, 'Detours', in James Banner Jr and John R. Gillis, eds, *Becoming Historians* (Chicago: Chicago University Press, 2009), 163.
7   Bill Schwarz, 'History on the Move: Reflections on History Workshop', *Radical History Review*, 57 (2002), 202–20.
8   Sheila Rowbotham, *Promises of a Dream: Remembering the Sixties* (London: Penguin, 2000). For other memoirs see: Bernard Levin, *The Pendulum Years: Britain and the Sixties* (London: Jonathan Cape, 1970); Jenny Diski, *The Sixties* (London: Profile, 2009). For an oral history reflecting on personal experiences of being young in the sixties see: Jonathan Green, *All Dressed Up: The Sixties and the Counterculture* (London: Pimlico, 1998). For broader contextual accounts of the 1960s see also: Arthur Marwick, *The Sixties: Cultural Revolution in Britain, France, Italy and the United States 1958–1974* (Oxford: Oxford University Press, 1998); Dominic Sandbrook, *White Heat: A History of Britain in the Swinging Sixties* (London: Little Brown, 2006). For analysis of 1960s politics see: Martin Klimke and Joachim Scharloth, eds, *1968 in Europe: A History of Protest and Activism 1956–1977* (London: Palgrave Macmillan, 2008); Geoff Eley, 'Future Imperfect', in *Forging Democracy: The History of the Left in Europe 1850–2000* (Oxford: Oxford University Press, 2000).
9   Samuel H. Beer, *Britain against Itself: The Political Contradictions of Collectivism* (New York: Norton, 1982); Harold Perkins, 'The Backlash against Professional Society', in *The Rise of the Professional Society* (New York and London: Routledge, 1989), 472; Meredith Veldman, *Fantasy,*

Equally, a surge in union militancy found itself both in and out of step with a proliferation of social movements for whom it was not class but gender, race, sexuality or the environment that occupied the central focus. Underpinning all of these diverse and disparate forms was a shared sense of optimism and faith that the world should and could be remade, that history could be rewritten and the silenced be allowed to speak. The HW, acting as a catch-all for all these contending strands, served as both product and producer of that hope.

Despite the variety of interpretations on hand concerning the HW's approach to history, on one factor all accounts are agreed and that is the centrality of Samuel in its creation and early years. Curiously, whilst this is everywhere acknowledged, it is nowhere closely examined. The focus of this chapter is to analyse more thoroughly the role that Samuel took in setting up the HW and the nature of his relationship to it. It contends that, to some extent, he moved across all three of Schwarz's political 'moments' and that the HW's underlying agenda – to expand the use of history as critical political tool – was also continuous with his earlier activities. This view further reinforces the importance of the biographical approach in understanding Samuel as a historian. In setting up and running the HW in its early form, he drew on the cues from his communist childhood, the ethos inspired by the Popular Front and the skills and behavioural practices required for the communist organiser in conjunction with his more recent experiences as a New Left activist. He proceeded to use and adapt these in close dialogue with the political atmosphere of the time as it manifested through the particular context of Ruskin College, Oxford.

The Ruskin tutor

Samuel was very reluctant to take a full-time job at Ruskin College. He did not take it out of idealistic zeal and desire to educate adult workers alone, but out of necessity. After the break-up of the first New Left he had fled to Ireland, despairing of Labour leader Harold Wilson's modernisation program. Whilst there, he had attempted to write some poetry and do some historical research but unable to find work had returned to England

the Bomb and the Greening of Britain (Cambridge: Cambridge University Press, 1994); John Burrows, 'Avantgarde', in *The Crisis of Reason: European Thought 1848–1914* (New Haven: Yale University Press, 2000), 234–53; Michael Löwy and Robert Sayre, with Catherine Porter, tr., *Romanticism against the Tide of Modernity* (Durham: Duke University Press, 2001).

quite literally starving. Once back in Oxford, he suffered from severe depression. Emotionally, physically and intellectually, he was at a very low ebb. His old comrade and mentor Christopher Hill had tried to help him find teaching work but in a show of bravado, he cancelled the interview.[10]

Eventually, he took a position as tutor in labour history and sociology at the trade union affiliated, adult education focused Ruskin College, Oxford, but even so he did this reluctantly with a sense of trepidation. This was a point in his life when he was deeply vulnerable, disappointed and disillusioned. Later he would say that by 1963 he was 'psychologically no longer a Marxist' and that during this period he became 'quite influenced by libertarianism, anarchism and self-management' and that he continued to foster 'a deep suspicion of any kind of political leadership'.[11] Nevertheless, there was still no simple straight line away or clean break from his earlier communist commitments.

Politically in a state of flux, Samuel was a man in search of something to believe in. It was his location at Ruskin, his position as an adult education tutor and the comradeship of Ruskin students that provided relief. He later spoke of:

> [being] enormously helped by the students there and really responding enormously to them, both intellectually and politically, because then for the first time since I left the Communist Party I could kind of see what political work should be about.[12]

This revived sense of purpose ultimately found expression in the HW.

His early students at Ruskin were predominantly, although not entirely, older men drawn directly from the unions and the labour movement, often with various kinds of hard physical labour under their belts, experiences which had shaped both their bodies and also their minds. One had, for example, wrestled and jostled with cattle for 30 years; another had 20 years of experience working on the railways.[13] Most had come to Ruskin

---

10   Brian Harrison, Interview with Raphael Samuel, 23 October 1979, 19 Elder Street, London, transcripts held in Raphael Samuel Archive (RSA), Bishopsgate Institute, London.
11   Brian Harrison, 'Interview with Raphael Samuel', 18 September 1987, 19 Elder Street, London, transcripts held in RSA, Bishopsgate Institute, London.
12   Brian Harrison, 'Interview with Raphael Samuel', 23 October 1979.
13   Raphael Samuel, 'Ruskin Historians', in Samuel, ed., *History Workshop: A Collectanea 1967–1991*, 67–70.

via various union-funded schemes. Some were involved in union politics, or aspired to be. Others were not so overtly politicised, but all of them had come to Ruskin with expectations to learn.

Despite these intentions, many of the students harboured misgivings. Many had not stepped foot in a classroom for years, and the memories still rankled from the last time they had. Teachers were figures of authority, much like the overseer or the boss, who seemed more preoccupied with belittling or controlling them.[14] What they had been forced to learn before had meant little to their lives. They were not always comfortable with reading or writing; not many of them did these things for pleasure. As a result, learning could be a fractious and highly sensitive process, one in which defensiveness masking wounded pride could be roused at the merest suggestion of condescension. Britain in the 1960s was still a place where social class retained a stranglehold on hopes and ambitions. The students came to Ruskin College, and sat defiantly amidst the splendour of the ancient colleges of Oxford University, because it was *their* college, sensitive to *their* needs. Or, at least, it was supposed to be.

As an institution, Ruskin College occupied a unique position in the history of adult education in England. Founded in 1899 by Americans Charles Beard and Walter and Amne Vrooman, it was named for the Victorian art critic and educator John Ruskin (1819–1900) whose philosophy of 'purposeful education', learning that was suitable and meaningful to an individual's situation in life, was taken as its primary ethos.[15] Conceived as an independent venture (not directly attached to an existing educational institutional or body), it was purposely designed as a working-class institution with the express intention 'to educate working men in order to achieve social change'. This did not mean providing working-class students with a means of ascending the social ladder through education but, in keeping with its namesake's ideals, equipping that class with its own thinkers and leaders, drawn from amongst its own communities. As Vrooman expressed it: 'knowledge must be used to

---

14   Dave Douglass, oral communication with author, December 2011, Newcastle, recording held in author's collection; John Prescott, 'Genuine Love for Others', *The Guardian*, 11 December 1996.
15   For more on Ruskin's ideas on education see: Sara E. Atwood, *Ruskin's Educational Ideals* (Surrey: Ashgate Publishing Ltd, 2011).

emancipate humanity, not to gratify curiosity, blind instincts and desire for respectability'.[16] Accordingly, the proposed subjects of study were specifically selected to:

> guide students in gaining the knowledge which is essential for intelligent citizenship to give them a conception of the forces of the past which have contributed to the making of modern civilization; to acquaint them with the social organism of which they are a part, with the political machinery of the English speaking nations, and to inspire them with a hope for still greater achievements by mankind along rational lines.[17]

These illustrious topics, upon which so much rested, included History (with courses on English Constitutional and Political History, the History of Christianity and American History with a separate course on English Biography), Philosophy (including a course on Comparative Religions), Literature and Art (Historical Novels), Political Science (Present Day Institutions, Industrial History, Sociology, Political Economy, Political Machinery of England and America) and Science (including Psychology and Sociology). In his later years, Beard, reflecting on the optimistic idealism that had propelled the initial venture, came to the view that it had been unrealistic to expect students, on completion of their studies, to return to their working-class lives rather than using their education to pursue their own individual ambitions.[18]

Ruskin's political and educational project did not go uncontested. In 1908, a conflict erupted following the publication of a report written by a group of Oxford academics outlining a proposal to enable Ruskin students to study for and sit Oxford Diplomas. In the eyes of the authors, this was a means of opening up Oxford University to working-class students, but for some amongst the Ruskin student body it represented an insidious attempt at neutralising or subduing the critical dimension of working-class education.[19]

---

16 Harold Pollins, *The History of Ruskin College* (Oxford: Ruskin College Library Publication, no. 3, 1984), 9–27.
17 'Short Prospectus of Courses of Instruction at Ruskin Hall, Oxford, 1899', RS 1: New Left/Ruskin College, 401, RSA, Bishopsgate Institute, London.
18   Ellen Nore, *Charles A. Beard, An Intellectual Biography* (Carbondale: Southern Illinois University Press, 1983).
19   See Lawrence Goldman, *Dons and Workers: Oxford and Adult Education since 1850* (Oxford: Clarendon Press, 1995), chapter 5; Jonathan Rose, 'The Whole Contention Concerning the Workers' Educational Society', in *The Intellectual Life of the British Working Classes* (New Haven: London: Yale University Press, 2001), 256–97. For an alternative account see Roger Fieldhouse, 'The 1908 Report: Antidote to Class Struggle?', in Geoff Andrews, Hilda Kean and Jane Thompson, eds, *Ruskin College: Contesting Knowledge, Dissenting Politics* (London: Lawrence and Wishart, 1999), 35–58.

A group rebelled, forming the 'Plebs League' and running their own classes based around the principles of Marxist political-economy, enthusiastically supported by the Ruskin principal Dennis Hird who lost his job (or was 'encouraged into early retirement') as a result. The governors responded by closing down the college for two weeks and then reopening its doors to students who agreed to abide by its regulations, prompting a number of the rebellious students to break away altogether and set up the Central Labour College, which ran until 1929.[20]

It was this spirit and these *principles* of independent working-class education and the sense of solidarity, of confidence, that it fostered in the worker students that inspired the young Oxford-educated former Communist tutor. Samuel was naturally captivated by Ruskin's history, carrying out substantial personal research into the college's history and the life stories of its early former students. The points that he felt to be particularly salient he picked out in a document entitled: 'Emphases one could bring into "The Story of Ruskin College" if one had time, inclination or felt them to be important'. These emphases included:

1. More stress on the founders' aims. One can get a feel for these aims by consulting: the principal's scrap-book of early press cuttings, the Oxford Chronicle's account of Vrooman's inaugural speech, early issues of Young Oxford.
2. Vrooman's ambivalent attitude to the university and academic standards. Scholarship applied to worthwhile practical ends was OK but the barren academic life was to be shunned. Seemed to fear possible effects of bringing working-men to Oxford. But also hoped the founding of Ruskin would bring a revolutionary resurgence to 'young Oxford' (hence title of the early magazine).
3. More stress on early combination of a strong sense of social purpose (college to train future leaders of working-class movement) plus adherence to non-doctrinal methods of teaching the social sciences. In this combination lay the seeds of the later strike depending on which was emphasised to the detriment of the other. Hird was all social purpose. Lees-Smith all liberal non-doctrinal education.
4. More stress on early days of Ruskin Hall as centre of Ruskin Hall movement.[21]

---

20 For a fuller account of this see: B. Jennings, 'Revolting Students: The Ruskin College Dispute 1908–9', *Studies in Adult Education*, 9, 1 (1977), 1–16.
21 Raphael Samuel, 'History of Ruskin College', RS 1: New Left/Ruskin College, other Oxford institutions and interests, 401, RSA. Ruskin Hall was the original name for Ruskin College.

The list continued further in the same vein. It is worth noting Samuel's interest in Vrooman rather than Beard. His notes further imply that he saw Vrooman as the more articulate on Ruskin's social purpose whilst Beard, the academic historian responsible for the composition of the curriculum, assumed the more dubious role of ensuring the 'liberal non-doctrinal' content.

Working as a Ruskin tutor was compatible with the earlier roles and political sentiments that had attracted Samuel as a younger man. The organiser, drawn from the rank and file of party membership and distinguished by their self-taught scholarly commitment and intellectual prowess, had pronounced parallels with the role of the adult educator. As he would later comment, demonstrating his own sensitivity to the connections between the organiser and educator: 'Recruiting – the only Party activity I was any good at – involved, I now realize, a tutor-pupil relationship, not least in its elaborate pretence of equality between the teacher and the taught'.[22]

Accounts from his former students suggest that he enjoyed considerable popularity as a tutor, and was remembered fondly for his eccentricities such as falling asleep whilst invigilating exams, or giving impromptu tutorials on a train.[23] More seriously, he was also renowned for his considerable skills as a teacher. Dave Douglass (at Ruskin from 1966 to 1971) recalled that: '[N]obody had ever succeeded in getting me to work in the way he did. Raph was able to prise out of me things I didn't know were there'.[24] A trait further acknowledged by his close friend Gareth Stedman Jones who noted that 'he led people on journeys of creative self-discovery by blowing away the walls which separated working people from literary culture'.[25]

His political background and general persona carried an air of radical glamour about it, which even translated into his physical appearance. One poetic account described him as follows:

---

22   Raphael Samuel, *The Lost World of British Communism* (London: Verso, 2006), 195.
23   Oral and written communications with author, 2011–12, recordings and transcripts held in author's private collection.
24   Dave Douglass, 'Ruskin Remembered', *Tributes to Raphael Samuel*, held at the Bishopsgate Institute, London.
25   Stedman Jones, 'Obituary: Raphael Samuel'. As a colleague, however, he was less popular, due to an uncanny ability to get out of tedious administrative responsibilities.

> [H]is long wildly straying hair and his narrow eager face were perfectly right for his fervent, restless personality ... In later years he was described as looking like a 1960s character, but perhaps he was more like a Bohemian of the era of Baudelaire.[26]

In addition to this, Samuel could be a charismatic speaker and compelling performer, with an extremely idiosyncratic lecture style. His papers were typically unscripted, with little regard for the formalities of time keeping, involving piles of notes and sources piled precariously by his side.[27] They were delivered with ardent passion; at their best, his oratorical talents were unsurpassed, matched only by E.P. Thompson.[28] American historian John Gillis recalled his time as a visiting graduate student in Oxford during the 1960s where he heard Samuel and Thompson speak: 'For the first time, I felt myself connected to history, moved to draw on my own experience to illuminate the generational relations that had become increasingly problematic in the 1960s'.[29]

On other occasions, however, his gifts as a speaker could fail him and he could miss the mark entirely. As former workshopper Sheila Rowbotham remembered:

> I went to hear Raphael again soon after, anticipating another tour de force. It didn't happen. This time he didn't pull it off. He spoke on Tawney but somehow lost the thread and simply rambled.[30]

Samuel treated his students seriously, showing great respect for and an inexhaustible interest in their lives and backgrounds.[31] As former Ruskin student John Prescott (1963–65) (later British Deputy Prime Minister) reflected:

---

26   Mervyn Jones, 'Raphael Samuel', *The Times*, 11 December 1996.
27   Chimen Abramsky, 'Raphael Samuel', *The Jewish Chronicle*, 17 January 1997; Bill Schwarz, 'Keeper of Our Shared Memory', *The Guardian*, 10 December 1996; Stuart Hall, 'Raphael Samuel: 1934–1996', *New Left Review* (*NLR*), I/221, Jan–Feb (1997), 119–27.
28   A lecture on the Irish famine was particularly exemplary of his prowess as a speaker. Noted by Shelia Rowbotham, 'Some Memories of Raphael', *NLR*, I/221, Jan–Feb (1997), 128–32. See also: Stedman Jones, 'Obituary: Raphael Samuel'.
29   Gillis, 'Detours', 163.
30   Rowbotham, 'Some Memories of Raphael'. See also Stedman Jones, 'Obituary: Raphael Samuel'. Samuel's delivery of the 1994 James Ford public lecture in British history, Oxford, was a notorious disaster in which he failed to reach any meaningful point or argument.
31   This seriousness has been the source of some of the accusations of romanticism. There have also been suggestions that it was not always sincere. Whether or not this is the case only the man himself could tell; perhaps what is more significant is that he made people *feel* valued.

3. THE WORKSHOP HISTORIAN

He had this tremendous understanding of the inner inferiority that mature students have in a society that tells them they've missed out. He learned from you and you learned from him. He was fascinated by other people's experience.[32]

Similarly, Paul Martin (a Ruskin student from 1986 to 1988) recalling the derisive general reactions to his idea for a study on the history and use of the lapel badge in the trade union movement remembered that: 'Raph was the only one who accepted [the project] at face value, as though its validity and interest were self-evident. As my supervisor, he was never less than enthusiastic and supportive'.[33]

He was also profoundly caring as a tutor, becoming deeply involved in his students' lives and supportive of them through difficult times. As one student wrote to him in the summer of 1967:

> Should I survive the course … you are the one I will owe most thanks, because you have been so very patient with me … I know this is something you would have done and will do for any pupil of yours … but as I also know there are very few tutors who would do the same, I am indeed very grateful.[34]

Or this from another student, writing in the previous year, which hints towards the extent that his support for his students could lead him into conflict with the college's management:

> If you ever need to justify what you are doing, and of course the very idea is stupid, but if you ever do, then simply think of me … for if you never achieve another success, then the joy and pleasure which you have given me make it all worthwhile.[35]

For all that he was an entertaining and kindly teacher, he was a conscientious one too, judging by the nature of his commentaries on student essays. These commentaries, written to provide feedback on student tutorial essays, were typically positive and encouraging (never unnecessarily rude or disparaging), but they were also meticulous in providing a detailed critique, often running to four or five densely typed pages, sometimes

---

32 Prescott, 'Genuine Love for Others'.
33 Paul Martin, 'Look, See, Hear', in Geoff Andrews, Hilda Kean and Jane Thompson, eds, *Ruskin College: Contesting Knowledge, Dissenting Politics* (London: Lawrence and Wishart, 1999), 146–47.
34 Letter from student to Raphael Samuel, Summer 1967, RS 1: The New Left/Ruskin College, 405, RSA.
35 Letter from student to Raphael Samuel, Summer 1966, RS 1: The New Left/Ruskin College, 405, RSA.

longer than the original essay. No mistake went unamended, no obscurity remained unclarified, no potential development unacknowledged. The gravity and rigour with which he treated all his students' work undermines any claim that he was uncritical towards them.[36]

All, however, was not quite so optimistic at Ruskin College during Samuel's early years there in the 1960s. The college was undergoing a crisis in its sense of identity and educational mission, reflective, in part, of a wider situation in the field of adult education. As Tom Steele has argued, in postwar Britain, independent workers' education was almost a moribund force. In an age enamoured with the ethos of modernisation and the languages of social planning, it was viewed as ad hoc, disorganised, and lacking in structure, clear objectives or tangible outcomes. Moreover, this time also saw a move away from 'workers' education' towards a more generalised notion of 'popular adult education', administered and organised within extramural university departments.[37]

Strong objections to this were voiced by figures such as G.D.H. Cole. Writing in 1952 he advised the Workers' Educational Association to vigorously resist handing over control to university departments, asserting that the WEA was at its healthiest when rooted in the local community and maintaining close ties with the labour movement.[38] The purpose of workers' education was at stake here, as it had been over half a decade earlier for the students of the Plebs League. There was a significant difference between educating workers to 'get on' in the society in which they lived or educating them in order to foster radical changes to that society, to expose and understand the structures of oppression and act as crucible for the formulation of independent ideas and practices. By collapsing workers' education in with the more generalised notion of 'popular liberal education', Cole argued, its critical edge was blunted: education in this guise served to ensure the stability and continuation of the status quo,

---

36   See for example: Raphael Samuel, feedback on student essays, RS 1: The New Left/Ruskin College, 407, RSA. Sheila Rowbotham also recalled his thoroughness in reading her handwritten PhD thesis (despite the fact she was not one of his students or even a student at the college) and responding with detailed commentary and, again, great enthusiasm, 'Some Memories of Raphael', 128.
37   Tom Steele, *The Emergence of Cultural Studies 1945–65: Cultural Politics, Adult Education and the English Question* (London: Lawrence and Wishart, 1997), 9–12. See also J.F.C. Harrison, 'The Search for Social Relevance', in *Learning and Living 1790–1960: A Study in the History of the English Adult Education Movement* (London: Routledge and Kegan Paul, 1961), 328–63.
38   G.D.H. Cole, 'What Workers' Education Means?', *Highway*, October 1952, 11.

the means for gratifying personal interest or, worse still, fracturing class solidarity by offering a chosen few, often those deemed 'the brightest', the means for individual advancement.

Cole had issued his warning in the early 1950s; by the 1960s and 1970s the reformers and modernisers were well underway with their plans. Adult education flourished, with large extramural departments at the universities of Leeds, Liverpool, Manchester and Nottingham, all offering regulated programs of study and corresponding frameworks for judging educational attainment based on performance in these programs. Further indications that adult education was becoming an established, professionalised field is suggested by the emergence of the first scholarly journal, *Studies in Adult Education*, and the formation of the Standing Conference on University Teaching and Research in the Education of Adults (SCUTREA) in 1970.[39]

The situation faced by Ruskin in the 1960s reflected these tensions. Its historic mission to provide independent working-class education rang ever more hollow amidst a cultural and political shift towards the more encompassing notion of 'adult education'. Furthermore, the professionalisation of adult education increased pressures to provide students with a more tangible outcome, such as qualifications, to justify their years of study. The result, in terms of both the curriculum and ethos of the college, was ambiguity. From Samuel's perspective:

> When I started to teach at Ruskin I was very shocked at the ways in which students were treated, adult students, worker students. And they were treated as being sort of under privileged, educationally retarded people who had somehow or other to be dragged up to the level of grammar school university entrance.[40]

The key point of contention amongst the staff and students at Ruskin was the college's attachment to the Oxford Special University Diploma qualification and examination system designed and administered by Oxford University. Samuel's notes from this time repeatedly questioned and critiqued the preoccupation with the diploma, which he felt to be 'an unnecessary obstacle which we place in the students' path'.[41]

---

39   J.E. Thomas, 'Innocence and After: Radicalism in the 1970s', in Sallie Westwood and J.E. Thomas, eds, *The Politics of Adult Education* (London: National Institute of Adult Continuing Education, 1991), 10.
40   Brian Harrison, 'Interview with Raphael Samuel', 23 October 1979.
41   Raphael Samuel, 'Notes towards reform of the diploma', RS 1: The New Left/Ruskin College, 408, RSA.

The content of the diploma syllabus also raised his ire. Economics claimed the privileged position. The liberal arts were afforded very little space. The labour history course dwelt at length on the trade union movement, industrial disputes and key legislative reform in industrial relations. Social history, meanwhile, focused on charting the rate and extent of industrialisation with its attendant technological advances and shifts in patterns of work, habitation and consumption.[42]

A demeaning examination system that provided no opportunity for independent research and the lack of student input into the governance of the college were the key issues that fuelled an outbreak of student unrest at Ruskin in 1966. Naturally, Samuel supported the protesting students. Penning an internal document, 'The Future of Ruskin', he argued that the college's enthrallment to the examination system had not only weakened its sense of purpose but was a betrayal of the hopes and expectations of the Ruskin student body. Using the polemical skills of the seasoned activist, he juxtaposed Ruskin's own radical history, the 'spirit of endeavour' amongst its founders and optimism of its early working-class students, against its lacklustre present situation saying:

> there is a real uncertainty about the purpose of Ruskin, and no clear view at all about its future educational role ... it may be seen in the disappointment that many of our second year students express with what the College has done for them, and on the part of the staff – when faced with the question of what Ruskin is for? – by a kind of dull unease.[43]

In this passage he made clear that as important an issue as Ruskin's lack of firm identity was, the shift from 'spirit of endeavour' to 'dull unease' and the loss of intellectual excitement amongst Ruskin staff and students was even more concerning.

Amongst the notes and drafts for 'The Future of Ruskin' document are proposals for reform. He suggested, for example, that in labour history:

---

42 For example: a 'Revision Paper' in social and economic twentieth-century British history from 1967 includes the questions: 'Compare and contrast the labour policies of the war time government in 1914–18 with that of 1939–45' and 'How do you account for decline in the rate of population growth during the first four decades of the twentieth century?' Raphael Samuel, 'Revision Papers for Labour and Social History 1966–1968', Samuel 097/Undergraduate teaching, RSA.
43 Raphael Samuel, 'The Future of Ruskin', 29 May 1968, RS 1: The New Left/Ruskin College, 408, RSA.

3. THE WORKSHOP HISTORIAN

> Our students have special strengths that can be brought to bear upon the subject. Many have strong local roots and come from communities rich in the history and historical materials of the subject … For project and vacation work – for making some creative contribution, however modest, during their period of time at Ruskin the subject is therefore one in which our students are particularly well-placed.[44]

Elsewhere, he recommended that economics not be a compulsory subject and that the liberal arts be better represented amongst the college courses:

> For anyone who goes on to teach liberal studies, as many of our students do, the reading of literature would be plainly of more importance [than economics]: indeed the narrow training of the diploma condemns our students to go to … the least imaginative training colleges … at a time when the best training colleges are teeming with experimental and new ideas.[45]

His allusion to 'liberal studies' and 'literature' makes a reference to one area where postwar extramural education had proved particularly dynamic. In his study of cultural studies and postwar adult education, Steele suggested that the space that opened up between the breakdown of confrontational class-based forms of adult education and the growth of the more inclusive concept of popular education provided a fertile niche for the early emergence of cultural studies. In the work of figures like Richard Hoggart, Raymond Williams and E.P. Thompson (all of them former New Left colleagues), cultural studies, in this guise, retained elements of oppositional social critique combined with a more expansive definition approach to the definition of people.[46]

His suggestions continued: on teaching practices, he suggested that exams be used to test *understanding* rather than used to judge ability. Above all, he urged repeatedly that substantial project work be incorporated into the students' studies. This, he added, would have the added benefit of challenging the tutor who risked 'growing too reliant on old lecture notes and losing their own intellectual creativity'.[47] Whilst he was not alone amongst the Ruskin staff in harbouring or advancing these criticisms,

---

44 Raphael Samuel, 'Notes on the future of Ruskin', RS 1: The New Left/Ruskin College, 408, RSA.
45 Ibid.
46 Steele, *The Emergence of Cultural Studies 1945–65*, 200–1.
47 Raphael Samuel, 'Notes towards reform of diploma: projects', RS 1: The New Left/Ruskin College, 408, RSA.

he was, perhaps, the most vocal. One fellow staff member wrote to him saying, 'You seem to be a born catalyst and how the history in the Dip needs one'.[48]

Neither Samuel's suggestions nor the staff–student protests against the diploma and the college's structure of governance yielded much response. The college authorities opted to contain, rather than address, the problems, which they did by establishing an internally examined diploma and a series of committees designed to keep student representatives tied up in an endless procession of meetings.[49] To those protesting, this seemed a rather dismal and unsatisfactory response on the part of the college. As he would later say, 'I found the educational regime at Ruskin profoundly offensive, and was looking around for ways [the students] could have a more dignified existence'.[50]

In an irresistible echo of the independent actions, although *not* the exact politics, of the earlier 'Ruskin rebels', the concept of the HW began to develop. It was, in the first place, 'an attempt to encourage working men and women … to become producers rather than consumers of their own histories'.[51]

The Workshop historian

In setting up the HW, Samuel was immediately confronted by a number of practical considerations which, for a former communist organiser, was familiar territory. He wanted to introduce forms of history that appealed and resonated with his worker students. He wanted this history to be 'useful' to them, to tell them something about how their own experiences of work and life connected with wider social structures and processes. Above all, he wanted to do this in a manner that showed respect for their innate intelligence and made them into active participants in the learning process; giving them the confidence to become producers of history.

---

48   Unsigned to 'Raff', RS 1: The New Left/Ruskin College, 408, RSA.
49   Bob Purdie, '"Long Haired Intellectuals and Busy Bodies": Ruskin, Student Radicalism, and Civil Rights in Northern Ireland', in Geoff Andrews, Hilda Kean and Jane Thompson, eds, *Ruskin College: Contesting Knowledge, Dissenting Politics* (London: Lawrence and Wishart, 1999), 59.
50   Brian Harrison, 'Interview with Raphael Samuel', 23 October 1979.
51   Raphael Samuel, 'General Editor's Introduction', in *Village Life and Labour* (London: Routledge & Kegan Paul, 1975), xx.

The problems that Samuel faced in achieving these objectives included the hostility shown from the college's authorities, particularly (in his view) to class-time being siphoned away from studying for the college's diploma qualification. Then there were also the problems of limited external sources of funding and the issue of the students' own low levels of confidence or experience in research and written work. On the other hand, Ruskin was positioned in close proximity to exceptional resources such as the Bodleian Library, not to mention the rich reservoir of the students' personal experiences and interests.

His first priority was to create an environment that broke down the 'barriers' and formality inherent within most academic institutions, but particularly those formalities associated with Oxford life. This was achieved by subverting many of the behavioural 'manners' implied by the conventional academic seminar and rejecting some of the conventional insignias of scholarly superiority. The cultivation of a 'dispassionate' research personality and emphasis on text-based sources of knowledge were replaced with an openly 'partisan' atmosphere in which all the participants pooled their respective forms of knowledge, often non-textual in nature, in the shared activity of history-making. This made the concept of the 'Workshop' so critical.[52]

It is worth reflecting briefly on the significance of the term 'workshop'. Historically, it conjured images of a pre-industrial form of production: a cottage industry, often informal and small-scale, involving one or more highly skilled craftspersons. Conceptually, it made reference to ideas of 'learning by doing' and of the intellectual journey from apprentice to skilled craftsperson during the course of which the former continually learned from the latter and the latter then continued to learn through ongoing practice.

He borrowed the name of 'workshop' from the Theatre Workshop (TW) (1945–67) set up by Joan Littlewood and Ewan MacColl (he later collaborated with MacColl on a HW book about working-class theatre movements).[53] Both former communists, MacColl and Littlewood had learnt their craft through agit-prop theatre and the TW was no less political in its theatre making. It became known for productions such as Shelagh

---

52 Raphael Samuel, 'Afterword', in *People's History and Socialist Theory*, 415.
53 Raphael Samuel, 'HWs 1–13', in Samuel, ed., *History Workshop: A Collectanea 1967–1991*, 97. Raphael Samuel, Ewan MacColl and Stuart Cosgrove, eds, *Theatres of the Left 1880–1935: Workers' Theatre Movements in Britain and America* (London: Routledge & Kegan Paul, 1985).

Delaney's *A Taste of Honey* (1958), which examined issues of gender and race in working-class lives, and the satirical musical *Oh, What a Lovely War!* (1963), which took a critical stance on the First World War.

TW was also the first British company to engage with the work of the German playwright Bertolt Brecht, staging *Mother Courage and her Children* in 1955 and introducing British audiences to Brecht's trademark dramatic technique of 'de-familiarisation' whereby the viewer is deliberately alienated from the unfolding drama.[54] In its working methodology, it cultivated an approach to drama that was intended to be experimental and participatory, with performances often developed through protracted processes of improvisation. Littlewood in particular was renowned for her openness as a director.[55] Samuel, who harboured a deep admiration for theatre as an art form, took great inspiration from the idea of creative production as a collaborative activity.[56]

Another openly acknowledged connection came from the Communist Party Historians' Group (CPHG). Samuel said later:

> the line, certainly, from the Communist Party Historians' Group to History Workshop is an <u>extremely</u> close one, because History Workshop is a fairly simple realization of what was one of the dreams of the Communist Party Historians' Group, which believed that history ought to be a democratized, popular thing.[57]

Whilst the fusion of history with an openly partisan political agenda undertaken in a collaborative and comradely working atmosphere certainly took its cue from the CPHG, this was uncoupled from any explicit Marxist framework. There was, he acknowledged, no conscious attempt to reformulate Marxism and its conception of history.[58]

---

54 John J. White, *Bertolt Brecht's Dramatic Theory* (New York: Boydell and Brewer Inc., 2004).
55 Robert Leach, *Theatre Workshop: Joan Littlewood and the Making of Modern British Theatre* (Exeter: University of Exeter Press, 2006); Nadine Holdsworth, *Joan Littlewood's Theatre* (Cambridge: Cambridge University Press, 2011). See also Joan Littlewood, *Joan's Book: Joan Littlewood's Peculiar History as She Tells It* (London: Methuen, 1994).
56 Alison Light, 'A Biographical Note on the Text', in Raphael Samuel, *Island Stories: Unravelling Britain* (London: Verso, 1998), xvi.
57 Brian Harrison, 'Interview with Raphael Samuel', 20 October 1987, 19 Elder Street, London, transcripts held in Raphael Samuel Archive (RSA), Bishopsgate Institute, London.
58 Samuel, 'Afterword', in *People's History and Socialist Theory*, 413.

3. THE WORKSHOP HISTORIAN

A less recognised cue for the HW came from Samuel's own educational experiences at various progressive schools such as King Alfred School (KAS) in Hampstead, North London. KAS was founded in 1898 by a group of residents from Hampstead Garden Suburb, itself the result of a progressive approach to social planning, concerned with creating an educational environment in which the student assumed a more active role in the day-to-day running of the school and in their own learning processes. The school was also concerned to expand student experiences beyond purely academic study. The young Samuel had been a rebellious student, critical of his schooling and the progressive political ideals that it espoused; nevertheless it accustomed him at an early age to the idea of alternative forms of education outside of the narrowly prescribed 'academic'.[59]

His sensitivity to and consciousness of alternative pedagogical philosophies and the politics of education were further honed through his teaching of the sociology of education. He was responsible for designing the rubric of the course, suggesting thorough knowledge and familiarity with the full range of ideological perspectives on education and pedagogical theory. The essay questions that he composed for the course reflected this: 'Are school and university textbooks value free?', 'Is the home a greater influence on educational achievement than the school?' and 'In what ways do teachers try and reinforce their authority over pupils?'[60] There can be little question that in setting up the HW he was fully conscious of the educational environment he was trying to achieve (making it slightly less of an 'organic' evolution than he would later depict).

Finally, inspiration came from his enthusiastic reading of the journal *Anarchy* (1961–70), edited by the British anarchist thinker and writer Colin Ward. He later described *Anarchy* as 'the only revolutionary reading around at that time' (giving some indication of his feelings towards the highly theoretical direction that the *NLR* had taken under Anderson's editorship).[61] The anarchism discussed in *Anarchy* was of a very different nature to the extreme, even violent, forms of revolutionary politics and

---

59 Raphael Samuel, 'Country Visiting: A Memoir', in *Island Stories*.
60 Raphael Samuel, 'Sociology of Education Course outline', RS 1: The New Left/Ruskin College, 1969, 407, RSA.
61 Raphael Samuel, 'Then and Now: A Re-evaluation of the New Left', in Robin Archer et al., eds, *Out of Apathy: Voices of the New Left 30 Years On* (London: Verso, 1989), 148.

direct action with which it is typically associated. This was a form of social anarchism based on principles of community, compassion and cooperation rather than cataclysm, chaos and carnage.

Under Ward's editorship, *Anarchy* emphasised the primacy of humans as social beings but rejected the need for any central controlling power such as the state or revolutionary vanguard. The journal carried numerous articles and features on various approaches to cooperative social organisation, including several case studies of non-authoritarian forms of education such as, for example, community 'workshop' initiatives.[62] This stress on the arts of cooperative organisation and community activism had obvious appeal to the former communist who had cultivated the skills required to organise and coordinate rather than dictate and lead. Samuel placed the principles of collective work, solidarity and autonomy at the heart of his vision of the HW. Ward would later acknowledge the HW as a good example of cooperative and collaborative education. Samuel, in turn, would also maintain an enthusiastic and receptive view of Ward's work and politics.[63]

The HW started life as an informal student seminar series on 'The English Countryside in the Nineteenth Century' (1966), later hosting a day event, 'A Day with the Chartists' (1967), in which established historians were invited to share with the students their insights into the research process. The second day event, 'Workers and Education in Nineteenth Century England' (1968), was the one at which the term 'Workshop' was formally adopted and Ruskin students began to co-participate in the event. By HW 4 (1969), attendance figures had swollen dramatically, with over half the papers coming from student contributions.[64]

---

62 Colin Ward, ed., *A Decade of Anarchy 1961–1970: Selections from the Monthly Journal Anarchy* (London: Freedom Press, 1987). Notably, the HW had a strong appeal to and enduring relationship with contemporary community-based creative writing and publishing initiatives, in particular the Brighton-based QueenSpark and projects such as the People's Autobiography of Hackney. See the program for HW 10, 'Adult Education and the Working Class' (1975); Raphael Samuel 'People's History', in Samuel, ed., *People's History and Socialist Theory* (London: Routledge and Kegan Paul, 1981), xv; Ken Worpole, 'A Ghostly Pavement: The Political Implications of Local Working-class History', in *People's History and Socialist Theory*, 22–32; Jerry White, 'Beyond Autobiography', in *People's History and Socialist Theory*, 33–41; Stephen Yeo, 'The Politics of Community Publications', in *People's History and Socialist Theory*, 42–48.
63 Colin Ward, 'Schools No Longer', in *Anarchy in Action* (London: Allen and Unwin, 1973); Raphael Samuel, 'Utopian Sociology', *New Society*, 2 October 1987.
64 HW 4, 'Proletarian Oxford' (1969), dedicated an entire day to student papers.

In the early manifestations of the HW, Samuel assumed the major responsibility for organising the meetings. The seminar sessions, for example, worked closely with the Ruskin history syllabus.[65] The subtlety of Samuel's influence in these events, familiar to those who knew, was acknowledged by a letter from a friend following 'A Day with the Chartists' who commented: 'I cannot pretend to have loved all the papers at the workshop but most were very interesting and some stimulating. The organisation and so on were a great credit to your alter ego'.[66] Later, as it developed, a student Workshop Collective was formed with Samuel as a 'guiding' presence,[67] still acting as the main point of contact for all HW communications concerning everything from details of proposed papers to enquiries concerning accommodation arrangements (which is not to say that he necessarily dealt with these himself).[68]

He canvassed his personal network of contacts – former comrades from the CPHG, friends from university, former New Left colleagues – for contributions to Workshop events. Dorothy Thompson, Eric Hobsbawm and Stuart Hall, for example, were all participants in early HW events.[69] One of the most memorable of these early contributors was E.P. Thompson who gave a rousing paper on eighteenth-century rural resistance in HW 3 (1968).[70]

Undoubtedly Thompson and the historical vision outlined in his book *The Making of the English Working Class* were extremely influential for the HW, although perhaps not as much as some commentators are apt to suggest.[71] The book had been written against the backdrop of the first New Left debates over working-class history and consciousness and bore within its eloquent pages much of the passion those debates had provoked.[72] Starting with the assertion 'I do not see class as a "structure", nor even as a "category", but as something which in fact happens (and can

---

65 This was particularly the case for the early seminar sessions such as 'The English Countryside in the Nineteenth Century' (1966).
66 'Richard' to Raphael Samuel, 'Letter following Day with the Chartists' 1967, RS 7: History Workshop Events/A Day With the Chartists 1966–1968, RSA.
67 An insight into the nature of this 'guidance' is discussed below.
68 See, for example, Samuel, 'HWs 1–13', in *History Workshop: A Collectanea 1967–1991*, 101–02.
69 Dorothy Thompson spoke at HW 1, 'A Day with the Chartists' (1967), Eric Hobsbawm spoke at HW 4 (1969) and Stuart Hall spoke at a Workshop on 'Popular Culture and Past and Present' hosted at the Centre for Contemporary Cultural Studies at Birmingham University (1971).
70 Rowbotham, 'Remembering 1967', 4.
71 Dworkin, *Cultural Marxism in Post War Britain*, 189.
72 Elements of the argument rehearsed in 'Commitment in Politics' and in his review of Williams's *Long Revolution*.

be shown to have happened) in human relationships',[73] Thompson unfolded a compelling narrative set at the early dawning of the labour 'movement'. He argued that far from being a product of nineteenth-century industrialisation, arriving promptly alongside the factory, the overseer and the machine, working-class consciousness was a living entity composed from shared experiences of exploitation and suffering but also a sense of injustice and defiance and drawing on the fragments of a once vibrant popular culture dispersed, but not lost, in the relentless advance of industrialisation.

As much as *The Making of the English Working Class* displayed a powerful historical imagination, it also captured the mood of the times (in particular the paperback version published in 1968). It was a call to arms, a defiant assertion of the capacity of people to create and, more to the point, to re-create their worlds. Following the positive reception to the book, Thompson had taken the directorship of the Centre for Social History at the University of Warwick (at which Samuel was an occasional guest speaker) where he continued to focus intently on the relationship between 'value systems' and class struggle.[74] Rather than progress through the formal development of the labour movement, the evolution of its institutions and its political vehicle, the Labour Party, Thompson turned backwards, intent upon retracing the prehistory of the movement expressed informally through culture, customs and collisions with authority. It was a timely project for a period increasingly characterised by disillusionment with party politics and the 'official' channels of government.[75]

Samuel described the bold political vision and historical methodology set out in *The Making of the English Working Class* as an influential 'starting point'.[76] He also insisted that the HW did not set out to pursue a 'Thompsonian' political or historical project, even going as far as to suggest that it had made a conscious attempt to 'escape' from the 'grand

---

73   E.P. Thompson, 'Preface', in *The Making of the English Working Class* (London: Victor Gollancz, 1963), 8.
74   Peter Searby, with John Rule and Robert Malcolmson, 'Edward Thompson as a Teacher: Yorkshire and Warwick', in John Rule and Robert Malcolmson, eds, *Protest and Survival: The Historical Experience – Essays for E. P. Thompson* (London: Merlin, 1993), 18–19.
75   'E. P. Thompson [interview by Mike Merrill]', in Henry Abelove et al., eds, *Visions of History* (Manchester: Manchester University Press, 1983), 20; E.P. Thompson, 'Time, Work-Discipline and Industrial Capitalism', *Past and Present* (*P&P*), 38 (1967), 56–97; E.P. Thompson, 'The Moral Economy of the English Crowd in the Eighteenth Century', *P&P*, 50 (1971), 76–136.
76   Raphael Samuel, 'Notes on proposed Ruskin Social History course 1966', RS 1: The New Left/Ruskin College, 405, RSA.

terrain' of Thompson's history.[77] The main point of distinction between the historical approach in his book and that of the HW was the latter's far more expansive interest in 'everyday life' and 'ordinary people', an expansiveness directly influenced by the Ruskin students, its primary participants.

Samuel took an extraordinarily enthusiastic interest in his students' lives and backgrounds. As his close friend Hall put it:

> He knew an astonishing range and variety of people each of whom at some point he had engaged in a searching conversation about their background, their families, their work, their life as if preparing everyone for the possibility of becoming an oral historical testimonial.[78]

This was not just natural curiosity but a highly conscious process, bearing traces of the methods once employed by the would-be party organiser. He would engage people in intense and searching conversations much like those conducted whilst attempting to recruit at university (the case of Denis Butt for example, see Chapter One). The effect of this was to make the individual feel valued and understood, often prompting an intimate sense of trust and confidence to develop.[79] Rather than use this as the grounds for a recruitment pitch, he now used the insights gained as a 'way in' to history-making, encouraging students to draw upon their own lived experiences, working in a coal mine or growing up in a rural town, as a point of departure for historical inquiry.

For others, he drew upon their interests. He encouraged Sally Alexander, a Ruskin student (1967–69), to draw on her passion for and knowledge of nineteenth-century novels to provide a point of entry into understanding the complex and shifting landscapes of working-class Victorian social and cultural life.[80] What, for example, could be drawn from Charles Dickens's representations of the world of children in contrast to the one of adults; what did this suggest about attitudes to childhood? How did changing

---

77 Raphael Samuel, *Theatres of Memory: Past and Present in Contemporary Culture* (London: Verso, 1994), 320.
78 Hall, 'Raphael Samuel: 1934–1996', 123.
79 Ibid.
80 Sally Alexander, oral communication with author, January 2011, London, recordings held in author's collection.

depictions of the Victorian heroine, as found in the works of Charlotte Brontë or Elizabeth Gaskell, reveal prevailing social attitudes to women or suggest changes to female self-identity?[81]

Unsurprisingly, a recurrent Workshop favourite were the novels of Thomas Hardy. In Hardy, the students found much to identify with both in his books' larger themes, such as the thwarted attempts of Hardy's tragic protagonist Jude to become an Oxford scholar, but also the 'incidental' components of the novels, the parts that nineteenth-century readers would have scarcely noticed but which stood out to twentieth century ones. Student Jennie Kitteringham drew upon her own family's rural roots to illuminate Tess's gruelling labour as a swede trimmer, Arabella's robust technique at pig killing and Marty's sleepless night making spars for thatching as insights into the tough physicality of female labour.[82] Elsewhere, the tensions between Henchard and Farfrae[83] provided generous scope for assessing changes in the culture and conduct of nineteenth-century business practices.[84]

Slowly 'investing' the student with such a direct sense of their own connection to the past was useful in kindling their curiosity, a key motivational factor for overcoming reticence towards libraries or archives, viewed by many of the students as the preserve of the cultural 'elite'. Given the Oxford location, the greatest example of this was the magisterial Bodleian Library, which many Ruskin students habitually avoided, despite their entitlement to use it. Emboldened by their interest and animated by the thrill of investigation, Workshop students were inspired to head into the Bodleian's silent catacombs.[85]

---

81 Raphael Samuel, 'Notes on the English Countryside in the Nineteenth Century Workshop seminar series', RS 7: History Workshop Events/The English Countryside in the Nineteenth Century 1968–1969, 013, RSA.
82 Tess: *Tess of the D'Urbervilles* (1891); Arabella: *Jude the Obscure* (1895); Marty: *The Woodlanders* (1887). Jennie Kitteringham, 'Country Work Girls in Nineteenth Century England', in Raphael Samuel, ed., *Village Life and Labour* (London: Routledge & Kegan Paul, 1975), 27–69.
83 Thomas Hardy, *The Mayor of Casterbridge* (1886).
84 Raphael Samuel, 'Notes on the English Countryside in the Nineteenth Century Workshop seminar series', RS 7: History Workshop Events/The English Countryside in the Nineteenth Century 1968–1969, 013, RSA.
85 Dave Douglass, oral communication with author, December 2011, Newcastle, recordings held in author's collection.

Once lured inside an archive or library, the sheer physical thrill of encountering documents, often untouched since their deposit, was a further potent force.[86] Close concentration on primary sources was a defining feature of Workshop history. Again, Samuel was personally implicated in this. He spent the summer of 1966 in the newly opened local records office in Lancashire, rummaging amongst a treasure trove of documents relating to local news, events, disputes and organisations, untouched since their original deposit. On his return to Ruskin, he shared the fruits of his investigations with his students, passing on his personal excitement at the pleasures and possibilities offered by original primary source research as he did so.

This personal enthusiasm was a vital tool. Highly infectious in nature, it extended far beyond the text-based document, reaching into the realms of visual and material culture, music, art, architecture, physical landscapes, photography and drama, all read as social documents inscribed with meaning, situated amongst overlapping webs of social and historical context.[87] Running in close conjunction with this was his eager interest in oral history. Instead of the quiet gloom of an archive and the faint rustle of ancient paper, the document was a living human being, the precious insights into the past etched in their bodies, strewn about their manner of speaking and stored up in their minds. His enthusiasm for this led to his close involvement with the formation of the Oral History Society (1971–) and the *Oral History Journal* (1971–) to which he was an early contributor.[88]

But the HW did not simply expand the range of subjects and approaches to history. Critical to the HW's *modus operandi* was its insistence on linking history to present-day events – further enhancing the sense of inter-connectedness between past and present, giving renewed emphasis to the relevance and urgency of historical research. Certainly there was no more appropriate time to be rewriting history, as the political landscape of Britain seemed electrified, with groups jostling to have their voices

---

86 Samuel, 'Ruskin Historians', in *History Workshop: A Collectanea 1967–1991*, 67.
87 Ibid., 76, 82; Samuel, *Theatres of Memory*, 337–49. Workshops would often conclude with an evening's entertainment of folk music. There was a performance of 'The Factory Lad' at the 1970 Workshop. Ruskin student and Workshop participant David Marson's research was also turned into a play, 'Fall in and Follow Me', performed at a Workshop in July 1973.
88 For an overview of the Oral History Society see: Graham Smith, 'The Making of Oral History', *Making History: The Changing Face of the Profession in Britain*, The Institute of Historical Research, www.history.ac.uk/makinghistory/resources/articles/oral_history.html (accessed 25 November 2014).

heard, their causes recognised, their political visions realised. These were irresistible conditions for the erstwhile activist with an exceptional talent for organisation and agitation.

Ruskin's close relationship to the trade union movement meant that much of the HW's early work was conducted in close dialogue with (and, through the students' often quite intimate knowledge of) the rising union militancy that dominated the political landscape of the period starting with the Seamen's Strike in 1966 and peaking with the Upper Clyde Shipbuilders' dispute (work-in) in 1971. Themes like 'Workers' control in Nineteenth Century England' complemented, and in some cases, anticipated union actions.[89]

Aside from the organised labour movement, there were further close connections between the HW and the flourishing student movement. Samuel's notoriety as one of the first New Left's primary instigators and his position as a tutor at what had traditionally been a workers' college made him an attractive mentor figure to the younger generation. As once he had canvassed the support of 'elder' figures, he too was now approached for support in 'new' ventures or for contributions to 'new' journals.[90]

Student political activity in Britain, whilst never quite reaching the ferocity or extremities seen in France or America, became a more vocal presence during the late 1960s, galvanised, in part, by the implementation of the Robbins Report into higher education (1963) that recommended both the expansion of access to existing institutions and the creation of new universities, which became the sites of dynamic student activism.[91] Even the tranquillity of Oxford was disturbed by lively protests against the Vietnam War and former Conservative MP Enoch Powell's 'rivers of blood' speech. On a more local scale, there was opposition to a 'colour bar' at a local hairdressers and to the regulatory powers that college proctors had over student personal lives. Ruskin students regularly joined forces with their (often) younger comrades at the university over the issues of

---

89 HW 5, 'Workers' Control in Nineteenth Century England', was held in February 1971, anticipating the Upper Clyde Shipbuilders' dispute, June 1971, by some months.
90 Examples of this can be found in: 'Assorted notifications, posters and pamphlets', RS 1: New Left/Student and other Revolutionary movements of the 1960s, 201–02, RSA.
91 Lord Robbins, *The Robbins Report: Higher Education* (London: Her Majesty's Stationery Office, 1963), www.educationengland.org.uk/documents/robbins/robbins1963.html (accessed 18 February 2015). Full-time student attendance in higher education increased from 3.4 per cent of the population in 1950 to 8.4 per cent in 1970. Paul Bolton, 'Education Historical Statistics', *Social and General Statistics*, House of Commons Library, 27 November 2012, 14.

3. THE WORKSHOP HISTORIAN

racism and Vietnam, and it was Ruskin students who took the lead in agitating for civil rights in Northern Ireland or in supporting the workers in industrial disputes taking place at the local Cowley car factory (an old favourite of Samuel's, see Chapter One).[92]

Part of this student ferment involved a renewed questioning and struggle over the politics of education and of knowledge itself, and it was here that the HW, 'guided' by Samuel, intersected most emphatically. Not only was the HW itself emblematic of an alternative, independent approach to education, it also addressed the subject directly in its choice of themes. Naturally, he took a particularly strong lead in instigating this topic, returning to it several times, firstly in HW 2 (1968) on 'Education and the Working Class' and again in HW 10 (1975), which was more specifically focused on the working class and adult education. As early as 9 May 1975 (one year before it was intended), Samuel began circulating his plans for HW 10, detailing objectives, speakers and topics as he had once detailed objectives, contributors and articles for the *Universities and Left Review*:

> If we do our job properly we ought to be able to raise some central questions on working class education, at the same time as opening up a serious historical inquiry into its various impulses. There is a considerable accumulation of work to draw upon as this is something that the Workshop has been engaged with, off and on, throughout its existence … There is also a possibility of a discussion on the present state of adult education in Britain; the crisis in the WEA, Open Universities, literacy programmes, Ruskin itself.[93]

A note addressed directly to the student Workshop Collective, dated a few days later, proposed further suggestions:

> First as to subject. We could define it much more generously to include <u>unofficial</u> sources of learning eg. apprenticeship and the practice of craft skills and also <u>indirect</u> contributions to adult education – eg. libraries. We could also frame the Workshop in a clearer statement of a central problematic: the relationship of adult education to class consciousness.

---

92 Purdie, '"Long Haired Intellectuals and Busy Bodies"', 58–79.
93 Raphael Samuel to History Workshop Collective, RS 7: History Workshop Events/Workers Education and Class Consciousness correspondence 1975–1976, 027, RSA.

Second, as to method. It would be possible to divide the Workshop into large sessions, having the character of lectures or addresses, and a parallel series of smaller ones inquiring into particular subjects and spending more than one session discussing them. For example, the class character, the ideological and cultural contribution of reading rooms …

Third, preparation. If we were to draw up some preliminary statements about each area – and a preliminary statement about adult education and history … we could canvas [sic] support from WEA branches and tutor organisers.[94]

Finally, a draft program for the event (dated 18 June 1975) (italics are my own):

Themes – working sessions

Below is a possible grouping which would cover, though not by any means all of, the planned papers. We could make, perhaps, two themes per day, one and two on Saturday, three and four on Sunday.

Religion and Politics

Eric Hobsbawm – Radical Shoemakers

Anna Davin and Raphael Samuel – Open Air Preaching in Mid Victorian London

Stan Shipley – Club Life and Socialism in Mid Victorian London

J.F.C. Harrison – Owenite Education

Alun Howkins – The Word of the Lord Made Flesh (Primitive Methodists and the Word of the Lord Made Flesh)

…

The Present State and Crisis of Adult Education

(No suggestions made)

Working Class Writers

David Goodway – Chartist Writers

Martha Vicinius – The Industrial Muse; Working Class poetry in 19th c Lancashire

…

Ken Worpole – Autobiography

Adult Students

Sheila Rowbotham – Early years of University Extension

---

94   Ibid.

Geoff Brown – Early Years of WEA
Paul Yorke – Early Years of Ruskin Students
Ruth Frow – The Labour Colleges in Lancashire

<u>Women and Education</u> *(added in a handwritten note)*
Jean McCrindle and Sheila Rowbotham *(no subject proposed)*[95]

These documents illustrate his organisational mind in action. Three observations might be ventured from these plans. Firstly, the desire to connect the HW to wider contemporary debates on the 'current crisis' within adult education (the erosion of its independent forms and structures, such as the Workers' Educational Association) was not an additional sideline to a Workshop on the history of education. It was a central strand, planned from the earliest stages and shaping the entire form and shape of the event. Secondly, following on from the first, the proposed content of the HW demonstrates the uses of historical inquiry in engaging with this debate. His suggested papers juxtapose studies of independent forms of working-class education (self-organised initiatives): 'Radical Shoemakers', 'Club Life and Socialism in Mid Victorian London', 'Chartist Writers' and so on, with papers on the points of intersection between the working classes and formal institutions (religion, the universities): 'The Word of the Lord Made Flesh', 'Early years of University Extension'.

Finally, the plans set out here did not stop at setting out an objective or settling upon subject matter, they extended into the very structure (ways of dividing the HW events for maximum effect) and dissemination (ways of attracting and recruiting participants and attendees) of the material. All this recalls strongly his detailed plans for shaping and extending the reach of the *Universities and Left Review* (see Chapter Two) proving, again, that for Samuel no organisational detail was too small or insignificant.

These themes, workers' control and workers' education, fell firmly within the former communist's familiar intellectual and political territory. There was, however, one major area of the HW's burgeoning interests in which he was not on such well-known ground and could not, therefore, be as interventionist: the HW's pivotal relationship with the Women's

---

95 Ibid.

Movement. The first British Women's Liberation conference was organised as a direct result of a Workshop meeting, with several of the key organisers of this event closely associated with the HW.

A major figure in instigating this was the historian and feminist activist Anna Davin.[96] She was born in 1940 to Winnie and Dan Davin and raised in Oxford.[97] In 1958 Davin married the British mathematician Luke Hodgkin with whom she had three children. She went on to study history at Warwick University (1966–69) where she encountered E.P. and Dorothy Thompson.[98] Following the breakup of her marriage to Hodgkin, Davin met Samuel and during the early 1970s the two formed a personal and working relationship, with Davin often laying aside her own research to take on the editing of Samuel's Ruskin students' papers.[99] Already a prominent figure in the women's movement, having set up a Women's Liberation group at Warwick in 1968, Davin, along with others including Sheila Rowbotham and Sally Alexander, was one of the key architects behind the first Women's Liberation Workshop held at Ruskin on the last weekend of February 1970, attracting over 500 participants.[100]

Subsequently, Workshops were held on 'The Child in History' (1972) and later 'Women in History' (1972). The effect of these was to move the HW more firmly into the history and politics of the personal. Looking at the histories of social groups such as women or children not only demanded more creative interpretation of historical sources, it also gave renewed significance to living history and oral testimonies to counteract the paucity or limitation of official sources and forced a closer examination of the relationship between private and public spheres in social life.

As fruitful as the relationship was, it also contained some of the seeds of Schwarz's collision of 'moments'. As Schwarz argued, the HW encompassed a range of political positions and agendas which, whilst often overlapping in their sympathies and revolutionary zeal, bore within them highly distinctive, even conflicting implications. Unsurprisingly, for many of the Ruskin students, many of whom were coming to the college

---

96   Rowbowtham, 'Remembering 1967', 5.
97   Dan Davin was a prominent New Zealand born author. Keith Ovenden, *A Fighting Withdrawal: The Life of Dan Davin, Writer, Soldier, Publisher* (Oxford: Oxford University Press, 1996).
98   Anna Davin, oral communication with author, January 2012, London, transcript held in author's private collection; Davin, 'The Only Problem Was Time', 239–40.
99   Samuel, 'General Editor's Introduction', in *Village Life and Labour*, xxi.
100 Rowbotham, 'Remembering 1967', 5; Davin, 'The Only Problem Was Time', 240.

through the largely masculine world of the trade unions, the concepts of class and class struggle were fundamental and all-encompassing. Within this, women's history was broadly acceptable provided it complemented and contributed to this agenda, restricting its comments to the experiences of women and children in labour.

As some, like Davin, began to probe more deeply into the realms of the private and personal spheres, this prompted a shift towards conceptualising gender as a *distinctive* form of politics in its own right, one that not only questioned the emphasis placed on class but in some cases challenged its sovereignty as the main site of political oppression.[101] Fractures and fission within the working class as a social group gave rise to the idea that the working classes were just as complicit in creating and perpetuating inequities on the basis of gender, race or sexuality. This was the crux of the division, noted by Schwarz, between the older political moments and the post-1968 generation, a shift from class as central focus towards a view of it as one of many imposed or constructed social identities and sites of struggle.

Samuel's position here was supportive. In his accounts of the HW, the Women's Movement is always respectfully acknowledged as a critical part of the HW story, a turning point in its trajectory. Elsewhere, he staunchly defended the need to probe into the relationships that operated *within* working-class communities against critics who thought this extraneous to the major political and economic issues of the day.[102] But his support had limitations. His own work never fully metabolised the deeper implications of a gendered approach to politics raised by some amongst the Women's Movement (by way of example, in his plans for HW 10 on the 'Working Class and Adult Education', discussed earlier, 'Women and Education' was, firstly, a handwritten note added on to the original document and, secondly, a theme for which he was able to identify possible contributors but *not* to propose a topic).[103] For Samuel, women and children were another group neglected from the official record, whose energies and creative potential were either squandered or crushed.

---

101 See for example: Anna Davin, 'Imperialism and Motherhood', *HWJ*, 5 (1978), 6–66.
102 Samuel, 'General Editor's Introduction'.
103 This view was broadly endorsed by Anna Davin, his partner during this time. Oral communication with author, January 2011, London, recordings in author's collection.

As the HW grew in size and ambition, several of the student papers were turned into pamphlets of around 20,000 words each (the realisation, in part, of a suggestion made in 1966 by David Selbourne, Samuel's Ruskin colleague, about publishing occasional papers by Ruskin students), compiled and published by the HW collective.[104] The first HW book collection of essays, *Village Life and Labour,* appeared in 1975.

Samuel was the 'General Editor' for the HW pamphlet and book series. The role and function of the editor shares parallels with that of his other roles; the organiser, the club chairman and, of course, the tutor. It was principally organisational in nature, overseeing the project and coordinating the individual components into a whole. Editorial work demanded the forging of close relationships with the respective authors in the development and evolution of their contributions. Drafts and re-drafts, comments and replies flew back and forth between writer and editor as the piece slowly took shape. In many respects, this process was similar to the critical feedback he had provided as a tutor but in other respects this relationship was far more intensive, effectively demanding a concession of the 'power' of the tutor to set questions or assign grades. Rather than *impose* arguments the editor could only (in theory) *offer* suggestions.

In making such an offering, he had also to exercise his creativity as a historian in connecting his own substantial knowledge of nineteenth-century British social and labour history to the student's specific research or particular case study. He worked, for example, with Alun Howkins to explore how the lingering of pre-industrial customs (the marking of the Whitsun holiday in nineteenth-century Oxfordshire) could reflect on the unevenness of the spread of industrialisation and the reluctance or antagonism of rural communities to the imposition of the industrialised working week and calendar.[105] Similarly, he encouraged Dave Douglass to 'mine' his intimate inside knowledge of pit life in County Durham

---

104 Raphael Samuel, 'Notes on the Future of Ruskin', May 1966, RS 1: The New Left/Ruskin College, 309, RSA. Early Ruskin HW pamphlets included: Frank McKenna, *A Glossary of Railwaymen's Talk*; Sally Alexander, *St Giles Fair, 1830–1914*; Bernard Reaney, *The Class Struggle in 19th Century Oxfordshire*; Stan Shipley, *Club Life and Socialism in mid-Victorian London*; Dave Douglass, *Pit Life in County Durham*; John Taylor, *From Self Help to Glamour, the Working Men's Club, 1860–1970*; Alun Howkins, *Whitsun in 19th Century Oxfordshire*; Dave Marson, *Children's Strikes in 1911*; Dave Douglass, *Pit Talk in County Durham*; Jennie Kitteringham, *Country Girls in 19th Century England*; Edgar Moyo, *Big Mother and Litter Mother in Matebeleland*.
105 Alun Howkins, *Whitsun in 19th Century Oxfordshire*; oral communication with author, May 2012, Diss, Norfolk, transcripts in author's collection.

to provide insights into both the physical experiences of the work and the ways in which the pitmen understood and organised it through their language and stories. It was not, however, inevitable that his suggestions or advice would be taken. Douglass, for example, recalled a terrific struggle between the two men over his insistent inclusion of a sea monster story in his work. (Convinced by Samuel to abandon it in early writings, he later, stubbornly, returned to it, convinced of its significance.)[106] Samuel subsequently continued with and expanded upon this editorial role through the *History Workshop Journal* (*HWJ*), which made its debut appearance in 1976.[107]

The historian of the Workshop

There is no greater proof of Samuel's centrality to the HW than the fact that he was its first and, for a long time, only historian (he remains the main source of Workshop accounts). If, as he professed, the writing of history was an innately political act, the power to endow an order, a shape and meaning on the facts of the past, then a close reading of his first attempt to construct and frame the HW story is revealing.[108]

The mood of this account was set by the epigraph, Brecht's poem 'Questions from a Worker Who Reads' (1935). The poem took well-known coordinates in world history, such as the building of Thebes or Alexander's conquering of India, and asked the reader to be curious about the people upon whose mundane labours, and sufferings, they were made possible: 'And Babylon, so often destroyed, Who kept rebuilding it?' It continually juxtaposed glory and power with the small, everyday acts that went into their realisation: 'Caesar beat the Gauls. / Without even a cook?'

The poem also asked the reader to recognise the humanity of these people beyond the contribution of their labour: 'Philip of Spain wept when his fleet went down. / Did no one else weep besides?' In this way, not only does the poem make an argument about the restricted view presented in so much of history as it was recorded and passed down, Brecht also

---

106 Dave Douglass, *Pit Life in Country Durham, Pit Talk in Country Durham*; oral communication with author, December 2011, Newcastle, transcripts held in author's collection.
107 See Chapter Five for a fuller discussion of the journal.
108 Samuel, 'General Editor's Introduction', xiii–xxi.

reminded his readers of the shared humanity between leadership figures and the people who laboured for them, served them, paid for them or were crushed by them. This spoke of a history that had wearied of 'great' battles and instead asked of the histories that were less apparent, concealed in the ordinary experiences and struggles of everyday life.

Set against this interpretive framework was the HW's 'story of origin'. In the first place, Samuel positioned the HW as an act of resistance against an authoritative force that undermined the confidence and self-esteem of the Ruskin students. This can be seen with most force through his choice of language in describing the situation (italics are my own): 'The Workshop began as an *attack* on the examination system, and the *humiliations* which it imposed on adult students'. This key theme of defiance and struggle was continued by his references to the sustained failure of educational institutions to support the HW in its endeavours: '[N]o grants from the SSRC [Social Science Research Council] facilitated [the students] in their work'.

This failure extended to the student's own college authorities, which in his view had come perilously close to an act of outright betrayal: 'in the early years, when such research activity was wholly unofficial, even – from the point of view of the curriculum – clandestine, there was not even recognition or support from their own college'.[109]

In contrast, failure on behalf of authority figures was juxtaposed by the determination and sacrifices made by the students: 'one student financed his research by cleaning the rafters in the British Leyland Motor Works at Cowley; another by selling his car; a third by living on baked beans; most by going short'. Here he echoed the technique used in Brecht's poem. The sheer mundaneness of the activities, cleaning rafters, eating baked beans, are imbued with nobleness and political significance. The students were willing to accept these physical discomforts in order to satisfy their desire to become independent learners. Further on, he continued with this theme of physical deprivation saying: '[A]ll that sustained them was the seriousness of their commitment, and the awakening pride that comes from mastering a craft for oneself'.[110]

---

109 This was later contested by H.D. Hughes (Ruskin principal 1950–79). H.D. Hughes, 'History Workshop', *HWJ*, 11 (1981), 199–201.
110 Samuel, 'General Editor's Introduction', xx.

Replacing a more varied diet or other material luxuries as the key sources for bodily nourishment or pleasure was the sense of 'commitment' and of 'pride'. The points made here were the significance of less tangible qualities, such as mental stimulation and independence, for nurturing a general sense of wellbeing. These sacrifices were small acts and choices made according to what these students could arrange out of the resources at hand in their everyday life. What he invoked in this passage was a sense of the 'innocence' and humbleness in the HW as a venture.

He concluded this early account with a few striking lines that hinted towards how he viewed his own relationship to the HW during this time. In speaking of the role that his partner, Davin, and he himself had played in putting together the papers for the HW book collections he, once again, referenced a profoundly domestic setting, his own home, to enforce the earlier invocation of 'everydayness':

> [T]he manuscripts line the passageways, crawl up the stairs to sleep at night, and invade the children's bedroom. For us, as for many of the contributors, they are the troubled product and labour of love.[111]

Manuscripts that line passageways where human beings pass to and fro as they go about the daily activities of domestic life, that, like the human inhabitants, head up the stairs to bed at night and crawl into the *children's* bedroom. The HW papers are depicted here as part of the fabric of his family life. Davin and Samuel are positioned in parental roles, presiding over and managing the day-to-day running of the household, caring for the students' work as they did for Davin's three young children, with love and hard work.

In this early account, the sentiments were heavy-handed, overly defensive or protective, but they do suggest the chief contours of Samuel's thought. The guiding motivation behind the HW was inextricably bound with the Ruskin students (arguably, symbolic for a general conception of 'workers') who, in turn, served as a metaphor for people who had been silenced, dismissed or ridiculed but were yet struggling to be heard. The initial motivation behind the HW was simply to make people into producers rather than consumers of their own history. This was the key principle embedded in his emerging sense of politics. His role, as tutor and Workshop organiser, was to guide and facilitate this process.

---

111 Ibid., xxi.

The time during which Samuel first arrived as a tutor at Ruskin College and initiated the History Workshop was a period of personal, political and intellectual 'recovery' and expansion. On the one hand, the adult tutor and later the HW's general editor were intellectual roles that were not far removed from his earlier aspirations, all of which involved working within given circumstances to encourage people to actively participate in political or intellectual work. On the other hand, the creative thinking and openness involved in finding and facilitating the links between his students' experiences, interests and wider historical frameworks in conjunction with the political mood of the times, actively forced him to expand his own ideas. This expansion could also be discerned in Samuel's own development as a historian, which is the subject of the next chapter.

4

The Secret Life of Headington Quarry: People's History in the Field

Raphael Samuel (second from right) and History Workshop students outside Ruskin, Oxford 1980

Raphael Samuel Archive, Bishopsgate Institute, London, courtesy of Alison Light and the Raphael Samuel Estate.

Masons Arms pub, Quarry School Place Road, Headington Quarry, Oxfordshire, 1969

In the summer of '69, the unobserved-observer, quietly ensconced in a snug in the Masons Arms pub, would have witnessed an intriguing spectacle. An unusual visitor had joined the usual array of Quarry drinkers that year. This was long before the days when village pubs arrayed their exteriors with hanging baskets and served gourmet seasonal lunches. The Masons Arms was still very much a 'local' place where newcomers were noticed. And this 'stranger' would have been particularly noticeable. This stranger was a historian, a tutor at the workers' college, in Oxford city. He and some of students had been visiting the Quarry for some time now. They all seemed to be absolutely fascinated by the place. On this occasion the newcomer was alone, conducting another one of his interviews. Whilst casually dressed, scruffy even, everything about him, from the poise with which he held himself to his educated accent betrayed him as different.[1] Even his name, 'Raphael Samuel', would have sounded exotic and different. Not from Oxford. Not a working man.[2] Yet so sincere was his interest that slowly the Masons Arms' locals had started to share with him their most prized memories and secrets.

What might those old Quarry boys have made of all this? Perched in their accustomed spots, hands rested on pint glasses or fingers nimbly rolling cigarettes, listening solemnly with rapt concentration as one or other of them recited their remembrances and spun out the old tales to the eager delight of this stranger and his cumbersome recording equipment.[3] Perhaps they were a little suspicious, unused to finding so receptive an audience amongst the younger generations. Perhaps they enjoyed the process, the opportunity to resurrect and reinvent their younger selves, to revisit old grievances and relive old triumphs:

---

1   Chimen Abramsky, 'Raphael Samuel', *The Jewish Chronicle*, 17 January 1997.
2   Samuel noted the 'class barriers' between himself and his interview subjects. Brian Harrison, 'Interview with Raphael Samuel', 23 October 1979, 19 Elder Street, London, transcripts held in Raphael Samuel Archive (RSA), Bishopsgate Institute, London.
3   Samuel remembers pint and cigarette fumes during the interview process. Ibid.

> [D]id old Crowy tell you? As when they used to have to come in Quarry – now I be going back ninety years ago – what I heard Granny Webb tell me – that when the policeman come in the Quarry on 'orses they took'm off the horse and put him down the well.[4]

It certainly made them think about things that they had not brought to mind for many years. As memories proved patchy or treacherous, the speakers pondered over whom amongst their connections and acquaintances would be able to fill in the spaces. Furthermore, could they convince these possible informants, their friends and relatives, to talk to this man?[5] This process of talking and remembering also caused arguments to break out amongst them about the way things used to be, but even when these squabbles broke out the historian Samuel was unperturbed.[6] In fact he seemed all the more enthralled. The contrast between the men's thick local Oxfordshire accent and the newcomer's University of Oxford English was almost comic, yet he could not have been a more attentive or appreciative audience.[7] He really seemed to be trying to piece together a picture of the Quarry back as it was before they put in the roads. Even back before old Bessie had opened up her shop and started selling all those delicious cheap pies.[8]

The picture that Samuel had been trying to construct went much deeper than a concern for the sequence of events that may or may not have taken place in the village all those years ago. Samuel was gleaning information from all manner of clues, not simply from the stories themselves, but from the very nature of their performance.

During the 1970s, Samuel published his first major *historical* publication. Now a well-established Ruskin tutor, and having gained some distance from the events and activities of the first New Left, he had spent the last decade or so learning his own historian's craft alongside his students. Taking his first major oral history essay 'Quarry Roughs' (published in the first History Workshop (HW) book collection *Village Life and*

---

4   Raphael Samuel, '"Quarry Roughs": Life and Labour in Headington Quarry, 1860–1920. An essay in oral history', in Samuel, ed., *Village Life and Labour* (London: Routledge & Kegan Paul, 1975), 151.
5   Samuel referred to 'little cousinhoods' as providing much of the core qualitative material. Brian Harrison, 'Interview with Raphael Samuel', 23 October 1979.
6   Samuel, *Village Life and Labour*, 247, note 85.
7   The quotes in *Village Life and Labour* are written out in full dialect. For an example of Samuel's speaking voice: Bishopsgate Library's channel, 'Raphael Samuel on history from below, 1990', uploaded 5 January 2012, www.youtube.com/watch?v=w96_Nf-RJHs (accessed May 2014).
8   Samuel, '"Quarry Roughs"', 243.

Labour, 1975) as its focus, this chapter explores the development of his historical imagination during the early 1970s. To further illustrate this, it also considers more closely the contrast between Samuel and E.P. Thompson as historical and political thinkers. This, it argues, lay as much in their distinctive personalities and backgrounds as in their generational difference.

Headington Quarry: Origins and influences

The research into the community of Headington Quarry was pedagogical in its origin. Since his arrival at Ruskin College, Samuel had been battling to force an experience of primary sources on his students, something missing from the college's existing history syllabus. As part of this attempt, he designed four- to five-week projects for the students to undertake before they wrote any history essays or read any textbooks. This was how Headington Quarry came about.

Samuel had found documents in the Oxfordshire County Record Office relating to a 30-year struggle between the Quarry community and local authorities, which had ended in an act of communal incendiarism in 1880. Not only were the documents relating to this study available and 'manageable', the subject matter and location of the project made it an attractive project to Ruskin students. Not only were first-year Ruskin students based out in Headington, but the poetic appeal of this common rights struggle happening right on the doorstep of Oxford University was attractive. He was delighted to have found a part of Oxford 'that wasn't Anglican and wasn't Tory and wasn't College and was historical'.[9]

During the course of this initial phase, some of the students visited the Quarry independently and returned with tales of its wildness, enhancing its potential for a more in-depth case study into 'living history'.[10] He described his own attraction to such an approach:

> I think the whole idea of the micro, of the small-scale, of seeing large things in miniature was important. I mean if you're kind of in revolt against abstraction, reductionism, systemisation – I mean wanting something that, as it were was congruent to how you actually experience life, I mean you could find a whole number of different ways in different subjects in

---

9   Brian Harrison, Interview with Raphael Samuel, 23 October 1979.
10 Ibid.

which people were reaching round, often, as I think in retrospect, quite unsatisfactorily, but I mean the effort was to produce something that was more life-like, more real, corresponded more to the human experience, the texture of human speech, the scale of human life i.e the community as studied …[11]

The roots of his 'revolt against abstraction, reduction and systemization' could be discerned in the New Left debates, in part a reaction against Stalinism, but also a response to the 'social science' turn that had begun to dominate intellectual culture. Some of his most polemical writing had been levelled against the application of sociological methodologies and modelling to explain social issues, such as the effects of affluence on voting behaviour or the causes of juvenile delinquency amongst adolescent boys.[12]

As a history tutor at Ruskin, he had also rallied against prevailing forms of social, economic and labour history. The substantial growth of social history, as championed by vehicles such as *Past and Present* (*P&P*), had done much to fracture the stranglehold of traditional political history, but whilst it had successfully expanded the subject matter on which historians worked, little inroad had been made into to the ways of thinking about history. In some incarnations, social history remained unreflective on the question of politics, content to accumulate facts in contribution to existing debates (such as rates of industrialisation or changes to standards of living and so on).

Where it did engage with politics (like at Ruskin, a self-identified workers' college), this was often on a literal level; the internal histories of unions, union leaders, the details of legislative reform in labour and industrial relations. In other forms, it drew upon simplistic sociological models, such as 'nineteenth century v. status models of class', for which it provided factual information. In short, it offered few satisfying answers to the nature of the relationship between material conditions and social-political consciousness.

If Samuel's activities during the late 1950s had informed his strong scepticism towards the reductive tendencies in sociological modelling, they had also suggested alternatives. Richard Hoggart's bestselling

---

11   Ibid.
12   See for example: Ralph Samuel, 'Dr Abrams and the End of Politics', *New Left Review* (*NLR*), I/5, Sep–Oct (1960), 1–8.

Uses of Literacy (1957) provided a strong example of a community study concerned with the impact of social structures on popular mentalities. In highlighting this relationship, Hoggart's work reached towards a sociocultural anthropological approach.

Despite its more formal alliance with sociology, the Institute of Community Studies's (ICS) early work also had an anthropological flavour. This came through the influence of Charles Madge, co-founder of Mass Observation (a popular ethnography movement), anthropologist Geoffrey Gorer and sociologist Edward Shils, all of whom were on the institute's advisory board.[13] The institute's publications, such as *Family and Kinship* (1957), had drawn upon elements of an, albeit 'unschooled', anthropological approach to illuminate the importance of kinship structures in shaping community life. Samuel's own work as a researcher and interviewer had brought him into close contact with 'Bethnal Green adolescents' and 'working-class Tory voters', and revealed the complexity between people's lived conditions and their understandings of their worlds.

His most conscious engagement with anthropology, as a distinct discipline, came initially through extensive independent reading. An early influence was Erving Goffman's *Asylum: Essays on the Social Situation of Mental Patients and other Inmates* (1961).[14] The book contained three essays charting the experiences of patients within mental institutions and one looking at the relationships between medical staff and other professionals. It was later described as an 'ethnography of the concept of total institutionalisation'.[15] What excited him about Goffman's study was the use made of the quotidian, the seemingly inconsequential details of everyday life, which were transformed into openings for whole new avenues of inquiry.[16] This was not an account of an institution's development but

---

13   For more detailed accounts of Charles Madge and the Mass Observation movement see: James Hinton, *The Mass Observers: A History 1937–1949* (Oxford: Oxford University Press, 2013). Samuel would later argue that Gorer and Shils were critical early influences for the ICS: Brian Harrison, 'Interview with Raphael Samuel', 23 October 1979; Asa Briggs, *Michael Young: Social Entrepreneur* (New York: Palgrave, 2001), 147.

14   'Most cited authors of books in the humanities, 2007', data provided by Thomson Reuters, ISI Web of Science, 2007, *The Times Higher Education Supplement*, 26 March 2009.

15   Gary Fine and Philip Manning, 'Erving Goffman', in George Ritzer, ed., *The Blackwell Companion to Major Contemporary Social Theorists* (Malden: Blackwell Publishing Ltd, 2003).

16   Brian Harrison, 'Interview with Raphael Samuel', 23 October 1979.

an examination of its impact on individual consciousness. Despite the focus on individual perception, the study did not rely on abstract theories alone, but based its arguments on detailed observation.[17]

During the mid-1960s, Samuel even designed and taught a course on social anthropology at Ruskin. Although retaining the title 'Sociology', it featured well-known studies by prominent anthropologists such as E.E. Evans-Prichard (*Kinship and Marriage Amongst the Nuer*, 1951) and Margaret Mead (*Coming of Age in Samoa*, 1928; *Growing Up in New Guinea*, 1930) and proposed tutorial questions such as: 'Compare the Kinship system described in any recent English study with that described by Evans-Prichard among the Nuer'. Other topics playfully subverted some of the sociologist's most favoured subject matters. In addressing urbanisation, he asked about the types of associations which developed amongst immigrants in industrial areas. Another section in this curious, explorative mixture used Christopher Hill's *Society and Puritanism in Pre-revolutionary England* (1964) as a core text for exploring the impact of Puritanism on the family.[18]

The attractions of anthropology as a discipline were familiar to historians, particularly those working within the flourishing field of social history. Keith Thomas's influential article 'History and Anthropology', published in 1963 in *P&P*, urged the case for a fruitful relationship between the two disciplines. This, Thomas acknowledged, was not new (a similar appeal had been made by R.H. Tawney in his Inaugural Lecture at the London School of Economics 30 years before) but in the present climate, where history seemed ever more fragmented into specialisms, it bore further pressing. Thomas welcomed new calls for a more integrated analysis of history's enduring relationships, the sort advanced through journals like *P&P*. At the same time, he critiqued over-reliance on 'a brand of vulgar Marxism' in attempting such a synthesis. Perhaps naively, he dismissed this as owing more to 'a lack of acquaintance with any other theoretical

---

17   Other examples of his readings include: Horace Miner, *The Primitive City of Timbuctoo* (Princeton: Princeton University Press, 1955); Conrad Arensburg and Solon Kimball, *Family and Community in Ireland* (Cambridge: Harvard University Press, 1948).
18   Raphael Samuel, Course Outline and Tutorial Notes for Sociology, RS 1: New Left/Ruskin College, Correspondence and Notes 1965–1967, 405, Raphael Samuel Archive (RSA), Bishopsgate, London.

attempts to effect that interrelation and mutual explanation of social facts which they would so much like to see' than a commitment to the doctrine itself.[19] Anthropology offered that alternative.

Drawing upon anthropology, the historian would find both the subject matter of their discipline greatly expanded and familiar historical problems given fresh perspective. The application of anthropological technique to an apparently paradoxical event, for example, might reveal a rationale not immediately apparent from an exclusively external perspective. Closer examination of myths, legends or histories read for their internalised attitudes to social and political authority could shed an intimate light on the dynamics of a society's organisation. Historians, Thomas concluded, could ill afford to ignore the insights offered by anthropology: '[T]he justification of all historical study must ultimately be that it enhances our self-consciousness, enables us to see ourselves in perspective and helps us towards that greater freedom which comes with self-knowledge'.[20] Following the publication of Thomas's article, Samuel wrote to Thomas (a former Balliol contemporary) expressing his enthusiastic support and agreement.[21]

The argument for anthropology was not conceived as a rejection of or antidote to social history but as an enrichment of its aims, which were only impoverished by a relative lack of conceptual resources. The recognition of a mutual concern to expand historical subject-matter and integrate its component parts into a more holistic form of analysis was important, but Thomas was too hasty in dismissing the potency of social history's political motivations. In the tumultuous years of the 1960s, others saw in the thorough-going study of the past, its structures, evolutions and points of transition, the key to the transformation of the present.

The work of E.P. Thompson also drew emphatically on anthropological insights. *The Making of the English Working Class* (1963) had demonstrated how the physical experiences of early industrialisation had fused with existing values, prompting direct confrontation with those in power, all of which had informed the emergence of a self-conscious English working

---

19   Keith Thomas, 'History and Anthropology', *Past and Present* (*P&P*), 24 (1963), 7.
20   See also: Keith Thomas, 'Should Historians be Anthropologists?', *Oxford Magazine*, 1 June 1961, 405–6; Keith Thomas, 'The Tools and the Job', *The Times Literary Supplement*, 7 April 1966; Keith Thomas, *Religion and the Decline of Magic: Studies in Popular Belief in Sixteenth and Seventeenth Century England* (London: Weidenfeld and Nicolson, 1971).
21   Brian Harrison, 'Interview with Raphael Samuel', 23 October 1979.

class and labour movement. As director of the Centre for Social History at Warwick University,[22] Thompson continued to focus on value systems and their role in stimulating conflict between the 'ruling' and 'ruled'. In a challenge to depictions of the eighteenth-century English collier who claps his hands spasmodically upon his stomach and responds to elementary economic stimuli, he pursued the shared 'moral assumptions' animating popular life, the outrage of which 'quite as much as actual deprivation, was the usual occasion for direct action', whether in the form of the flouting of poaching laws or the staging of food riots.[23] Elsewhere, he considered how the imposition of new technologies of time measurement, the physical restructuring of the working day, week, year to align with the requirements of factory and market place, struggled against, and eventually rewrote, preexisting conceptions of time and production.[24]

For Samuel, however, the most important training ground for his historical thinking was the Social History Group (1964–74) which he established alongside recent Oxford graduates Gareth Stedman Jones and Tim Mason, both of whom would go on to be critical figures in the *History Workshop Journal*.[25] A generation younger than Samuel, the two men had already voiced strong critique over the existing state of Oxford history teaching as they had encountered it during their student days. Mason had joined a growing chorus bewailing the 'Anglo-centric', chronological and narrative-based history syllabus. He had supported a student campaign towards a reduction of compulsory English history, the option of presenting a thesis in finals, and the introduction of more courses in social, cultural and intellectual history (including, for the future historian of Nazi Germany, subjects with texts in foreign languages).[26]

---

22   Thompson held this position from 1965 to 1971. John Rule, 'Thompson, Edward Palmer (1924–1993)', *Oxford Dictionary of National Biography* (Oxford: Oxford University Press, 2004).
23   E.P. Thompson, 'The Moral Economy of the Crowd', in *Customs in Common* (London: Merlin Press, 1991), 187–88.
24   E.P. Thompson, 'Time, Work-Discipline and Industrial Capitalism', *P&P*, 38 (1967), 56–97; E.P. Thompson, 'The Moral Economy of the English Crowd in the Eighteenth Century', *P&P*, 50 (1971), 76–136; E.P. Thompson, *Whigs and Hunters: The Origin of the Black Act* (New York: Pantheon Books, 1975); Douglas Hay, Peter Linebaugh, John G. Rule, E.P. Thompson and Cal Winslow, eds, *Albion's Fatal Tree: Crime and Society in Eighteenth Century England* (Harmondsworth: Penguin, 1977). Collected together in: Thompson, *Customs in Common*.
25   Raphael Samuel, 'The Social History Group 1965–1974', in Samuel, ed., *History Workshop: A Collectanea 1967–1991* (Oxford: History Workshop 25, 1991), 85–86.
26   Tim Mason: 'The Teaching and Study of History', *Isis*, 31 May 1961, 20–21; 'Reform of the History Syllabus', *Isis*, 5 December 1962, 15; 'The History Syllabus: The End of the Road?', *Isis*, 13 March 1963.

Stedman Jones, active in student left-wing politics and a student member of a first New Left Club, put the case more strongly in his article, 'The Pathology of English History', published in *NLR* in 1967. Denouncing the prevalence of a Liberal bias in English academic history, he argued that the discipline's unswerving commitment to empirical inquiry failed to recognise its own ideological positioning. The splintering of the profession into so many sub-disciplines reinforced this with few attempts 'made to fuse this aggregate of specialist routines into a meaningful historical totality'. The article ended with a war cry: socialist historians must form their own institutions, be 'aggressive and iconoclastic'. '[O]nly vigorous intellectual imperialism and collective assault' would make a mark.[27]

The Social History Group was, however, not intended to be the vanguard of a historiographical revolution. The intention, more modestly, was to bring together champions of a broad range of new historical methods, 'united mainly by a common ambition to break out from the narrow confines of political and constitutional history'.[28]

The group took an initial interest in the social history of religious belief, under the guidance of John Walsh, a senior history tutor at Oxford and a historian of eighteenth-century religious history.[29] The first text to be studied by the group was Blaise Pascal's *Pensees* (1669) which the group subjected to close textual examination attempting to pay particular attention to how the nuances of language, phrasing and reference provided a glimpse into that brilliant but deeply conflicted thinker situated amidst his life and times in seventeenth-century France. This text, in which Pascal struggled between competing forms of knowledge and seemingly contradictory values, was quite appropriate for the mid-1960s, also caught amidst its own maelstrom of contending ideas and sentiments.[30]

An early project that Samuel initiated in conjunction with the Social History Group historians and the Ruskin Workshop historians was on 'Nineteenth Century Cromwell', an ambitious and expansive project attempting to 'read' political mentalities through the various

---

27 Gareth Stedman Jones, 'The Pathology of English History', *NLR*, I/46, Nov–Dec (1967), 43.
28 Gareth Stedman Jones, 'History and Theory', *historein* [Athens], 3 (2001), 111.
29 Ibid.; Brian Harrison, 'Interview with Raphael Samuel', 23 October 1979; Stuart Hall, Alun Howkins, Sally Alexander and John Walsh, 'Raphael Samuel 1934–1996', *History Workshop Journal* (*HWJ*), 43 (1997), x–xi.
30 See Blaise Pascal, *Pensees and Other Writings* (Oxford: Oxford University Press, 1995).

representations of Oliver Cromwell in Victorian popular culture. Despite a substantial amount of work, the early yields of the research were turned down for publication by the editors of *P&P* (a critical informing prompt for the creation of the *History Workshop Journal* (HWJ)).[31]

Against this backdrop, Headington Quarry, whilst originating as a pedagogical exercise, was also an opportunity to utilise and apply the techniques of social anthropology in order to gain a deeper sense of the internal relationships that shaped life in the community. Aside from the close scrutiny of the documents, another way of achieving this was through oral history and the use of living memory and oral testimony as a primary source. The first student project on the common rights struggle was presented at a Workshop held in 1968 which was also attended by Paul Thompson, a pioneering figure in British oral history who was instrumental in founding the Oral History Society and *Oral History Journal*.[32]

Thompson was a social and labour historian who had become interested in libertarian traditions, in particular the political thought of William Morris about whom he wrote his own study, *The Work of William Morris* (1967). Thompson was struck by Morris's sensitivity to the domestic dimensions of life, which made him unique amongst socialist thinkers.[33] Whilst working as a sociology lecturer at the University of Essex during the late 1960s, Thompson became involved in a project looking at the social history of Britain from 1900 to 1918. During the course of this project he had become aware of the lack of direct evidence relating to the everyday life of the Edwardian working class. Funded by a grant from the Social Science Research Council (SSRC) (who Samuel would pointedly note did not contribute towards the Headington project), he embarked on a large-scale project conducting some 450 interviews with men and women, by then very elderly people, who had lived during that time.[34]

The interviews were conducted by part-time researchers and followed a loose structure that included gathering information relating to domestic routines, household roles, meals, upbringing, family values, relationships with the wider community, courtship, school, politics and experiences

---

31 Trevor Ashton to Raphael Samuel, 'Letter Concerning 19th Century Cromwell', in Samuel, ed., *History Workshop: A Collectanea 1967–1991*, 94.
32 Brian Harrison, 'Interview with Raphael Samuel', 23 October 1979.
33 Paul Thompson, *The Work of William Morris* (London: Heinemann, 1967).
34 Raphael Samuel, 'General Editor's Introduction', in *Village Life and Labour*, xx.

of work.³⁵ The result of this project was *The Edwardians: The Remaking of British Society* (1975). This project also formed the basis for *Voices of the Past* (1978), Thompson's methodological textbook on oral history.

Recognising the close parallels with his own work, Thompson responded supportively to the HW's approach to historical research.³⁶ The Headington Quarry project had already made some use of oral history as a key methodological technique. Alun Howkins, who had not spoken at the first Workshop, had already undertaken one long interview with Crowy Kerry, a Quarry poacher. The insights gained from this interview had not, as yet, been worked into the papers on the common rights struggle. Thompson's enthusiasm, along with the inherent interest that this little community had aroused in some of his students, encouraged Samuel towards a more sustained turn to oral history.

During the course of 1969, Samuel, along with some of his Ruskin students including Sally Alexander and Howkins, undertook three projects on Headington Quarry.³⁷ Alexander's work concentrated on the relationship between the local St Giles fair and the industrial revolution. Howkins focused on the importance of poaching to the informal economic life of the Headington community. Samuel's work on life and labour in the Quarry was intended to provide an overview and background context to these papers through the more concentrated use of oral history. The three also planned a future Workshop meeting to be held in November 1969 showcasing the student work on 'Proletarian Oxford'.

The Quarry, with its apparently lawless, wild inhabitants, its transient gypsy population, its defiant poaching activities and its unique traditions of Morris dancing, resonated with the restless spirit of rebellion and radicalism that characterised the late 1960s. Yet, despite the Quarry's inherent 'wildness', the project was not consciously about an 'outsider' community and the research not about finding an 'ancestry' for the next appointed revolutionary social group. Samuel's expressed intention was more about telling the histories of the 'other Oxford'.

---

35 H.J. Dyos et al., 'The Interview in Social History Part 1: General Discussion', *Oral History*, 1, 4 (1972), 126–28; Paul Thompson, Edwardian online: www.qualidata.ac.uk/edwardians/original/method.asp (accessed May 2014).
36 Brian Harrison, 'Interview with Raphael Samuel', 23 October 1979.
37 Alun Howkins, email communication with author, October 2013, transcript held in author's private collection.

Inside the Quarry

Samuel did not embark on his Headington Quarry research in a state of starry-eyed innocence, ready to believe whatever was told to him. He approached the project having already conducted substantial documentary research into the area, and through his training in social and labour history he was already aware of some of the established patterns and trends in labour processes. In the course of his interviews, he carefully framed his questions around factual details, such as family history and work life, rather than directly addressing more subjective matters of belief and opinion.[38] During the research process for his essay on the Quarry, he continually performed a complex intellectual operation of sifting and interplaying the different sources, forms and registers of historical evidence.[39]

How did this work 'in the field'? During the course of one of the interviews a reference was made to the casual nature of work in the Quarry, even amongst skilled labourers like stonemasons. The 'manner' in which it had been mentioned, matter-of-factly, suggested that it was not an uncommon occurrence but an accepted feature of village life. Samuel then checked such an assertion against the locally available documentary evidence. In the case of the Quarry research, this had included the discovery of a diary written by a Quarry stonemason in 1883.[40] The diary's contents did not address the matter of 'casual' employment directly, but noted that during the course of one year this stonemason gained and lost work six times. It also recorded the location of these jobs allowing for further verification in official records. This erratic employment pattern supported the idea that work life was not stable whilst the sparse and factual manner of writing, in conjunction with the original casual reference made to this form of work life in the interview, reinforced the idea that this was typical, not worth commenting on in depth. He had then to reference this against his wider knowledge about temporary, seasonal, or piecemeal labour practices in nineteenth-century British economic life to make

---

38 Samuel in Dyos et al., 'The Interview in Social History Part 1', 133.
39 Samuel would write about some of the challenges – perils – of conducting oral history and of the research undertaken on the Quarry. Raphael Samuel, 'Perils of the Transcript', *Oral History* 1, 2 (1971), 19–22; 'Headington Quarry: Recording a Labouring Community', *Oral History* 1, 4 (1972), 107–22.
40 Brian Harrison, 'Interview with Raphael Samuel', 23 October 1979.

a convincing argument.⁴¹ In this way, he validated the comment made in the interview and, in turn, identified a highly specific example or case study against which to attach a discussion about wider economic trends.

It was not only the residents of Headington Quarry that were teaching him about the art of the oral interview, its uses for historical research and its potential pitfalls. In the early 1970s he also embarked on another project, a life history of Arthur Harding, an old criminal figure from the East End of London.⁴² The six-years-long series of interviews with Harding, at the time a man in his nineties, continued some of the themes and questions that had emerged during his time working at the ICS. Young and Willmott had placed a strong emphasis on the way in which structures of thought and feeling were imparted through familial and kinship relationships in their landmark study *Family and Kinship in East London* (1957).⁴³ His own work, both for the ICS and later undertaken independently, had further reinforced this concern and sensitivity towards the importance of social relationships in mediating political and moral consciousness.⁴⁴ His work with Harding swept up all these various components and coordinates as they had manifested in and shaped the lived experience of Harding as an individual.

The two made an unlikely pairing. Harding had been raised in the slums of East London. He was a former criminal, strike-breaker, Conservative voter, and former bodyguard to fascist politician Oswald Mosley. Samuel by contrast had been raised in the genteel surrounds of Hampstead Garden Suburb. He was from a Jewish family, a former member of the Communist Party of Great Britain (CPGB) and still a committed man of the radical left. Yet despite the social and ideological chasm between them, they struck up an instant rapport, another testimony, perhaps, to Samuel's capacity to engage with a wide range of people.⁴⁵

The interview process, however, had been far from straightforward. It must have been quite a strange situation with both participants 'performing their parts' on multiple levels. Samuel entered the process with 'concealed'

---

41 Demonstrated to strong effect in Raphael Samuel, 'Comers and Goers', in H.J. Dyos and Michael Wolff, eds, *The Victorian City: Images and Realities* (London: Routledge, 1973), 123–60.
42 For a background to this project see: Stan Newens, 'The Genesis of *East End Underworld: Chapters in the Life of Arthur Harding* by Raphael Samuel', *HWJ*, 64 (2007), 347–54.
43 Acknowledged in the preface to the subsequent book. Arthur Harding and Raphael Samuel, *East End Underworld: Chapters in the Life of Arthur Harding* (London: Routledge and Paul, 1981), vii–viii.
44 See for example: Ralph Samuel, 'The Deference Voter', *NLR*, I/1, Jan–Feb (1960), 9–13.
45 Newens, 'The Genesis of *East End Underworld*', 349.

intentions: to relate Harding, as an individual, to the wider social conditions which led to 'delinquency'. In order to gain Harding's trust, however, it was important that he was not made fully aware of Samuel's agenda. Meanwhile, Harding entered into the process with his own set of intentions: the opportunity to 'present his story as being a fight against the unjustified charges of the police'.[46] And so ensued a battle of wits between the interviewer and interviewee, the agenda of one clashing with the agenda of the other. 'I mean', Samuel would say of this project later, 'one couldn't be naïve on that because he was…certainly being very political himself in handling the interview […]'.[47] If Samuel had not been equally 'political' in interviewing Harding, the result would have had little use as a form of social documentary.

The end result, *East End Underworld: The Life of Arthur Harding* (1981), bore the scars of this struggle between the two men. His precarious balancing act between situating Harding's testimony in historical context and allowing Harding, as a subject, a voice, pleased no one. Harding allegedly disliked the book, feeling it did not represent his story well.[48] Critics, such as historian David Cannadine, felt the heavy inclusion of 'anecdotal' evidence obscured the strength of the argument.[49]

As embattled (and embittered) as this particular project was, it did, however, indicate the potential of such an approach. In this instance, as Cannadine argued, Samuel had not been able to fully integrate all the diffuse sources into coherent form, but the richness of the material and fluidity with which multiple dimensions of insight were traversed showed promise.[50]

This process of shifting between different sources and registers of information was supported by his habitual style of note-taking and research.[51] One observation or note was written on a single, loose sheet of paper along with assemblages of related material, supporting documentary evidence and secondary sources – journal articles or book chapters – compiled into one large collection. Out of this, he would compose draft paragraphs or passages from which an essay or article would be

---

46 Brian Harrison, 'Interview with Raphael Samuel', 23 October 1979.
47 Ibid.
48 Oral communication with author, Stefan Dickers, Head Archivist of RSA, Bishopsgate Institute, London, December 2011.
49 David Cannadine, *The Pleasures of the Past* (New York: WW Norton & Company Inc., 1989), 190–92.
50 Samuel, *East End Underworld*.
51 Light, 'A Biographical Note on the Text', xv–xxii.

constructed. Although outwardly chaotic as a working methodology, one of the great benefits of this approach was that these discrete facts could be continually shuffled and reshuffled, arranged and rearranged in relation to different perspectives, questions and positions. Accordingly, one encounter or observation had the potential to splinter outwards into multiple contexts, dependent on what aspect of the information was placed in central focus.[52]

How, then, did he set about reintegrating this mass of facts, gleaned from multiple sources, identified and extracted by direct and indirect means, into the organised whole of an essay? The first major clue lies in the title itself: '"Quarry Roughs": Life and labour in Headington Quarry, 1860–1920. An essay in oral history'. The title starts by borrowing from a description of the Quarry residents taken from an article published in 1905 in a local newspaper. It then goes on to state the subject matter, 'life and labour'; the place where this matter is being studied, 'Headington Quarry'; and provide the time frame for the study, '1860–1920'. Finally, the essay informs the reader of its own methodological approach: 'an essay in oral history'. All this information is factual, relating to specific coordinates. This makes the title 'descriptive', rather than 'argumentative' in nature. It is designed to give the impression that what follows is an investigation that might lead to the suggestion of some provisional conclusions rather than an argument that will either be 'proved' or 'disproved' by the evidence.

The essay continued on in this investigative mode; its sections were thematic, addressing the different economic relationships at work in the community which moved in ever-decreasing circles drawing on more intimate perspectives of life in the Quarry. He opened the essay with a broad overview of the village and its situation, the function of which was to sketch a view of the Quarry in terms of the interplay between the natural environmental features of the landscape (the quarry itself) and the built human settlement – the intersection of which informed the basis for the Quarry community's distinctive internal character and its conflicted relationship with Oxford City (and the outside world more generally).

---

52 Keith Thomas, 'Diary', *London Review of Books*, 10 June 2010, 36–37. Thomas also described his use of a similar practice of note-taking. Thomas acknowledged that, whilst never formally taught this approach, he took his cues, in part, from the working methods of Christopher Hill, the tutor that Thomas and Samuel shared as undergraduate students at Balliol College, Oxford University, during the early 1950s.

Having equipped his reader with mental coordinates of the Quarry as a place, he proceeded to address quarrying, the primary economic activity in the area. Samuel did more than just describe this activity, he explored the implications of this form of occupation. The nature of the employment combined with the location of the village created a sense of fluidity in working roles and relationships. Quarry labourers suffered from an unreliability of work, but enjoyed more freedom in their activities. As for the work itself, it was characterised by its hard and physical nature. Activities like brickmaking were largely male dominated and the Quarry labourers gained a reputation for being good workers who were physically strong.[53]

One might think that this would imply a highly dominant masculine culture in the village, and consequently a predominantly masculine focus to the essay, but Samuel dedicated as much space to the work undertaken by Quarry women whose primary occupation was laundry work. This was characterised by the hard physical nature of the labour processes involved. He noted how this work was often done in all-female groups or coordinated through families, citing an example of a family in which grandmother, mother and granddaughter all worked in the laundry together fostering close all-female relationships.[54] He commented on how laundry offered the potential for an independent income, providing widowed women with an alternative to Parish relief.

The analysis then moved to consider the community's 'secondary' forms of income generation, reflecting first on the need for a secondary economy. He suggested that the seasonal nature of building or brickmaking work forced the Quarry's inhabitants to find other means of supporting themselves and their families. He demonstrated how these were often determined by the natural resources available (produce from kitchen gardens and allotments or the keeping of pigs for example, which then became the basis for swaps, exchanges and bartering amongst the villagers) and pointed to the ways in which this 'informal' economy had a major influence on everyday village life, structuring family life through the organisation and distribution of labour, which shaped the relations between the genders and generations.[55] It also informed personal

---

53   Raphael Samuel, '"Quarry Roughs"', 168.
54   Ibid., 180.
55   Ibid., 200, 203.

preoccupations. A series of entries in the stonemason's diary, for example, detailed both the work he had done in the garden and the clemency of the weather (a continual source of anxiety for the keen gardener).[56]

Not content to rest at this, he probed ever further into these 'unofficial' realms exploring those activities conducted in a legally 'ambiguous' manner through the opportunistic uses of natural resources, such as the acquisition and selling of firewood, the catching of birds and the poaching of rabbits.[57] Again, his interest in these activities was not just for their own sake but also for the ways in which they provided an insight into the sociocultural life of the village. He cited the ways in which these 'goods' became an additional contribution to the household coffers, noted the manner in which the 'fruits' of poaching transformed the local diet; and observed how these 'unofficial' economic practices informed the village's relationships with both authority figures and community 'outsiders', such as the gypsies who camped in the local woodlands during the winter.[58]

Within all these sections, the most striking feature of the writing was the use that he made of his oral sources. Quotes taken from the oral testimonies were written out in full and original dialect, which had the effect of invoking the sound and sense of the speaker:

> Old Uncle George – Pedgell Webb – used to have a big 'llotment up there and 'ee used to have plenty of carrots, plenty of swedes – well that was a good feed, good rabbit-they'd ketch their own rabbits.[59]

By contrast, Samuel's own voice, as the historian, took a back seat. This did not mean that his commentary was cold or disinterested. It was friendly, free from technical language but for the most part avoided making its 'presence' too demonstrative. This was done partly in order to allow the voices to 'speak for themselves' and partly to avoid the 'superiority' implied by the researcher more intent on their personal interpretation than responsive to the information being given to them. The quotes were not just used as an illustration of the essay's analysis. They were *integral* parts of the study's analytical process. Samuel and his interview subjects worked in a dialogue with one another, the quotes providing certain informative cues that the commentary went on to explain.

---

56 Ibid., 193.
57 Ibid., 210.
58 Ibid., 209–25.
59 Ibid., 225.

The information provided by the oral testimonies also provided him with a compelling methodological argument as to why the use of qualitative sources was so crucial to the study:

> So far as the standard of life is concerned, it is difficult to assess the value of these extras in monetary terms, to 'quantify' in a way that the economic historian might feel professionally obliged to demand, or to incorporate them in the week-by-week household budget.[60]

Not only was this a general 'challenge' to the sociological tool kit of 'standards' and modes of 'assessment', it also reinforced the idea that understanding these 'unofficial' forms of economy demanded a close perspective. Little trace of them, or their central importance to village life, would have emerged from the documentary record alone.

Whilst the quotes used in '"Quarry Roughs"' were often taken on the basis of their direct informational content, some of his observations utilised the oral testimony more indirectly. He used the accounts told to him by villagers of that unfortunate policeman who had met with a watery drop down the village well less for their literal content and more for what the story, and its popularity amongst the villagers, could tell him about village attitudes to authority figures. He did not attempt to adjudicate over which of the many available versions of the story was true, nor did he attempt his own version of the actual incident; he simply took the telling of the story as a source of evidence in itself.[61]

As rich, in-depth and intriguing as his treatment of community life in Headington Quarry was, the essay also advanced a large political argument. Drawing on the prevalence of small-scale enterprise and non-accumulative capitalism in the Quarry's economy, he ventured an insight into the socioeconomic life in late Victorian and Edwardian English society as a whole:

> Capitalism in the nineteenth century was an uneven development, in the countryside no less than in the towns, and Quarry was one of those dark corners of the kingdom – like the East End of London – which had been imperfectly colonized, from an economic and industrial as well as from a cultural and social point of view.[62]

---

60   Ibid., 219–20.
61   Ibid., 151.
62   Ibid.

The implications of viewing capitalism as an uneven development, unconsolidated even as late as the twentieth century, posed a stark challenge to notions of class emerging as a political identity in response to an industrialised, capitalist society. This linked back to the New Left debates where he had rejected an overly simplified 'nineteenth-century class model'. But the argument here felt tenuous, additional rather than central.[63] It could hardly be said to have been plied with force. In fact, it was almost subdued, lingering in the background, drowned out by the colour and vibrant detail of Samuel's internal study of community life.

This argument emerged with more clarity in a later article '"The Workshop of the World": Steam Power and Hand Technology in Mid-Victorian Britain', an astonishingly detailed ethnographic study of the heterogeneity of labour experiences during this time, emphatically demonstrating a protracted history of fragmented and disjointed encounters with industrialisation amongst the mid-nineteenth-century labour force.[64] The article gave chapter and verse to the paucity of existing views about the historical development of capitalism. Its forms were more diverse and its spread more uneven than typically assumed.

The personal politics of Raphael Samuel and E.P. Thompson

"'Quarry Roughs'" was a fascinating exploration of community life. As an insight into nineteenth-century capitalism it was more limited. It bore the heavy imprint of Samuel's concerted drift towards left-libertarian politics, evident in this concluding comment:

> There was plenty of individual enterprise in Quarry, but it was apt to be dispersed in a variety of directions rather than concentrated in a single whole. The villagers were good at making ends meet, often in trying conditions, but not, it seems at making money. They lacked the capitalist instinct for getting rich at other people's expense, or on the basis of other people's labour. They made the best of their environment, but they did not overstep its limits, or treat it as a point of take-off.[65]

---

63 Samuel later acknowledged that he could have done more to develop this point. Brian Harrison, 'Interview with Raphael Samuel', 23 October 1979.
64 Raphael Samuel, 'Workshop of the World: Steam Power and Hand Technology in Mid-Victorian Britain', *HWJ*, 3 (1977), 6–72.
65 Samuel, '"Quarry Roughs"', 234.

4. THE SECRET LIFE OF HEADINGTON QUARRY

This celebration of a fiercely independent people, unmotivated by greed, felt a little idealised, too willing to overlook those who had willingly taken up the security of a reliable wage packet when the opportunity, in the form of the Cowley car plant, had arisen. This was the view taken by a number of critics for whom the HW's approach to history often lacked clarity in its political and theoretical framework.[66] One of the first people to advance this sort of critique was one of the HW's original and major sources of inspiration, E.P. Thompson.

It might appear puzzling that Thompson should criticise the HW's historical endeavours given that his own historical methodology and research interests had been so informative of it. In fact, there were many parallels between Thompson and Samuel. Both took their stance on 'history from below', concentrating their interests on popular life and culture.[67] Politically, both drew inspiration from English traditions of libertarianism and ethical socialism, emphasising the role of human agency and preferring the popular movement to party politics. Methodologically, both drew upon the insights and techniques of social anthropology but retained their fidelity to the empirical methods of historical inquiry. Yet despite all these similarities in interests and approach Thompson regarded Samuel, and the HW, with a sternly critical eye.

In Thompson's view, the HW's principal flaw was the extent of its immersion in popular life which, he felt, verged at times towards 'evacuating large territories of established political and economic history'.[68] At best, he would allow that the HW could be seen as part of a wider resurgence of libertarianism, which he welcomed.[69] By contrast, Thompson's sense of the politics in his own historical project was clear. *The Making of the English Working Class* had set out a bold account of suffering and struggle. Later essays delved even more deeply into the concealed and subversive 'theatres' in which such struggles took place. For Thompson, the driving preoccupation of his historical interests was

---

66 Dennis Dworkin, *Cultural Marxism in Postwar Britain: History, the New Left, and the Origins of Cultural Studies* (Durham and London: Duke University Press, 1997), 192.
67 E.P. Thompson, 'History From Below', *The Times Literary Supplement*, 7 April 1966. Samuel, 'General Editors' Introduction: People's History', in *Village Life and Labour*, xiii–xxi.
68 Quoted in Samuel, 'General Editor's Introduction', xix. A viewed echoed by subsequent critics including: Dworkin, *Cultural Marxism in Postwar Britain*, 187. Harvey Kaye, *The British Marxist Historians* (Cambridge: Polity Press, 1984).
69 Terry Hott, 'Interview with E. P. Thompson', *The Leveller*, 22 January 1978, 22.

the relationship between value systems and class struggle, and his interest in popular culture was, therefore, continually subjugated towards the politics of struggle.[70]

Samuel's response to Thompson's critique was to argue that there was nothing intrinsically 'micro' or 'macro' in the study of history. He teased his old comrade, asserting the validity of travelling the historical terrain by foot rather than 'in armoured car or tractor' (Thompson had been a tank commander the Second World War and was known to traverse the Worcester countryside, where he lived, by tractor).[71] In a further jibe, a cheeky misquotation of William Blake (Thompson was a notorious connoisseur of Blake), he contended that it *was* 'possible to hold eternity in a grain of sand'.[72]

In an article, 'Local History and Oral History', published the following year and appearing in the first edition of the *HWJ* (1976), Samuel advanced a clearer and more articulate statement of his historical methodology. Rejecting the view of the local study as myopic, dry or antiquarian, he argued that the demands imposed by the 'local' framework challenged overarching concepts such as 'class', 'community' or 'place', forcing them to shed some of their apparent cohesiveness when viewed 'up close'. With regards to oral history, he insisted that:

> The value of the testimonies depend on what the historian brings to them as well as on what he or she takes, on the precision of the questions, and the wider context of knowledge and understanding from which they are drawn.[73]

Here, he deftly shifted the onus of value onto the imaginative capacity of the historian. It was not the subject matter itself that determined its worth, but the way it was handled, interpreted and drawn out into a wider network of connections.

---

70 'E. P. Thompson [interview by Mike Merrill]', in Henry Abelove, Betsy Blackmar, Peter Dimock and Jonathan Schneer, eds, *Visions of History* (Manchester: Manchester University Press, 1983), 20.
71 Samuel, 'General Editor's Introduction', xix; W.L. Webb, 'A Thoroughly English Dissident', *Radical History Review*, 58 (1994), 162.
72 William Blake's famous stanza should read: 'To see the world in a grain of sand, And a heaven in a wild flower, Hold infinity in the palm of your hand, And eternity in an hour'. William Blake with David V. Erdman, ed., *The Complete Poetry and Prose of William Blake* (Berkeley and Los Angeles: University of California, 2008). Samuel, 'General Editor's Introduction', xix; E.P. Thompson, *Witness against the Beast: William Blake and the Moral Law* (New York: New Press, 1993).
73 Raphael Samuel, 'Local History and Oral History', *HWJ*, 1 (1976), 206.

4. THE SECRET LIFE OF HEADINGTON QUARRY

Samuel clearly considered the HW, and by extension himself, to be pursuing a distinctive intellectual and historical agenda to the 'grand terrain' occupied by Thompson.[74] How best to understand this distinctive agenda? Whilst Thompson's 'people's history' retained the centrality of class struggle and stressed the role of people in shaping that struggle, Samuel's historical interests were diffuse, stretching widely across popular life in all its guises and splintering off into many different avenues. Like Thompson, he shared the view of people as creative agents but was beginning to approach this more expansively, as interested in those not so explicitly engaged in forms of class struggle (the Arthur Hardings and deference voters of this world) and in the struggles that took place amongst and between members of a group.

In part this difference was informed by the influence of their respective generations on their intellectual dispositions and emotional sensibilities. Thompson was born in 1924, 10 years earlier than Samuel. Numerically this is not a long period of time, but, as Perry Anderson would later comment, between Thompson's generation and Samuel's lay the unbridgeable gulf of the Second World War; a sentiment echoed by the novelist Doris Lessing, a former comrade and contemporary of Thompson's who said of her generation: 'For that is how I see our lot now – war crazed – even if we were hundreds or thousands of miles from the actual fighting'.[75]

Thompson's adolescence was conducted in the shadow of the threat of fascism and impending war.[76] He went up to Cambridge as a student in 1942, a point where university life and student politics were, inevitably, dominated by both the intellectual and the practical implications engendered by being a nation at war. In 1944, aged 20, he undertook active duty, serving as a tank commander in Italy and North Africa.[77] He would later acknowledge that he had been 'forged in the forties', the decade of heroes, a time fuelled on the sort of sentiments to be found in the (early) works of figures like W.H. Auden, and when a British newspaper could say in all seriousness:

---

74   Raphael Samuel, *Theatres of Memory: Past and Present in Contemporary Culture* (London: Verso, 1994), 320.
75   Perry Anderson, 'Diary', *London Review of Books*, 21 October 1993, 24; Doris Lessing, *Walking in the Shade: Volume Two of My Autobiography* (New York: Harper Collins, 1997), 290.
76   'E. P. Thompson [interview by Mike Merrill]', in Abelove et al., eds, *Visions of History*, 11.
77   Rule, 'Thompson, Edward Palmer (1924–1993)'.

> At moments like this it is especially fitting that we should pay homage to poets ... for the sake of that clearer vision which their eyes, superimposed upon our own failing sight, can restore to us.[78]

The Carritts, neighbours and close friends of Thompson and his family, provided one example of this sort of heroism. Three of the boys, Gabriel, Anthony and Noel Carritt, became actively involved with resistance movements in the Spanish Civil War (Anthony was killed fighting with the International Brigade in 1937).[79]

The greatest symbol of the idea that the poet could also be a hero, however, lay even closer to home. Thompson's elder brother, Frank (1920–1944), was an exceptionally gifted linguist and poet, gaining mastery over 10 modern and ancient languages by the age of 23. Frank won a scholarship to Winchester College and later to New College, Oxford, to read Mods and Greats (classics). Thompson lacked his brother's gift for languages or aptitude for classical literature. Unlike Winchester, Thompson's school Kingswood had had no pretensions to elitism. He later described his own cultural and political drive as 'low-brow, moralising – perhaps even Methodistical – and self-consciously demotic'.[80] Frank's intellectual strengths were not matched by physical ones. He was tall, quite frail and uncommonly clumsy, very far from the physical perfection of the classical heroes that had so captured his imagination.[81] Thompson, of a stronger build and an enthusiastic sportsman, would often assume the role of his protector.[82]

During his years at Oxford, Frank became increasingly politicised, frustrated by the British Government's lack of firm response to the rising threat posed by fascism. Influenced by the future philosopher and author Iris Murdoch, he joined the CPGB in 1938. His attraction to communist politics, however, did not equate to a full acceptance or even a thorough understanding of Marxist theory but was an extension of his poetic sensibilities blended with his innate good nature and courage.[83] When

---

78   E.P. Thompson, *The Poverty of Theory and Other Essays* (London: Merlin Press, 1978), 264. This was also acknowledged by Raymond Williams in *Politics and Letters: Interviews with New Left Review* (London: New Left Books, 1979), 135–36. Quote taken from *The Times*, 26 September 1938.
79   Peter Conradi, *A Very English Hero: The Making of Frank Thompson* (London: Bloomsbury, 2012), 84–86.
80   E.P. Thompson, *Beyond the Frontier* (Stanford: Stanford University Press, 1997), 52.
81   Ibid., 51.
82   Ibid.
83   Ibid., 57; Conradi, *A Very English Hero*.

war was declared in September 1939 Frank was amongst the first to join up, disregarding the position of the British Communist Party. Ultimately this led him to a dangerous mission aiding communist partisan fighters in occupied Bulgaria. The mission ended tragically with Frank executed alongside several of the other partisans by a fascist firing squad in 1944.[84] Thompson and his mother, Theodosia Thompson, later published a collection of Frank's poetry entitled *Spirit in Europe*, taken from a letter by Frank sent to his family the Christmas before his death, in which he had written:

> There is a spirit abroad in Europe which is finer and braver than anything that tired continent has known for centuries, and which cannot be withstood ... It is the confident will of whole peoples, who have known the utmost humiliation and suffering and who have triumphed over it, to build their own life once and for all.[85]

Thompson's preoccupation with the relationship between value systems and class politics could be read as an attempt to reconcile the nobility of this spirit with the rigours of political-economic structural analysis.[86]

Following the war and the defeat of European state fascism, there was a sense of hope amongst socialists that a new world could be constructed. Thompson and his partner Dorothy travelled out to Yugoslavia (which voted to become a 'People's Republic' in November 1945) to join a group of international youth workers on a railway-building project. This was an important experience. The internationalism of the youth workers reinforced the sense of socialism as a universal politics, whilst the close-knit life of the group had demonstrated the small-scale cooperative community in action. What this experience also highlighted was the distance of the Soviet Union from this form of communist politics. Little support or interest was shown in the project by the Soviet Union and there were no Soviet people amongst the youth group.[87]

---

84 Roderick Bailey, 'Thompson (William) Frank (1920–1944)', *Oxford Dictionary of National Biography* (Oxford: Oxford University Press, 2004).
85 Frank Thompson, *There is a Spirit in Europe: A Memoir of Frank Thompson*, collected by T.J. Thompson and E.P. Thompson (London: Gollancz, 1947).
86 'E. P. Thompson [interview by Mike Merrill]', in Abelove et al., eds, *Visions of History*, 20.
87 Sheila Rowbotham, 'The Personal and the Political: Interview with Dorothy Thompson', *NLR*, I/200, Jul–Aug (1993), 87–100; E.P. Thompson, ed., *The Railway: An Adventure in Construction* (London: British-Yugoslav Assocation, 1948); 'E. P. Thompson [interview by Mike Merrill]', in Abelove et al., eds, *Visions of History*, 12.

Thompson's formative intellectual years took place in dramatic and disruptive times where the line between life and death, good and evil was vividly apparent. Samuel, meanwhile, a child on the British home front during the war, came into intellectual maturity in the postwar years. His student days at Oxford had been conducted in the political landscape of the 1950s, dominated by the inhibitive politics of the Cold War. These years were further characterised by successive Conservative governments, a welfare state entering the first decade of its existence and beginning to reveal the limitations of its vision, the resurgence of a consumer-based capitalism and the politics of affluence. All this had given rise to a decade categorically defined in its intellectual and artistic culture by a retreat from (and often mockery of) the heroic, taking instead the ordinary and the everyday as its major aesthetic. The tenor of political debate was transferred from the bloody theatres of conflict in a war-torn world and repositioned in the finer points of social planning and welfare policy.[88]

It was not, however, only generational difference that distinguished the two men but also a question of personal temperament informed by their respective upbringings. Thompson was raised in Boars Hill, a small settlement on the outskirts of Oxford. The community of Boars Hill constituted a 'self-conscious intellectual elite', renowned for its concentrated population of academics, writers and artists, conscious of their position as cultural figureheads and leaders in English society.[89] This was certainly applicable in the Thompson household. Thompson's father, E.J. Thompson, a former Methodist missionary in India who had become a lecturer in Indian languages at Oxford University, remained an articulate voice against British imperialism in India, and eminent figures from Indian politics and literature, such as Gandhi, Nehru and the Bengali poet Rabindranath Tagore, were known to have graced Scar Top, the Thompson's villa, with their presence.[90] It was generally agreed that all the Thompson family were highly informed and articulate in their political knowledge.[91]

---

[88] Tony Judt with Timothy Snyder, *Rethinking the Twentieth Century* (London: William Heinemann, 2012), 325.
[89] Conradi, *A Very English Hero*, 53. John Masefield, Gilbert Murray and Sir Arthur Evans were all neighbours of the Thompson family. Webb, 'A Thoroughly English Dissident', 161.
[90] Thompson, *Beyond the Frontier*, 47.
[91] Conradi, *A Very English Hero*, 99–100.

4. THE SECRET LIFE OF HEADINGTON QUARRY

Thompson shared his family's passion for literary culture and awareness of global politics, but a trait that developed more distinctively in him was an acute sense of moral seriousness, something that could on occasion worry his father and something that he recognised and acknowledged in himself.[92] This was partly informed by the strong influence of Methodism on his early education. Kingswood's Methodism, with its strong emphasis on public demonstrations of faith, infused the school day and the curriculum. 'Methodism is not far wrong', E.J. Thompson once wrote to his teenage son, 'when it reminds you that your job is to "serve the present age"'.[93] Whilst Thompson would later vehemently reject the Methodist church as an institution, he retained this sense of personal moral duty and public obligation, transferring it instead to the secular sphere of politics.[94]

By contrast, Samuel's childhood was entrenched in a direct experience of a communist culture in a way that Thompson's had not been (Thompson joined the Communist Party, aged 18, in 1942; Samuel was raised in a, albeit unique, North London communist 'community'). He had learnt to be suspicious of anything resembling individual aggrandisement, preferring to subjugate everything to the notion of the collective. Within this, the intellectual role he had aspired to was that of the organiser, which depended on working amongst the rank and file membership, gaining trust, persuading and facilitating whilst never *appearing* to be authoritative. In fact, as he later commented, many of the party roles, like the organiser, depended for their success on 'elaborate pretences of equality' between the organiser and the organised, the recruiter and the recruitee.[95] The most effective means of achieving this was to be able to communicate with people on their own terms and in their own environments, not from any sort of platform of superior knowledge or insight.

A further point to consider is the developmental trajectory of the two men's working lives as historians, which also had significance for their ideas and uses of history. Both Thompson and Samuel became historians more through circumstance than by conscious intention, discovering in

---

92 Mary Lago, *India's Prisoner: A Biography of Edward John Thompson 1886–1946* (Colombia: University of Missouri Press, 2001), 294; Conradi, *A Very English Hero*, 74.
93 Lago, *India's Prisoner*, 294; Thompson, *Beyond the Frontier*, 52.
94 Particularly evident in his treatment of it in his book, *The Making of the English Working Class* (London: Penguin books, 1991), 405. See also Samuel's reference to Thompson's Methodism in: Raphael Samuel, 'British Marxist Historians 1880–1980', *NLR*, I/120, Mar–Apr (1980), 54.
95 Raphael Samuel, *The Lost World of British Communism* (London: Verso, 2006), 195.

history an important medium with which to develop their political and philosophical ideas. Thompson's early passion was for literature, which he studied for a year at Cambridge after his demobilisation, conceiving a particular passion for Elizabethan and Jacobean writing.[96] As a tutor in the extramural department of Leeds University in Halifax, Yorkshire (1946–65), he predominantly taught classes in literature.[97] His first historical work on William Morris (notably a biography of a literary figure) was published in 1955. *The Making of the English Working Class* followed eight years later.

Evidence of Thompson's passion for English literature was on clear display in *The Making of the English Working Class*. The book was a carefully crafted narrative, a 'biography' of a class.[98] As the unseen 'narrator' of the piece, Thompson was nevertheless an unmistakable presence. The rich baroque style of his prose made the sufferings and, more importantly, the struggles of 'ordinary people' compelling and noble (notably, many of Thompson's 'ordinary' people were often *extra*-ordinarily radical in their ideas and active in their politics). It told their story with great pathos, generously illustrated with choice passages of poetic and literary quotation, leavened with sharp parries of wit, reinforced elsewhere with impassioned polemic. Not once did Thompson transgress too far or lose sight of his main subject but continually drew the great expanse of his vision back to its central theme and powerful conclusion. Blending tragedy with the seeds of hope, he made his plea for the courage of those early pioneers *not* to have been in vain. Compare this with '"Quarry Roughs"', where the words of *the Quarry residents* bear most responsibility for the writing's vibrancy and, as narrator, Samuel retained a more modest distance.[99]

The success of *The Making of the English Working Class* prompted Thompson's move in 1965 from adult education to the directorship of the Centre for Social History at the newly created University of Warwick. As an established historian in his early forties and the director of a research centre, he was able to shape and determine much of the centre's research activities, and it was during this time that he furthered some of the lines of inquiry first intimated in his book. Thompson's Warwick students were mostly young graduates, some of whom collaborated with him on his

---

96   Dorothy Thompson, 'Introduction', *The Essential E. P. Thompson* (New York: The New Press, 2001).
97   Andy Croft, 'Walthamstow, Little Gidding & Middlesborough: E.P. Thompson, Adult Education and Literature', *Socialist History*, 8 (1995), 24.
98   Raphael Samuel, *Island Stories: Unravelling Britain* (London: Verso, 1998), 218.
99   I am indebted to Carolyn Steedman for this observation.

research projects.[100] He was renowned for being a tough, uncompromising teacher, determined that his students be academically rigorous and dispensing such career advice such as, 'If you want to teach, then TEACH, and don't put on a great fraternal anti-authoritarian act pretending that snotty-nosed 18-year-olds know as much as you do'.[101]

In 1971, Thompson left the centre at Warwick to become a full-time writer. His political articles regularly appeared in mainstream media outlets such as the *New Statesmen* and *The Times Literary Supplement*.[102] At a point when the HW was just beginning to develop its historical interests, he had served his time as a teacher and was largely preoccupied with his own independent writing, typically on political issues.

Samuel also held an influential role in the organisation of the HW, and yet for all his centrality, his ability to control all of the HW's activities was subject to certain limitations (perhaps curtailed by the performance of a 'great fraternal anti-authoritarian act'). The HW started life as an informal pedagogical exercise designed to encourage his worker students to write their own histories. Workshop projects were, therefore, largely dependent on the students' residual interests and experience. As the HW received little financial support from the college, it also depended on what materials were readily to hand. Unlike Thompson, Samuel was not an established, published historian. On his arrival at Ruskin he was learning his own historian's craft directly alongside his students. This meant that he did not have a clear research agenda that he was attempting to develop.[103]

Whilst Thompson's historical interests were concentrated intently on the eighteenth and early nineteenth century, Samuel focused on a much later period which, as his work on Headington Quarry demonstrates, allowed him to make extensive use of oral history. This meant encountering his historical 'subjects' face-to-face, inevitably restricting some of his interpretive 'freedoms'. There was no way, for example, that he could have easily transformed Harding into a well-intentioned libertarian rebel![104] Similarly, the HW's close relationship with the women's movement had prompted considerable revision of concepts such as 'class' and 'class

---

100 Hay et al., *Albion's Fatal Tree*.
101 Peter Linebaugh, 'From the Upper West Side to Wick Episcopi', *NLR*, I/201, Sep–Oct (1993), 23.
102 Collected in E.P. Thompson, *Writing by Candlelight* (London: Merlin, 1980); E.P. Thompson, *The Heavy Dancers* (New York: Pantheon Books, 1985).
103 First significant publication in history: Samuel, 'Comers and Goers'.
104 Newens, 'The Genesis of *East End Underworld*', 348.

struggle', which were inadequate for dealing with marginalisation on the basis of gender (or, equally, sexuality, age or race). This relationship had also fostered, inevitably, a more concerted focus on everyday, domestic life. Notably, one of the main criticisms to be levelled at Thompson addressed his lack of sensitivity towards the distinctive politics implied by the oppression of cultural identities such as gender.[105]

Whilst Thompson and Samuel shared many similarities in their historical interests, methodologies and political influences, they were distinguished by the different trajectories of their lives giving rise to their distinctive politics of performance as intellectuals. Thompson had been raised in an atmosphere steeped in high literary culture and infused with a solemn sense of duty to offer moral leadership. As a historian, no one surpassed his ability to tell the heroic story in which 'the people' (or a select few of them) were the central protagonists in the making of 'History'. But for all its undisputed power and prowess, *The Making of the English Working Class* still performed a species of ventriloquism: the people's story selected, crafted and given meaning by another.

Samuel, by contrast, had grown up deeply suspicious of overt displays of leadership. At an early age he had taken to heart the organiser's insight that in the battle of ideas for change, a heroic story alone was not sufficient. Change was more profound when individuals had a personal stake in creating it, when they were more than just readers of the story but its writers as well (recall his description of the party's recruitment processes which, in his view, were most effective when the sympathiser was directly 'involved' in party work[106]). He had cultivated the subtle arts of achieving this. As the moving spirit behind the HW he drew on these skills to facilitate history-making, thus deepening the extent of personal investment in the stories of the past. 'The people' in '"Quarry Roughs"', for example, were not just the subject matter of the piece, they were co-collaborators in the writing of it.

---

105 Catherine Hall, 'The Tale of Samuel and Jemima: Gender and Working Class Culture in Early Nineteenth Century England', in Harvey Kaye and Keith McClelland, eds, *E. P. Thompson: Critical Perspectives* (Philadelphia: Temple University Press, 1990), 78–102.
106 Ibid., 125–26.

4. THE SECRET LIFE OF HEADINGTON QUARRY

Naturally, the work on Headington Quarry was the product of its time, place and conditions of production. As those times always appear differently when viewed from a distance, so do the ideas and work produced in them. Alun Howkins, one of the original student researchers on the project, later reflected that whilst they 'had got a lot right, they had also got quite a lot wrong' about turn of the century Headington Quarry.[107] This is an inevitable feeling for historians who revisit a project over 30 years after it was first begun. From the distance permitted by an elapse of time, the subject matter of '"Quarry Roughs"' does have its restrictions. It rejoices too uncritically in the 'organic community', intimating its roots in the political atmosphere of the late 1960s and 1970s.

What is of greater interest is what the '"Quarry Roughs"' essay reveals about how Samuel was starting to think about and practise history. There was the painstaking excavation of the relationship between social consciousness (as expressed in the oral testimonies) and the material experiences of daily life in the Quarry. There was also the attempt to pick out the threads of connection between the details of the micro study and the wider, overarching historical theme or question. For some commentators, history-writing like '"Quarry Roughs"' with its sheer density of detail suggested a lack of clarity in the HW's political framework. What made this 'Socialist' history? Was it enough for the subject matter to focus on working-class life or was something more substantial needed?

The publication of the first HW book took place in the same year that the idea for a HW journal was developed. The journal was initially conceived of as a space where some of these issues could be worked out and addressed, whilst still retaining the general spirit of experimentation and democratisation of history enshrined in the HW meetings. Its manifesto, echoing so much of the HW endeavour, was hugely optimistic and vastly ambitious presenting would-be readers with a vision of a harmonious exchange between vigorous inquiry and a democratic ethic of participation. Whilst this ambition did not 'fail', it certainly found itself on a different path. The journal quickly became caught up in the epistemological debates that had been taking place across the political and intellectual left, growing ever more intensely contested. These debates would ultimately reach a crisis point at a HW meeting in December 1979.

---

107 Alun Howkins, email communication with author, October 2013.

5
The Socialist Historian?

Raphael Samuel (far right) with students, London History Workshop Group, 1980
Raphael Samuel Archive, Bishopsgate Institute, London, courtesy of Alison Light and the Raphael Samuel Estate.

Saturday evening, St Paul's Church, Oxford, 1 December 1979

Even by the History Workshop's (HW's) usual hectic standards, it had been a long day. In the evening, an audience into the hundreds gathered in the cavernous old body of St Paul's Church, Oxford, a former church turned arts centre.[1] This was not how it was supposed to have been. The HW collective had intended to use Ruskin's more spacious site out in Headington, which came with proper seats and central heating.[2] A combination of miscommunication and the new principal's desire to assert his leadership had forced them to take St Paul's for their venue.[3] Clustered together in the available spaces, people huddled, cold, uncomfortable and slightly anxious, awaiting the final plenary session of the day and anticipating drama.

The general mood of Workshop meetings was always expectant, but on this occasion it was infused with a very palpable sense of tension. The front 'stage', lit up by bright spotlights, seemed to reinforce the mood. The day's events had been difficult. In addition to the usual problems involved in coordinating such a large-scale event, such as time keeping, lunch provision and faulty equipment, this conference, more than the previous 12, had been overtly marked with conflict. The sheer volume of attendees and the task of marshalling them about had lost some of the fun of earlier occasions. The conference papers, once exciting, adrenalin-fuelled accounts from the forgotten realms of people's history, were increasingly dominated by critical theory.

Many of the speakers, eager to get to the discussion at the end, had rattled through their papers, assuming audience familiarity with their material. Many of the Ruskin students found themselves unable to follow the complicated concepts and theorists knowingly alluded to. They became bored and resentful. In the spirited discussions that followed, they grew even more alienated from the proceedings.

---

1 Martin Kettle, 'The Experience of History', *New Society*, 6 December 1979, 542.
2 Having outgrown its premises on Walton Street, Oxford, Ruskin College acquired 'The Rookery', Headington, Oxford, in 1948. www.headington.org.uk/history/listed_buildings/rookery.htm (accessed 14 February 2015).
3 Raphael Samuel, 'Post-Mortem of HW 13', RS 7: History Workshop Events/039, Raphael Samuel Archive (RSA), Bishopsgate Institute, London.

5. THE SOCIALIST HISTORIAN?

In their own contribution to the conference, a plenary session on history as a weapon of struggle, the students presented research on worker historians in the 1920s. It had been an uninspiring affair, with the students never enthused with the project. They had wanted to hold a Workshop on the state and repression (which had seemed appropriate with Margaret Thatcher and the new Conservative Government already making their presence felt) but had been talked into having it on socialist theory, and given a project they did not much care about.[4]

The session got underway.[5] Taking the stage, 'heavily disguised as the spirits of Theory, Culture and History', was Richard Johnson of the Centre for Contemporary Cultural Studies (CCCS) and two veterans of the first New Left: Stuart Hall (also from the CCCS) and the historian Edward Thompson, fresh from the publication of his polemic 'The Poverty of Theory'.[6] Hall, now a prominent figure in British sociology and cultural studies, was the first to speak. He was a good orator, and an old hand at sparring with Thompson. His paper was critical but reasonable, agreeing with his former comrade on the 'poverty of *theoreticism*' but also suggesting that few had taken French social theorist Louis Althusser's theoretical claims that seriously.[7] He entered a plea for the necessity and importance of cultural theory, adding that Thompsonian-style polemic was unhelpful in addressing the complexities of the issues at hand.[8]

Richard Johnson followed. Johnson had already provoked Thompson's ire by suggesting that he represented the first 'turn' towards cultural analysis in Marxist political thought but had been unable to develop a more substantial theory of cultural materialism.[9] Beside the other two men, he was not as accomplished a 'performer'. The force of his argument was better expressed in his writing.[10] His main point was that theory did express real social problems and was therefore important to engage with.[11]

---

4   Ibid.
5   Raphael Samuel, '1ˢᵗ Dec. evening', RS 5: History Workshop audio recordings/024, RSA.
6   Stuart Hall, 'Raphael Samuel: 1934–1996', *New Left Review* (*NLR*), I/221, Jan–Feb (1997), 124.
7   Stuart Hall, 'In Defence of Theory', in Raphael Samuel, ed., *People's History and Socialist Theory* (London: Routledge and Kegan Paul, 1981), 379–80. This argument was also advanced in: Perry Anderson, *Considerations of Western Marxism* (London: New Left Books, 1976).
8   Kettle, 'The Experience of History', 543.
9   Thompson had responded by criticising Johnson's understanding of the historical context surrounding the first New Left. E.P. Thompson, 'The Politics of Theory', in Samuel, ed., *People's History and Socialist Theory*, 397.
10 Kettle, 'The Experience of History', 543.
11 Ibid.

Tentatively, he also suggested that Thompson himself had elements of the 'absolutist' in his intellectual posture, as much as any 'theorist' could be said to have.[12]

But then came Thompson, a compelling physical presence with his 'wild good looks' and powerful speaking voice.[13] On that evening there was a particularly hunted air about him, born out of frustration with the British left in all its forms.[14] He was impatient with the 'niceties', the cosiness, of the HW's general approach and weary with the theory debate. He had said what he wanted to say in *The Poverty of Theory*, but still they demanded that he explain it again, when he wanted to move on to more serious political issues, such as the revival of the Campaign for Nuclear Disarmament (CND).[15]

With all this bubbling just below the surface Thompson turned on his opponents, upbraiding the 'theorists' for performing a 'psycho drama within the enclosed ghetto of the theoretical left'.[16] The overall effect of Thompson's contribution and manner was an atmosphere that left further 'discussion' virtually impossible. Hall and Johnson were hurt and annoyed. There was outrage and upset amongst the audience, with one woman angrily rejecting the 'booming male voices' on the stage.[17] All the tensions and divisions that had been just about held at bay during the course of the day were suddenly laid bare. Ugly and exposed.[18] Even the evening's proposed entertainment of folk song did little to lift the mood.[19]

What of Raphael Samuel, the HW's organiser? Many expected him to do something, to intervene in some way. But he seemed to do nothing.[20] There was a scheduled plenary session, 'Socialist history, past, present and future', due to be held at 5pm the next afternoon.

---

12   Richard Johnson, 'Against Absolutism', in Samuel, ed., *People's History and Socialist Theory*, 386–96.
13   References to Thompson's personal appearance and style of speaking: Perry Anderson, 'Diary', *London Review of Books*, 21 October 1993, 24; Penelope J. Corfield, 'E. P. Thompson, the Historian: An Appreciation', *NLR*, I/201, Sept–Oct (1993), 10; Sheila Rowbotham, 'Remembering 1967', in Raphael Samuel, ed., *History Workshop: A Collectanea 1967–1991* (Oxford: HW 25, 1991), 4.
14   E.P. Thompson, 'Foreword', in *The Poverty of Theory and Other Essays* (London: Merlin Press, 1978), ii.
15   Thompson, 'The Politics of Theory', 396.
16   Kettle, 'The Experience of History', 543.
17   Samuel, '1st Dec. evening', audio recording, RS 5: History Workshop audio recordings/026, RSA.
18   Samuel received a considerable number of letters complaining about the session. 'HW 13 correspondence', RS 7: History Workshop Events/039, RSA.
19   Alun Howkins, oral communication to author, May 2012, Diss, Norfolk.
20   Stuart Hall, oral communication to author, May 2012, Hampstead, London.

Mysteriously, this was cancelled.[21]

Given the drama of the events, it is unsurprising that commentators have viewed HW 13 as symbolic of the 'tectonic shift from social history to cultural history';[22] the collision between the cultural politics of a 1968 left and the social politics of the 1950s New Left.[23] This, however, tends to reduce the full complexity of the debates into a 'generation game', a tedious power struggle amongst left-wing intellectuals, which, in turn, obscures the importance of the issues addressed.[24] At stake were questions concerning the relationship between mind and body, the possibilities and limits of historical knowledge and the role of the historian in respect to this.

This chapter focuses on Samuel's response to these debates, both in terms of his direct contribution and also his actions. It argues that this period marked a significant turning point in his personal intellectual development, political sensibilities and his perception of himself as a public intellectual and educator.

Agency and structure

The year 1979 had been a gruelling one for the political left not least because of the re-election of a Conservative Government, led by Margaret Thatcher, earlier in the year. This had not appeared in a vacuum; it was the result of an accumulation of simmering fractures and tensions. The escalation of union militancy, greeted with enthusiasm by some in the late 1960s, had increasingly turned in upon itself leading to bitter inter-union disputes and damaging conflicts between work groups, undermining any sense of class solidarity. Moreover, the so-called 'winter of discontent' (1978–79) – the series of strikes at hospitals, in refuse collection and in public transport – had most affected members of the public, in particular

---

21 Carolyn Steedman, oral communication to author, May 2013, University of Warwick.
22 Geoff Eley, *A Crooked Line: From Cultural History to the History of Society* (Michigan: University of Michigan Press, 2005), xii–xiii.
23 Dennis Dworkin, 'The Politics of Theory', in *Cultural Marxism in Postwar Britain: History, the New Left, and the Origins of Cultural Studies* (London and Durham: Duke University Press, 1997), 232–45.
24 Thompson, 'Foreword', in *The Poverty of Theory*, ii.

working-class people, *not* the workers' employers.[25] As Eric Hobsbawm commented in his 1978 Marx Memorial lecture 'The Forward March of Labour Halted', 'We now see a growing division of workers into sections and groups, each pursuing its own economic interest irrespective of the rest'.[26]

Division was not confined to internal disputes amongst an industrial workforce but equally present amongst the emerging social movement groups. It was especially evident in the HW's often tense relationship with the women's movement.[27] With its base at the trade union affiliated Ruskin College, the socialist politics of many of Ruskin's students, and Workshop participants, were deeply rooted in the highly masculine world of the labour movement and union politics. The women's movement challenged the 'received wisdom' implied by this form of socialism. The Workshops on 'The Child in History' and 'Women in History', which grew out of the Women's Liberation Workshop (1970), had been both exciting but also difficult affairs where tensions had run high.

Confronted with the confusion and fragmentation of its most important concepts and vehicles, class solidarity and unionism, those amongst the intellectual left naturally turned their attention towards conceptual questions: what was 'class'? To what extent had its meaning changed, why had it done so? How were the political insights implied by other cultural identities, such as gender, race, or sexuality, to be connected? These were important questions to ask in the rethinking, redefining, of socialism. History had an important role to play in addressing why particular ideas emerged, how they developed and, critically, what, if any, common ground lay between them. This had been the motivation for hosting the HW in the first place.

Of further significance was the breakdown of independent forms of workers' education and the move towards a broadly conceived 'adult education', embedded within university extramural departments. Such a move naturally changed the conditions in which political debate could take place, inevitably introducing formalised structures into

---

25 David Cannadine, *Class in Britain* (London: Penguin, 2000), 171–80; Robert Taylor, 'The Rise and Disintegration of the Working Classes', in Paul Addison and Harriet Jones, eds, *A Companion to Contemporary Britain 1939–2000* (Oxford: Blackwell, 2005), 380–82.
26 Eric Hobsbawm, 'The Forward March of Labour Halted?', *Marxism Today*, September 1978.
27 See Bill Schwarz, 'History on the Move: Reflections on the History Workshop', *Radical History Review*, 57 (2002), 202–20.

the learning process. The general expansion of higher education and the fracturing of subjects into multiple subdisciplinary specialisms meant that much of the important work of self-examination was being conducted amongst increasingly enclosed, self-referential academic groups. Working so intensively within a competitive academic culture, still largely sceptical towards 'radical' political views, also meant that a considerable amount of energy was required just to be taken seriously as a professional thinker. So, whilst the political left had always 'wrestled' amongst itself, generation against generation, activist against intellectual, never before had divisions been so complex and so many.

The confrontation between Thompson, Hall and Johnson was set against these tensions and went straight to the core of them, addressing two distinct but related issues: what was the key crucible of social consciousness? What degree of agency did the individual have? From its earliest articulations, Marxism had always stressed the means of production as the critical determinant in sociopolitical organisation and change over time. In the century and more since Marx had first set out his evolutionary schema, its all-encompassing logic had shown some limitations. In step with an economy moving away from secondary industry, components of the left also shifted attention towards structures of meaning. This was not a simple move from body to mind, the tensions lay in the traffic between the two.

The relationship between structures of meaning and social structures was not the only contentious strand of the debates. A recurrent and unresolved issue for the intellectual left was the question of human agency. With the individual buffeted on all sides by determining forces, what, if any, scope was there for effective action? It was on this issue that Thompson had taken a firm stance in the 1950s and, subsequently, made the connecting thread throughout his later work.[28] *The Making of the English Working Class* had, in part, constituted a more sustained working out of his ideas about the relationship between class consciousness and material conditions of being. It had, however, been anything but the last word on the subject.

During the 1960s, Thompson engaged in a protracted exchange on the subject with Perry Anderson and Tom Nairn, the new, young editors of the *New Left Review*. Viewing their predecessors as lacking in a systematic

---

28   For Thompson's critique of Raymond Williams: E.P. Thompson, 'The Long Revolution I', *NLR*, I/9, May–Jun (1961), 24–33; 'The Long Revolution II', *NLR*, I/10, Jul–Aug (1961), 34–39. For an example of his critique of Stuart Hall and Richard Hoggart: E.P. Thompson, 'Commitment in Politics', *Universities and Left Review (ULR)*, 6 (1958), 50–55.

cultural sociology, Anderson and Nairn had set about addressing this in a series of bold articles intent on rethinking the past and present of English socialism to take better account of perpetuating ideological frameworks.[29] Thompson's replies were dense and sceptical. Drawing upon the depth of historical knowledge set out in *The Making of the English Working Class*, he further pressed his case for the presence of a dynamic and democratic popular culture in the English past. It's 'failure' to translate into a dominant power structure, he contended, had lain in the inability of the left to link together the different components within itself.[30]

In the late 1970s, Thompson's ferocity found a new target, Louis Althusser, a French theorist whose creative revision of Marxism drew inspiration from linguistic structuralism. Althusser argued that human consciousness was ensnared within a matrix of autonomous ideological discourses that coexisted in a constant state of conflict and contradiction, one occasionally gaining dominance over the others. These discursive codes were disseminated through participation in social life, in particular contact with state apparatus (religion, civil law and education). Ideology functioned to induce an illusionary consciousness of a coherent, unified reality, which did not in fact exist.[31]

For Thompson this was a species of repackaged economic determinism that significantly diminished the role of the popular movement and greatly inflated that of the theorist in left-wing politics. When not shuffling mindlessly between discursive formations, 'the people' were left dependent on eagle-eyed intellectuals to diagnose and remedy the erroneous beliefs conjured through prolonged ideological exposure. Furthermore, here was a theory that for the most part relegated historical context to providing the conditions in which one discursive formation (otherwise comparatively untouched by its broader context) gained precedence over the others. Thompson's response came in *The Poverty of Theory* (1979), a blistering polemic which lampooned Althusser's 'arid academic scholasticism unleavened by any vital tension with a point of reference beyond itself',

---

29   Perry Anderson: 'Origins of the Present Crisis', *NLR*, I/23, Jan–Feb (1964), 26–53; 'Socialism and Pseudo-Empiricism', *NLR*, I/35, Jan–Feb (1966), 2–42; 'Components of the National Culture', *NLR*, I/50, Jul–Aug (1968), 3–57; *Arguments in English Marxism* (London: Verso, 1980). Tom Nairn: 'The British Political Elite', *NLR*, I/24, Mar–Apr (1964), 19–25; 'The English Working Class', *NLR*, I/24, Mar–Apr (1964), 43–57.
30   E.P. Thompson, 'The Peculiarities of the English', *The Socialist Register*, 2 (1965), 311–62.
31   Louis Althusser, 'Ideologies and Ideological State Apparatuses: Notes Towards an Investigation', *La Pensee*, 151 (1970). I used a reprinted version in Aradhana Sharma and Akhil Gupta, eds, *The Anthropology of the State* (Malden: Blackwell, 2006), 86–111.

enamoured of the aesthetic perfection of its own internal logic.[32] The empirical approach, so despised by theorists, could often present stark challenges to the assertions of these conceptual categories.

So, whilst Samuel had been developing his historian's craft, first through the Social History Group and later in the HW, Thompson had been battling on the frontline of the epistemological debates. *The Poverty of Theory*, far from being an intervention or entry into the debates, had, therefore, been intended as his last word on the matter, a final payment of dues to 1956.[33] By the time of HW 13 Thompson was weary and irritable with the infighting and divisions amongst the various factions of the left, worn down by the continual defence he was forced to make of his position.

The fierceness of Thompson's polemic had the effect of obscuring the finer points of his argument. But in judging his performance, alongside his weariness with the issue, it should also be remembered that he was a veteran political activist (with a particular taste for the theatrical) as much as he was an experienced scholar.[34] The political platform is different to the scholarly lectern and utilises different performative skills – colourful and relentless demolition of one's opponents being just one of them. The extravagant force of his polemical arguments certainly bore more relation to the former than the latter.[35] In a letter to Samuel dated 5 December 1979 Thompson seemed unaware of the drama he had caused (italics are my own words):

> Sorry not to have more time to talk at w/e, and sorry also to be so flustered … It is just that I loathe the cult of the historiographical individual, whether for applause or attack. I thought the evening's discussion went off less well, and I am still confused as to whether I or the chairman or all of us were at fault. I had intended to say almost nothing until I got the 'position papers', and Richard J's made me cross.

A line crossed out at this point reads 'what riled me was (in effect) being admonished'.

---

32 Thompson, *The Poverty of Theory and Other Essays*, 291–94.
33 Ibid., 384.
34 Thompson's mother, Theodosia, encouraged her youngest son at the age of 17 to attend the Royal Academy for Dramatic Arts! Peter Conradi, *A Very English Hero: The Making of Frank Thompson* (London: Bloomsbury, 2012), 74.
35 Thompson's use of polemic as a critical rhetorical device noted by: Anderson, 'Diary', *London Review of Books*, 21 October 1993, 24; Jonathan Ree, 'A Theatre of Arrogance', *Times Higher Educational Supplement*, 5 June 1995.

> Here is a corrected and expanded version of what I said ... otherwise the rumour may go around that I said unfraternal things, which I did not say. The text is a writing-up of my notes with one or two unnecessary acid-drops taken out.[36]

In a second letter dated 18 December 1979, Thompson remained unrepentant, saying dismissively:

> Oh I don't think there was anything very tragic that Sat night at the Workshop. I was sorry to learn that tensions had grown up between the Ruskin students and the journal operation – inevitable I suppose but very sad.

The letter continued, offering some small crumbs of self-reflection and explanation:

> I was perhaps a bit too blunt.
>
> I agree that there we all were, arguing or discussing together in some manner, as we haven't for a long time and this was a gain of sorts. The only bad thing was the way John Saville[37] got received – he shouldn't have come "uncle" over people – this provoked a savage generational response ...
>
> I am obsessed with politics at the moment the sense that we could be in the last year or two of our own peculiar Weimar, the cruise missile and Trident affairs and so on. I just wish people could get rid of the inward-turning mentalities and look out again. And I get so cross when I hear again and again the received modish wisdom about the moralistic, bourgeois character of the CND – which did actually impinge for a moment upon the world of power.[38]

Aside from the literal content of these letters, the general tone of them reveals Thompson's frame of mood, his impatience with the lingering sensitivities between the respective leftist generations and his emerging political priorities. But what of its recipient? Where did Samuel stand in relation to these debates about socialism, critical theory, history and the role of the socialist intellectual?

---

36   E.P. Thompson, 'Letter to Raphael Samuel', 5 December 1979, RS 7: History Workshop Events/History Workshop 13, People's History and Socialist Theory, 1979, 039, RSA. See Thompson, 'The Politics of Theory', 405.
37   John Saville was a fellow speaker at the event who received a hostile reception for his critique of cultural theory.
38   E.P. Thompson letter to Raphael Samuel, 18 December 1979, RS 7: History Workshop Events/History Workshop 13, People's History and Socialist Theory, 1979, 039, RSA.

His most intensive engagement with these matters came through the *History Workshop Journal* (*HWJ*). Launched in 1976, the journal had started out in the much 'colder' political climate of the mid-1970s than the optimistic birth of the HW in the late-1960s. Nevertheless, the original intention behind the *HWJ* was to act, in effect, as an extension of the HW meetings, one that retained its radical and experimental spirit but also enabled a closer engagement with the issues that time and the format of the meetings could not accommodate. This intent was reflected in the manifesto:

> Like the Workshop, like the pamphlets and books in the Workshop series, the Journal will address itself to the fundamental elements of social life – work and material culture, class relations and politics, sex divisions and marriage, family, school and home. In the Journal we shall continue to elaborate these themes but in a more sustained way …[39]

The founding editorial board was made up of a mixture of historians, including former Ruskin students Sally Alexander, Alun Howkins and Stan Shipley, and former participants of the Social History Group, including Tim Mason and Gareth Stedman Jones. Samuel and Anna Davin (now separated as a couple) occupied bridging positions between the combined spirits of activism and scholarly critique.[40]

To gain a clearer sense of the *HWJ*'s intellectual, educational and political positioning it is useful to consider it in contrast to two other journals to which it was closely related: *Past and Present* (*P&P*), established in 1952; and its close contemporary *Social History* (*SH*), also launched in 1976. The relationship to *P&P* was a close one; not only had Samuel been the youngest member of Communist Party Historians' Group (CPHG) and a student member of the P&P society at Oxford University but Mason worked as an editor on the *P&P* journal. Moreover, the HW owed a considerable intellectual debt to *P&P*, partially responsible, as it was, for advancing and propagating the 'new' social history.[41] In other respects, however, the *HWJ* deliberately started out with the intent of assuming a far more expansive and experimental approach to history-making. A brief anecdote concerning the early relations between the two 'camps' illustrates this.

---

39 Editorial Collective, 'Editorial', *HWJ*, 1 (1976), 1.
40 Alun Howkins, oral communication with author, May 2012.
41 Jim Obelkevich, 'New Developments in History in the 1950s and 1960s', *Contemporary British History*, 14, 4 (2000), 125–42.

In 1968 following HW 2 'Education and the Working Class' Samuel and others drawn from the HW and Social History Group had embarked on a collaborative research project on 'Nineteenth Century Cromwell' reported by Mason as a project that, in an echo of Hill's 'The Norman Yoke' (1954), sought to explore nineteenth-century political ideologies through depictions and representations of the Puritan leader Oliver Cromwell.[42] As it unfolded, its vast cast of contributors uncovered an immense array of intriguing but deeply conflicting sources. The emphasis of the work shifted towards a more expansive concern with popular perceptions of the national past. When the enormous quantity of diffuse and eclectic findings was offered to *P&P* for publication in 1972, the startled journal's editorial board refused them. The rejection prompted the project's key coordinators, Mason and Samuel, to reflect on the need to create their own vehicle for publication, one more accommodating towards the experimental and to documenting the actual process of historical research.[43]

The relationship between the intellectual positioning of *HWJ* and *SH* was more complex. *SH* captured something of the evangelical mood rising amongst social historians in the 1970s. Its stated intention was to pursue 'not a new *branch* of historical scholarship' but 'a new kind of history', one that cut across the various fields of historical analysis, privileging no single branch in particular, not even class.[44] However, as Jon Lawrence and David Feldman noted, having made this declaration, *SH* proceeded to make its name through publishing a considerable body of significant work on class formation, class consciousness and class struggle in eighteenth and nineteenth-century England.[45]

The *HWJ*, by contrast, continued to openly assert the primacy of 'working-class experience' (a term left undefined and unexamined) to its historical interests and its objective to relate this to 'an overall view of capitalism as a historical phenomenon, both a mode of production and

---

42 Tim Mason, 'Nineteenth Century Cromwell', *Past and Present*, 40 (1968), 187–91.
43 Raphael Samuel, 'Nineteenth Century Cromwell', in Samuel, ed., *History Workshop: A Collectanea 1967–1991*.
44 'Editorial 1', *Social History*, 1, 1 (1976), 1.
45 David Feldman and Jon Lawrence, 'Introduction: Structures and Transformations in British Historiography', in Feldman and Lawrence, eds, *Structures and Transformations in Modern British History* (Cambridge: Cambridge University Press, 2011), 1. Feldman and Lawrence note amongst others: F.K. Donnelly, 'English Working-Class History: Edward Thompson and his Critics', *Social History*, 1 (1976), 219–38; A.E. Musson, 'Class Struggle and the Labour Aristocracy', *Social History*, 1 (1976), 335–56; John Foster, 'Some Comments on "Class Struggle and the Labour Aristocracy"', *Social History*, 1 (1976), 357–66.

as a system of relations'. Its first editions, accordingly, carried lead articles addressing class and the labour process.[46] On the other hand, the journal also expressed its interest in the 'internationality of class experience', its desire to 'expand the area of enquiry in new directions' taking up 'popular culture, literature, music and art' and to address 'theoretical questions in history more explicitly', carrying an editorial on 'feminist history' and a 'work-in-progress' essay on homosexuality in the nineteenth century in the first edition.[47] The two journals were united in assuming an interdisciplinary posture towards the respective areas of historical analysis, but whilst *SH* pursued this as a primary and self-conscious objective *HWJ* did so less from a deliberate intention and more as a result of its nature as a publication.

In its early form, the *HWJ* occupied a very different cultural space from either *P&P* or the later *SH*. Its roots lay firmly in an extramural and activist culture, openly partisan in its politics, aspiring to promote grassroots historical research as well as provide a vehicle for history scholars. It differed from a 'scholarly' journal in a number of ways: the space it devoted to the reprinting of original documents and discussion of archival collections, the section on 'Enthusiasms' instead of book reviews (intended as a means of 'practical solidarity' with the readers, who included labour activists and amateur historians alongside students, teachers and researchers).[48] In its physical appearance the contrast was also marked; it carried 'Fraternal Greetings' and advertisements from trade unions, notices of events within the left movement, a liberal quantity of lively cartoon illustrations, all calculated to eschew any resemblance to a conventional academic journal. As Stedman Jones later remarked, 'Its most important characteristic was the pluralism that was built into it from the start'.[49]

HWJ started off on its mission enthusiastically. An early and immediate point of concern was the relationship between history and sociology, a long-standing issue for Samuel stemming from his days in the first

---

46 Rodney Hilton, 'Feudalism and the Origins of Capitalism'; Frank McKenna, 'Victorian Railway Workers', *HWJ*, 1 (1976), 9–25, 26–73.
47 For example, there were sections dedicated to 'History on Stage' and 'History on Film'. See also Anna Davin's essay 'Children's Historical Novels', *HWJ*, 1 (1976), 121–26, 127–35, 154–65. For articles relating to feminism and homosexuality see: Sally Alexander and Anna Davin, 'Feminist History'; Jeffrey Weeks, 'Sins and Diseases: Some Notes on Homosexuality in the Nineteenth Century', *HWJ*, 1 (1976), 4–6, 211–19.
48 Raphael Samuel, 'History Workshop Journal', in Samuel, ed., *History Workshop: A Collectanea 1967–1991*, 108.
49 Gareth Stedman Jones, 'History and Theory', *historein* [Athens], 3 (2001), 115–16.

New Left, and here he formed an important and influential working partnership with Stedman Jones. The first edition carried a joint editorial by the two men announcing the establishment of a working group to scrutinise the relationship between sociology and history.[50] Despite an earlier call for socialist 'intellectual imperialism' in history-making,[51] Stedman Jones was never fully aligned with the theoretical position of Anderson and the *NLR*. Nor did he welcome the tendency to sweep history up in the service of sociological theory. Rather than proclaim and pursue the 'failure' of socialism, his interest lay in the 'triumph' of liberal ideas and assumptions among the mass population, which he sought to explore through an integrative, or 'totalising', form of historical analysis that brought the social, economic, political and cultural into conversation with one another.

The first substantial product of this inquiry was Stedman Jones's book *Outcast London* (1971) which sought to explore the gap between Thompson's heroic radical culture in the early nineteenth century and the uninspiring, deeply conservative working-class community recreated by Richard Hoggart in *Uses of Literacy* (1957) in the mid-twentieth century. Focusing on working-class life and experience in London during the late nineteenth century (incidentally, a similar topic to that of Samuel's abandoned PhD, 'unskilled labour in London between 1871–1891'[52]), he argued that the estrangement from political activity was a product of the material realities of their lives. The uncertainties and spasmodic nature of casual labour and increased domesticity, for example, informed an 'escapist culture' of sports, entertainments and drinking (a contrast might be drawn here with Samuel's irascible, irrepressible Quarry folk whose response to unreliable casual labour was to establish for themselves a thriving 'secondary' economy based on what they could glean from their environment, coloured by a robust dislike of authority figures – suggestive perhaps of the subtle distinctions in outlook between the two).[53]

---

50 Raphael Samuel and Gareth Stedman Jones, 'Sociology and History', *HWJ*, 1 (1976), 6–8. The group's critical stance towards sociology meant that it was initially known as the counter-sociology group. Anna Davin 'The Only Problem Was Time', *HWJ*, 50 (2000), 244.
51 Gareth Stedman Jones, 'The Pathology of English History', *NLR*, I/46, Nov–Dec (1967), 29–43.
52 Brian Harrison, 'Interview with Raphael Samuel', 23 October 1979.
53 Gareth Stedman Jones, *Outcast London: A Study of the Relationship between Classes in Victorian Society* (Oxford: Clarendon Press, 1971).

Despite the intentions expressed in the manifesto, *HWJ* soon found itself drifting more emphatically towards the intellectual and theoretical side of the equation.[54] For a journal which took such an openly political stance in relation to its approach to history, it was inevitable that it would soon be drawn into the epistemological storms that dominated discussion amongst the intellectual left. It would have been strange, irresponsible even, for the journal not to have acknowledged and engaged with the questions being posed.

The 1978 publication of Richard Johnson's article (*HWJ*, 6) marked this more definitive entry into the realms of the theoretical. Johnson's article amounted to a developmental trajectory, or generational narrative, of British Marxist historiography. In Thompson, he proposed, there had been a fundamental break from an older school of Marxism, represented by Maurice Dobb, primarily applying a Marxist critique and analysis of British history. *The Making of the English Working Class* had signalled an important departure by examining the role of culture in actively constituting social and political consciousness. This 'turn', however, had been limited by the 'humanist moralism' of his 'generation'. Johnson urged the need to consider this more fully from the other direction, how consciousness was constituted in the interests of ruling ideologies, how it was imposed and disseminated through social life and everyday practices. In short, he proposed a synthesis of the analytical 'long view' typical of Dobb's older generation, with astute attention to cultural moments as a site of political struggle.[55]

The article prompted a wave of critical articles in response. Some, like Keith McClelland and Tony Judt, saw too great an artifice and over-reliance on social theory in the 'positions' sketched out in Johnson's trajectory.[56] Others, such as Simon Clarke, found points of agreement with the outline proposed by Johnson but differed on the question of its significance – arguing that Thompson had represented a break with older

---

54 Samuel, 'History Workshop Journal', in *History Workshop: A Collectanea 1967–1991*, 109.
55 Richard Johnson, 'Edward Thompson, Eugene Genovese, and Socialist-Humanist History', *HWJ*, 6 (1978), 79–100.
56 Tony Judt, 'A Clown in Regal Purple: Social History and the Historians', *HWJ*, 7 (1979), 66–94; Keith McClelland, 'Towards a Socialist History: Some Comments on Richard Johnson, "Edward Thompson, Eugene Genovese, and Socialist-Humanist History"', *HWJ*, 7 (1979), 101–15.

forms of Marxist historiography, not simply through his engagement with culture, but in restoring an essentially moral character to political analysis, a reminder of its roots in lives of *real* people.[57]

In the mid-1970s Samuel was still uncertain of his ideas about the nature of the relationship between history and theory. The editorial in the edition that carried Johnson's paper expressed a similar scepticism towards the reliance on critical theory in history. But his thoughts on this matter were not as yet fully resolved. When asked 'what is socialist history?' in an interview with Brian Harrison in October 1979, he stumbled and evaded the question: 'It's an awfully big question, Brian. No, I think it'll lead us off into a different track to this. It's too big a question'.[58]

What he made clear was his rejection of an earlier definition of 'socialist history' offered in the first HW book collection:

> I mean, I say 'the job of the socialist historian is *keeping the record of the oppressed* ...' and I don't know how that came about, and it certainly wasn't one that we'd been using before then quite explicitly like that ...[59]

As these debates rumbled on, grappling with increasingly complex theoretical positions, the gap between the concerns of the intellectuals and academics and those of the Ruskin student constituency widened. The Ruskin students, so central to the ethos and organisation of the Workshops, felt increasingly alienated by the more rarefied tones that the debates were taking and as a result a sense of distance developed between the student collectives responsible for organising the Workshops and *HWJ*'s editorial collective. This was reinforced by the failure of members of the editorial collective, due in part to overwhelming academic workloads, to actually attend many of the HW meetings and conferences.[60]

HW 13, 'People's History and Socialist Theory', was conceived to address these issues. Not only was it an opportunity to bring these strands of debate into a shared space for mutual discussion, it was also an opportunity for the *HWJ* editorial collective to restore relations with the Ruskin students

---

57 Simon Clarke, 'Socialist Humanism and the Critique of Economism', *HWJ*, 8 (1979), 138–56.
58 Brian Harrison, 'Interview with Raphael Samuel', 23 October 1979.
59 Raphael Samuel, 'General Editor's Introduction', in Samuel, ed., *Village Life and Labour* (London: Routledge and Kegan Paul, 1975), xix; Brian Harrison, 'Interview with Raphael Samuel', 23 October 1979.
60 Raphael Samuel, 'Post Mortem of HW 13', RS 7: History Workshop Events/History Workshop 13, People's History and Socialist Theory, 1979, 039, RSA.

by working more closely with them in the organisation and running of the HW; but, despite the good intentions, this was problematic from the very start. The Ruskin student collective had intended (Samuel noted waspishly, 'for once off their own initiative')[61] HW 13 to be on the theme of 'State and Repression', but after a meeting with Samuel and Mason, representing the collective, they were persuaded to change themes. Despite their acquiescence, the students had misgivings. There were further problems and tensions throughout the organisational process for the HW. Both students and speakers alike missed meetings. The students also failed to raise much enthusiasm for their own contribution to the conference, 'Worker-Historians in the 1920s'.

What eventually transpired was a hugely ambitious conference that sprawled across multiple issues, and involved a vast cast of intellectuals, historians and students who spanned multiple interest groups and generations. Whilst there were strands on the methodological issues relating to local and oral history, and discussions devoted to the availability or conditions to be found in labour archives, all questions and issues that the HW 'movement' had made so much their own, there were also strands dealing more directly with the theoretical conceptions of colonialism, of feminism, of fascism and their relationship to history. There was also a far greater sense of internationality at this Workshop than at previous meetings, with a number of the speakers, such as the French philosopher Jacques Rancière, travelling from overseas to participate and entire streams devoted to 'African History' or 'Socialist History in Europe'.

The Saturday-evening session between Thompson, Hall and Johnson had been shocking, but it was far from this alone which had caused such heightened tensions. Feeling that the conference was becoming increasingly preoccupied with theory, the disgruntled Ruskin students, in true Ruskin tradition, had proposed to break away and set up an independent Workshop to focus more exclusively on labour history.[62] The bad feeling stirred up by the conference was not confined to the students but went so far across the broad array of the HW participants that it really seemed to throw genuine doubt as to whether any sort of unified and constructive conversation could be achieved. Either way, it spelt the end of the HW's home at Ruskin College.

---

61 Ibid.
62 Ibid.

The sheer size, scope and ambition of the conference had seen variations of Marxist critical theory converge and combine with history and other forms of left-wing politics in multiple forms. It had also involved the collision of generations, of social backgrounds, and intellectual disciplines. It had been both tremendously exciting in its scope and diversity, but also intimidating and overwhelming for many of its participant members. Even for its moving force and driving spirit, Samuel, the arch-organiser, the problem of retrieving from the intellectual and emotional fragments some basis for common ground, some shared position from which to move forward, was an extremely complex, almost impossible, task particularly when he was far from assured on the questions himself.

History and theory

The extent of the fragmentation in evidence and the high emotional context in which this played out posed no greater test for Samuel's organisational skills. His position was a delicate one. He felt a strong sense of loyalty to the students but equally he felt this loyalty to the editorial collective and was not uncritical of some of the students' hostile attitudes to 'intellectualism' and theory. In terms of the 'debate' that had taken place, Hall was an old friend dating back to his student days at Oxford. Thompson too was also a long-standing comrade. In regard to the wider conflicts and disputes, several of the feminist positions advanced, for example, came from his close friends or even former partners. Moreover, his concern was not simply to navigate the politics of friendship and alliance, but to attempt to find the basis of common ground between the disparate positions in order for the 'left' as a whole to move forward as an effective voice and force for social critique and change.

In his initial response, Samuel avoided becoming a direct 'protagonist' in the debates as Thompson had been. He had not directly intervened during the conference, although it is suspected that he was responsible for the cancellation of the scheduled plenary session due to take place the following day.[63] An indication of his views can be discerned in a drafted readers' letter for the *HWJ* in which he appeared broadly to align with Thompson (as he had, broadly, in the Sense of Classlessness debate in 1959):

---

63 Carolyn Steedman, oral communication with author, May 2013.

5. THE SOCIALIST HISTORIAN?

> Dear Comrades,
>
> The Making of the English Working Class originated not, as Richard Johnson supposes, from a disenchantment with Stalinism, or economism, but from a split in the old New Left. This split saw Edward Thompson representing 'history', the labour movement, and class struggle on one side of the divide, Stuart Hall ... and Raymond Williams ... representing 'culturalism' on the other. ...
>
> After taking Williams to task ... he ended up by declaring that the 'sociologists' had given their version of the ... it was now for historians to offer their alternative.
>
> ...
>
> Then would follow some 2,500 words on the The Politics of the Making of the English Working Class[64]

This signalled his essential agreement with Thompson's argument against Johnson (if not the style in which it was made), but the details of his interpretation of *The Making of the English Working Class* did not materialise. The 2,500 words never followed and the letter was not published, quite possibly a tactful decision considering the steady stream of complaints from distressed workshop participants in response to the confrontation.

What Samuel did do in the immediate aftermath of the HW was a detailed 'post mortem' on the event where he called upon the analytical and reflective skills of the experienced organiser (and social historian) to systematically dissect the various long- and short-term factors that had contributed to the calamity. As detailed as this document was, he deliberately avoided mentioning the 'confrontation', stating in a handwritten 'PS' on the document: 'I have not speculated on the effects on the HW of the Saturday night debate on The Poverty of Theory'.[65]

This indirectness of his initial response, however, did not mean that he did not have a position on the relationship between history and theory. Whilst a gesture towards this can be discerned in his discarded readers' letter,

---

64 Raphael Samuel, 'Draft Letter to *History Workshop Journal*', RS 7: History Workshop Events/History Workshop 13, People's History and Socialist Theory, 1979, 039, RSA.
65 Raphael Samuel, 'Post Mortem on HW 13', RS 7: History Workshop Events/History Workshop 13, *People's History and Socialist Theory*, 1979, 039, RSA.

something more of it can be seen in his editorials 'People's History' and 'History and Theory', written for the book collection of the conference papers, *People's History and Socialist Theory* (1981).

Whilst the content of these editorials had first been published as the editorial for *HWJ*, 6 (which carried Johnson's critique of Thompson's socialist humanism) and accredited to the *HWJ* 'editorial collective', they appeared in *People's History and Socialist Theory* under Samuel's name alone. Ostensibly, they were dedicated to outlining the subject matter of the book but at the same time they were also highly strategic documents. Given the HW 'general editor' was first and foremost an educational role, the editorials had a pedagogic function in explaining to an uninitiated student readership the complex terms and ideas invoked in the course of the debates and doing so in a straightforward style of prose. At the same time, they also went some way towards smoothing over the ruptures that had emerged between contending political–intellectual positions. By contextualising the various perspectives on offer, tracing their development and acknowledging both their strengths and weaknesses, he gave a subtle reminder that all ideas were products of their times and that they were inevitably subject to change. The subtext for these documents was that history, as a form of critical social knowledge, could, and should, accommodate a wide range of approaches without the need for one to dominate.

The editorial on 'People's History' took the form of a historiographical survey of the term's various European incarnations. Starting out from the early nineteenth century (considerably pre-dating the recent 'discovery' of 'history from below'), he surveyed its uses and appropriations at different times and from different political perspectives. Out of this diverse, politically and culturally pluralist set of incarnations, he discerned subtle linking filaments:

> People's history, whatever its particular subject matter, is shaped in the crucible of politics, and penetrated by the influence of ideology on all sides ... Each in its own way represents a revolt from 'dry as dust' scholarship and an attempt to return history to its roots, yet the implicit politics in them could hardly be more opposed.[66]

---

66   Raphael Samuel, 'People's History', in *People's History and Socialist Theory*, xx.

Samuel concluded with a repeat rendition of the totemic Brecht poem 'Questions From a Worker Who Reads' (1935) to re-emphasise his point that people's history was, fundamentally, a claim for recognition, a voice for the otherwise muted figures condemned to the backdrop of history's *tableau vivant* that not only expanded upon the weave of history but actually changed its course. The contrast between his account and Peter Burke's paper 'People's History or Total History' is illuminating. Burke, at that time a tutor at Emmanuel College, Cambridge, and member of the *HWJ* extended editorial committee, followed in recognising the roots of people's history in early nineteenth-century Europe. The limits of this project, he argued, lay in its lack of integrated analysis between social life and politics (not remedied until before Marx and Engels), and a selective reading of 'the people', endowing one particular group with an 'epical' historical role or destiny, at the exclusion of others. On this second issue he saw some parallel with contemporary forms of people's history:

> The epic approach to people's history still survives. The work of Edward Thompson, Christopher Hill and Raphael Samuel has this epic quality, a quality which is one of their great virtues. … At the same time, this epic approach involves some grave dangers. It's terribly easy to slide into a struggle between virtue and vice …[67]

He concluded with three cheers, the first for the recognition of social structures as political, the second for restoring the dignity to 'ordinary people', the third he reserved for a future move towards 'total history', 'in which the distinction between them and us is at last obliterated',[68] Where Samuel (the former activist) had seen 'people's history' by its very definition as intrinsically and inescapably political, a tool in a battle of ideas, Burke (the professional academic historian) felt that, as an intellectual project, people's history was hampered in its development by such partisanship.

Samuel's editorial on 'History and Theory' was a recapitulation of the position that he had worked out with Stedman Jones in their joint editorials on 'History and Sociology'. Theory could have a narrowing effect referencing a small number of canonical texts used as a talisman. It could be self-referential, leading to exclusivity and esotericism, involving a 'good deal of posturing'; the purpose of which, he could only surmise, was 'that of keeping an uncomfortable world at bay' unchecked by anything

---
67 Peter Burke, 'People's History or Total History', in *People's History and Socialist Theory*, 7–8.
68 Ibid.

outside of itself. It could lack critical self-awareness of its own historical context of production: 'theory is not something ready-made, waiting for us to adopt in the form of 'hypotheses', 'models' or protocol. Like any other intellectual artefact, it has its material and ideological conditions of existence'.[69]

That said, critical theory had performed an important role in opening up historical research and challenging the dominance of a complacent empiricism, expanding both the range of subjects studied and the analytical approaches with which to view them. It had also provided an important critical tension necessary in the writing of people's history:

> Left to itself, people's history can enclose itself in a locally defined totality where no alien forces intrude. It can serve as a kind of escapism, a flight from the uncertainties of the present to the apparent stabilities of the past.

Provided theory was used as a *tool*, a point of departure rather than the central object of historical analysis, then it had value. As Samuel phrased it: 'The theoretical worth of a project is not to be gauged by the manner of its expression, but by the complexity of the relationships it explores'.[70]

British Marxist historians

Complex relationships were the focus of Samuel's essay 'British Marxist Historians 1880–1980', which appeared in *NLR* four months after HW 13.[71] Whilst the essay responded directly to the debates which had played out in *HWJ* and HW 13, the work had a much longer genesis, reaching back to the proposed articles 'The Marxist Interpretation of History – Can it be rewritten?' and 'The Liquidation of the Thirties', promised for the earliest editions of the *Universities and Left Review* and never fulfilled. Some 20 years on from that time, both question and proposition were no less difficult and emotive.

Samuel broached the attempt by suggesting a different framework for the debate that abandoned such an intensively text-based focus:

---

69 Samuel, 'People's History', in *People's History and Socialist Theory*, l.
70 Ibid., li.
71 Raphael Samuel, 'British Marxist Historians 1880–1980', *NLR*, I/220, Mar–Apr (1980), 21–96.

> In recent years there has been vigorous debate amongst Marxists on fundamental questions of theory but the debate has turned largely on the epistemological status of Marxist concepts, rather than their historical or political determinations ... Such exegeses while opening up a space for theoretical disagreement within the Marxist tradition, have also served to reinforce the notion of texts which exist, in some sort, independent of their time and place.
>
> [S]o far from being immune to exogamous influences, Marxism may rather be seen – in light of its history – as a palimpsest on which they are inscribed.[72]

Drawing upon his encyclopaedic knowledge of Marxist culture and history, his investigation unfolded through thematic sections, allowing him to tease out entangled issues: 'I Mutations in Marxism', 'II Radical Democratic History', 'III Protestantism and Non Conformism' and 'IV Scientific Rationalism'. His concern was not British Marxist historiography as a single entity advancing through various developmental stages, but as an ensemble of ideas inhabiting distinct social, political and cultural spaces:

> The Marxist notion of scientific explanation in history may be said to have gone through a whole number of epistemological breaks. In one phase it was associated with a paradigm of biological necessity, in another with notions of technological determination, in a third with a sociology of class.[73]

The significance given to particular periods in British history was equally shaped by external contexts: '[F]orty years ago the heaviest concentration of Marxist historical work was in the field of 16th and 17th England' or '[T]he preponderance of classical history in early Marxist work, may be said to reflect, in some sort the centrality of classics in literary discourse and higher education'.[74] Furthermore, Marxist historiography had not existed in a political-intellectual vacuum but in conjunction with other radical traditions. The 'people's history' of the 1930s and 1940s, for example, was inherited from an earlier 'liberal-radical version': A.L. Morton's *A People's History of England* (1938) was modelled directly on

---

72   Ibid., 21–24.
73   Ibid., 24–25.
74   Ibid., 26, 30.

J.R. Green's *Short History of the English People* (1877). Similarly, the work of prominent historians such as R.H. Tawney, the Hammonds and the Webbs, none of whom were Marxists, had all provided major stimulus.

Radical religious traditions had also shaped British Marxist historiography. Dissenting and non-conformism was a recurrent preoccupation: 'Puritanism itself and the study of religious sectarianism ... has been responsible for some of the most interesting work within the Marxist tradition in Britain'.[75] More than this, religion had also been a deeply informing factor for individual Marxist historians:

> Three of the most widely-read Marxist historians writing today – Christopher Hill, E.P. Thompson and Sheila Rowbotham – had a Methodist or part-Methodist upbringing, being educated at leading Methodist schools, and it may well be that a study of personal formation would show many other Marxist writers and historians with a non-conformist or evangelical background only a generation away.[76]

This recognised the importance of the psychological and emotional landscapes of Marxist historians and even some purchase on their behaviour: 'Thompson has always used history as his pulpit. His opening salvoes are often no less exhortatory than his concluding apostrophes ... there is always, in the end, a fundamental moral issue at stake'.

The article answered the question he had posed in 1956: could Marxist history be rewritten? Yes, it had been in a constant state of rewriting since its inception. The matter of 'the thirties' however, still hovered in the air. In his concluding passages he seemed to reach towards it:

> The Communist Party Historians' Group of the 1940s and early 1950s saw history essentially as an epic with classes fulfilling (or failing to fulfil) their historically appointed mission. The science of history was pivoted on laws of development: humanity moved forward in a progression from point to point, until with the achievement of socialism, pre-history ended and real history began. To-day's Marxist historians have abandoned such overall evolutionary schemes, without offering any comparably unified view in its place. But they have not abandoned the materialist explanation of cause.[77]

---

75 Ibid., 42.
76 Ibid., 43.
77 Ibid., 95.

He went on to say that rather than approaching this in terms of 'cause and effect' analysis, contemporary Marxist historians found it more fruitful to reflect on disjuncture; why what was expected to happen did not. But if Marxism as an evolutionary schema was no longer convincing, as a mode of materialist critique it still had much to yield. What brought Marxist historians together across the ages, affiliations, and conceptual languages was the ethical intention behind their respective analyses: to bring to light concealed relationships that underpinned conditions of social being; that shaped, or organised social consciousness and gave rise to social inequalities and injustice.

The treatment was disappointingly brief. The article, admittedly 'part one', had furnished a rich background up until the 1950s, but there were still only glimpses of his views on the CPHG, obscured by being scattered amongst the thematic headings. The current state of Marxist historiography was little more than a concluding thought (or a point of departure for a later instalment).

Inevitably, the second article did not appear, but in Samuel's notes and drafts for the topic, material discarded from the first and draft passages clearly intended for the second, there are some clues as to what his thoughts on the subject were, not least of which can be gleaned from the manner, as much as the content, of his prose. Whilst his editorials and article had, necessarily, taken a moderate tone, with barbed remarks subdued for the sake of comradeship, in his personal notes there was a glimpse of a steelier, angrier side to the otherwise genial Workshop historian.

His notes on the CPHG reflected as much upon the fractures amongst the group as it did upon its unity, critically pointing to the divide between middle-class aspiring academics and the wider socialist movement:

> There is no doubt that the Party Historians' Group completely underestimated the potential of labour history, the major growth point of socialist work in the following years …
>
> This was partly, and in an ultimate sense, because of the uncertain relationships with what was an overwhelmingly middle class body, with very few members recruited from the working class or the labour movement homes … the great majority were first generation socialists drawn from

> the comfortable middle class and despite their utter devotion to the labour movement there remained a huge cultural distance ... The group studied the revolutionary tradition but they did not study strikes.[78]

Elsewhere:

> Another great weakness which was also the site of division with the group was local history. Betty Grant almost alone when she joined the group produced a remarkable document ... Lip service was paid to this and she soldiered on with Our History.
>
> But if one compares the local history bulletin and Our History ... this looks a very poor relation compared to the ambitious Past and Present.
>
> Thus at two points where the group might have helped out of the Party's political isolation they failed. The only bridge which had been successfully built in the Cold War years was that to the non-party scholarship ... it is not surprising that in the following decade, numbers of members crossed it.[79]

A handwritten note of an oral conversation with Dorothy Thompson (dated 20 January 1980) records Thompson's description of Grant as 'a nutter'. The question of a growing tension between the 'academic' and 'popular' agendas of the group recurred elsewhere: 'This gravitational uppull to the universities was also a cause of considerable strain within the historians' group. It proved difficult and indeed impossible to contain the pressure of research within the group's boundaries'.[80]

Further handwritten asides dwell further on the nature of the ambitions animating some amongst the founders of *Past and Present*: 'P&P [Past and Present] epoch making [*another sentence not legible*] Belligerently professional'.[81] This belligerent professionalism, he conjectured, arose directly from the deeply defensive position that Marxist historians working within the universities found themselves in and, as a result, were forced to expend considerable energy in addressing:

---

78   Raphael Samuel, 'Notes on Communist Party Historians Group', Samuel 134/British Marxist Historians, RSA.
79   Ibid.
80   Ibid.
81   Ibid.

5. THE SOCIALIST HISTORIAN?

> [W]hen it came to the discussion about bourgeois histories there is no doubt that the historians considered themselves engaged in a species of ideological class struggle, in which Marxist truth was engaged in heroic combat with bourgeois error.[82]

Samuel's notes on the contemporary situation within British Marxist historiography shifted even more emphatically in tone towards argument rather than analysis:

> The creation of an alternative history has much to offer and has already achieved much. But an oppositional history, one which would challenge both bourgeois thought and reach out to a wider constituency has still to come ... they will need to take a lesson from the CPHG ... find more collaborative methods of work, be more supportive to each other and deliberately map out major themes. The HW [History Workshop] is doing this but it is too infrequent ...[83]

It is clear from this that a springtime of disjointed histories was not the summit of Samuel's ambition. These, whilst important, had still, somehow, to be brought together, their differences transformed from so many internal divisions into a shared, multilayered, social critique. On the means towards achieving that, however, his subsequent notes betrayed a depth of feeling yet to be 'edited' for public consumption:

> The Marxist history that emerges from the Birmingham Centre of Contempt Studies [Birmingham Centre for Contemporary Cultural Studies] – a hot house of theoretical – self consciously setting out naturalise French Marxist structuralism will necessarily be very different from the one that emanates from the kitchens of Spitalfields and L. Pimlico or the terraces of World's End and Wolwroth – the characteristic habitats of the History Workshop Collective.

Part of the handwritten addition here read: 'Urgently need to be empirically as well as conceptually informed'.

---

82 Ibid.
83 Raphael Samuel, 'Notes on British Marxist Historiography', Samuel 100/British Marxist Historians, RSA.

The next paragraph continued:

> In recent years the scholarly mode has been no less influential on all kinds of books which bear the marks of the PHD even when they take on an explicitly Marxist problematic as with RQ Gray and Gareth SJ ...[84]

The use of metaphor in the passage bears further comment. The reference to the 'kitchen', the 'terrace' and 'the characteristic habitats' invoke warmth and a homely everyday-ness. Furthermore, they are common spaces used or traversed by many. In contrast is the 'hot house', creating, under controlled conditions and under great pressure, an artificial, self-enclosed environment for the growing of things that are not organic (indigenous) to the area. Similarly, 'the scholarly mode' and the capitalised 'PHD' gesture towards a formalised approach, the warmth of the former juxtaposed to strong effect against the coldness of the latter.

Above all, these notes repeatedly identified the disconnection between intellectuals and the wider movement (or, more expansively, the wider constituency) as the most pressing issue on his mind. Tucked away at the bottom of a page riddled with sentences trialled and discarded in the struggle for expression ('None of this can be done if historians regard their prime interests...', 'All this depends on who history...'), one lone line reads poignantly: 'Epistemological question that is also a political one: who are you writing for and why?'[85]

These were, of course, just notes and drafts. It would be unfair to infer too much from them, after all he did not publish them in this form. They do, however, reinforce something of the complexity of Samuel's positioning in relation to the British Marxist historiographical tradition and the generations of the left. On the one hand he was, quite literally, a physical connecting thread throughout the generations, the schoolboy member of the CPHG, a key New Left organiser and activist, the HW historian. His major historical project, an oppositional people's history, had its roots deep in the politics and political agenda of the Popular Front. Like his account of British Marxist historiography, his historical imagination had been continually revised, his histories rewritten, in relation to the wider contexts in which he lived and worked.

---

84 Raphael Samuel, 'Notes on British Marxist Historians', Samuel 135/British Marxist Historians, RSA.
85 Ibid.

On the other hand, these notes demonstrate the insufficiency of generations as a dividing concept on its own. It was not only his age but his entire set of priorities that were distinctive. Samuel was first and foremost a communist activist. Whilst hardly from a conventional 'labour movement home' himself, from his childhood he had been entrenched in a highly disciplined party life in a way that others amongst his contemporaries had not. Some of his phrases even recall those of Rajani Palme Dutt (italics my own): 'The intellectual who has joined the Communist Party … *should forget that he is an intellectual and remember that he is a Communist*'.[86] In many respects, this was exactly what Samuel was, not through slavish adherence to a particular view of history or incarnation of a social theory, but in his commitment to work within, amongst and for a wider movement, however diffuse and elusive in definition that movement had become.

Left reflecting

This reflectivity on left-wing cultures continued throughout the following decade, gaining greater urgency by events such as the formation of Solidarity in Poland (1980), the first trade union not to be controlled by the ruling Communist Party. Samuel recalled of this:

> I think that Poland was very shocking to me, the Solidarity. I think that was a kind of a firmer point of rupture with me: of seeing that Communism actually didn't have anything particularly to do with the mass movement any more, and to that extent I [felt] much colder towards it.[87]

It was not only events in Europe. Domestically, the ongoing internal disputes amongst the Labour Party raised further questions amongst the left. In 1981, Samuel and Stedman Jones collaborated on an article, 'The Labour Party and Social Democracy', which set out to challenge:

---

86 Rajani Palme Dutt, 'Intellectuals and Communism', *Communist Review*, September (1932), 421–30.
87 Brian Harrison, 'Interview with Raphael Samuel', 20 October 1987.

> [T]he overwhelming sense among the Party faithful that it had, from the moment of its foundation, been fundamentally the same sort of people, the same sort of struggles, the same geography of power, the same organisations.[88]

In place of this, they called for work towards a more complex account that took as its starting point the history of Labour Party politics as 'a perpetually shifting fulcrum between contending and initially extra-party pressures from left and right'.[89]

Both men made good on their own critique, going some way towards pursuing this in their own work. For Stedman Jones, the fruits of this could be seen in *Languages of Class* (1983) in which he drew upon cultural and linguistic analysis to show the different ways in which conceptions of class and class politics had been constituted and reconstituted over time.[90]

Samuel, characteristically, plied his histories through non-academic mediums such as *The Guardian* and journals the *New Statesman* and *New Socialist*. He penned letters challenging the ancestral appeals and omissions made by the Labour Party and the newly formed Social Democratic Party (SDP). The Labour MP Tony Benn, he argued, was too quick to claim the party as inheritor for all the various and contradictory traditions of opposition and dissent. In invoking R.H. Tawney as a political forefather, the SDP were wrong not to acknowledge the Christianity that had underpinned the former's socialist vision. He wrote articles such as 'The Vision Splendid' on the utopian roots of late nineteenth-century socialism and 'Enter the Proletarian Giant' on the early twentieth-century shift towards the 'muscular' language and aesthetic of the industrial worker, both further contributions towards an expansion and contextualisation of the 'socialist tradition'.[91]

Across this body of work, Samuel's theoretical conceptions were largely implicit, evident in the nature of his approach rather than clearly stated. He did, however, return to the question of theory in a two-part article,

---

88 Raphael Samuel and Gareth Stedman Jones, 'The Labour Party and Social Democracy', in Samuel and Stedman Jones, eds, *Culture, Ideology and Politics* (London: Routledge and Kegan Paul, 1982), 320–31.
89 Ibid.
90 Gareth Stedman Jones, *Languages of Class: Studies in English Working Class History 1832–1982* (Cambridge: Cambridge University Press, 1983).
91 Raphael Samuel: 'Religion and Politics: The Legacy of R.H. Tawney', *The Guardian*, 29 March 1984; 'Ancestor Worship', *The Guardian*, 4 October 1984; 'The Vision Splendid', *New Socialist*, 27, May (1985); 'Enter the Proletarian Giant', *New Socialist*, 29, July (1985).

'Reading the Signs', addressing the implications of the cultural and linguistic turn more fully.[92] His arguments were familiar: this debate was not new but had 'echoes of the dispute between nominalist and realists in the middle ages or for that matter the Sophists and Plato in Ancient Greece'; reading the signs could be an overdetermined exercise placing the intellectual in an elevated position of authority; representation should not be the sole object of historical research; 'getting up stuff' was what historians did best.[93]

His treatment of Michel Foucault, the French cultural theorist turned historian, revealed more of his own position. If Thompson had used Louis Althusser as a point of comparison, Foucault served a similar function for Samuel. Foucault used history to illuminate the relationships between knowledge, truth and power. It was not, he argued, the traditional elites that now wielded this power but the emerging 'professional' ones: managers, administrators, teachers, doctors, lawyers, psychiatrists and officials. Adopting an 'archaeological' approach, his radical histories of psychiatry, medicine, criminology and sexuality charted how each generated complex discursive systems which served to regulate human behaviour and legitimise social control. This innovative approach proved influential but it was also a bleak perspective.[94] In his hands, historical analysis did not offer alternatives but served only as a tool for puncturing the illusion of unity by revealing the interplay of discursive structures in the production of knowledge.

Samuel sounded caution against an unexamined embrace of Foucauldian intellectual history, suggesting, provocatively, that for all the emphasis on rupture and difference it had an ironic tendency towards the sort of universalism it claimed to reject, with all pathways leading towards modernity (or post-modernity). What riled the former grassroots activist most was that Foucault's approach failed to recognise the capacity of (so-called) 'ordinary people' to engage selectively and reinterpret what they were told.[95] By contrast, Samuel's preferred means of disrupting discursive

---

92 Raphael Samuel: 'Reading the Signs I', *HWJ*, 32 (1991), 88–109; 'Reading the Signs: Fact Grubbers and Mind Readers II', *HWJ*, 33 (1992), 220–51.
93 Samuel, 'Reading the Signs', 99, 105, 251.
94 See Jeffrey Weeks, 'Foucault for Historians', *HWJ*, 14 (1982), 106–19.
95 For a similar argument see Michel de Certeau, *The Practice of Everyday Life* (Berkeley and Los Angeles: University of California Press, 1988).

unities was through *expansion* as much as deconstruction. By allowing a greater range of voices and perspectives, other histories, he could deflate the supremacy of any one particular claim to truth just as effectively.

He used such an approach in response to the Miners' Strike (6 March 1984–3 March 1985). The strike, perhaps the most bitter industrial dispute in the twentieth century, shocked the country with its ferocity, tearing communities apart, exposing, again, the deep fractures amongst the political left. In a sign of the changing times, the Communist Party of Great Britain (CPGB) withheld official support from the striking miners and penalised party members who failed to comply with the party line. The result was a split, the first in the party's 60-year history.[96]

Samuel reacted by hosting a Workshop with the mining communities affected by the action. The intent was not simply to present an alternative account of the strike, but to provide the people involved the chance to construct their own histories of the event. As the report following the weekend read:

> A lot of the people that attended the weekend thought at the beginning that we at Oxford wanted the information off them to do the recording ourselves, this showed with comments being made early in the week-end such as you will have to come to Grimethorpe to get the feeling of the place. But by the Sunday morning they realised that they were capable of doing it themselves with a little help and backup from the History Workshop Centre.[97]

This 'help and back-up' was provided directly by the event's key organisers: 'On a more practical side Raph Samuells [sic] and Anna Davin gave talks showing how peoples history could be recorded by various means such as pictures, pamphlets, books, audio cassettes and video'.[98]

In the book collection which followed the weekend, Samuel's introduction did not shy away from advancing sharp insights into the 'radical conservatism' shown by some of the miners, noting, for example, the desire to conserve jobs despite the increasing inefficiency of coal mining in 1980s Britain. But he also showed sensitivity (betraying something of

---

96   See Geoff Andrews, *Endgames and New Times: The Final Years of British Communism 1964–1991* (London: Lawrence and Wishart, 2004).
97   'Report Back on Miner's Weekend', RS 5: Miners Dispute Weekend, 77, RSA.
98   Ibid.

his own sympathies as he did so) to the bonds of loyalty underpinning the mining communities and the disruption to deep structures of identity that the pit closures had precipitated.[99]

The strike and its repercussions had stirred up other ghosts lurking in Samuel's sense of identity. The aggressive reaction of the CPGB to the miners and their supporters affected him strongly. Despite the fact he had not been a party member for almost 30 years, he felt that it 'called into question the worth of my own political commitments'.[100] So, just as he had offered the mining communities, he too sought a voice in the debate through history. The 'Lost World of British Communism' essays, published in the *NLR*, were the means by which he finally confronted his view of the CPGB as it was and, more importantly, as it had been in his youth.

Following their publication, the essays were criticised for their chaotic style. His former New Left colleague, John Saville, described them as an incoherent personal sociology and was moved to venture his own memoir about life on the left.[101] Dorothy Thompson found them 'folksy' and wasted no more of her time on them.[102] Certainly, the essays were scattered in nature, often reading like a stream of consciousness in which distinct points became hopelessly entangled. Despite this, the essays constituted an original perspective. Rather than judging the political decisions taken by party management figures, Samuel concentrated on the ways in which political convictions were developed and perpetuated 'from below'.

Taking as his point of departure the 1940s (Popular Front), the high point of unity within the party and its followers, Samuel examined how that unity had been made possible, the ways in which class politics had been able to colonise bodies; minds and emotions effectively.[103] In one section, 'Metaphysical Space', he explored communism in terms of its quasi-religious properties; the all-embracing determinism of Marxism replacing the role of providence, the continual appeals made to 'liberation' and 'justice', the promised redemption of workers' revolution.

---

99   Raphael Samuel, 'Editorial preface', in Raphael Samuel, Barbara Bloomfield and Guy Boanas, eds, *The Enemy Within: Pit Villages and the Miners' Strike of 1984–5* (London: Routledge and Kegan Paul, 1986), 1–39.
100 Raphael Samuel, *The Lost World of British Communism* (London: Verso, 2006), 44.
101 John Saville, *Memoirs from the Left* (London: Merlin Press, 2003).
102 Dorothy Thompson, 'On the Trail of the First New Left', *NLR*, I/215, Jan–Feb (1996), 93.
103 Samuel, *The Lost World*, 9.

The CPGB itself he contrasted with the functioning of a 'crusading order', 'church militant'.[104] Elsewhere, in sections entitled 'The Disciplines of Organization' and 'The Vocation of Leadership', he traced how moral strictures were transformed and translated into the physical structures of party life, the distribution and nature of managerial roles assumed by party members, the demands placed upon its rank and file for sustained political activity and intensive political education.[105]

As important to Samuel's analysis was the CPGB's relationship to external forces and factors, the historical context of the Second World War providing 'a sense of burning necessity',[106] the correlations with the wider cultural 'moment' of the 1940s, 'the zenith of mass society' where organisation, standardisation and planning were fetishised in a broad ideology of 'fair shares'.[107] The party not only inhabited these historical spaces, it intermingled with the personal histories of its individual members. In 'Family Communism' he offered the experience of his own family by way of example: his mother who found in the party a freedom from the 'ghetto' and married life in 'The Suburb'; communism's impact on his own fledgling sense of social identity.[108]

Through these distinct but converging contexts, a structure of belief had been generated, made plausible by its positioning within and amongst the contexts that had fashioned it. During the postwar decades the integrity of this structure had come under attack at its connecting points. The events of 1956 had undermined the CPGB's moral credibility. More critically, class, as the major category of analysis, had become decentralised from political discourse. What had once seemed indisputable was now the source of bitter division.

Whilst not shying away from recognising the delusional mentalities and behaviours implicit in this communist world, he also recognised its valuable qualities: the sense of comradeship and solidarity that developed amongst the members. The essays were littered with Samuel's fond memories of former comrades who provided mentorship, kindness and guidance to others, including to him (he had only left the party out of loyalty to his

---

104 Ibid., 45–58.
105 Ibid., 100–20, 121–38.
106 Ibid., 35.
107 Ibid., 9.
108 Ibid., 59–68.

5. THE SOCIALIST HISTORIAN?

friends rather than from genuine desire). He acknowledged the levels of commitment and dedication shown by party members, particularly in the spheres of self-education. Speaking of these self-taught comrades he said:

> [T]heir correspondence … their class syllabuses and lecture notes … testify to their intellectuality, that of a generation of autodidacts, bred in vernacular Marxism, who within the limits and particularities of British national culture have some claim to being considered as an 'organic' intelligentsia, of a kind which the Designer Socialists of today, for all their noisy references to Gramsci, can hardly tolerate.[109]

This comment echoes his first account of the origins of the HW in which he had extolled the levels of commitment shown by the Ruskin students, for no other reward than for the sake of mastering a craft. This sort of independent action, often undertaken against the odds, in a spirit of collaboration, was a recurrent and valued ideal. Out of the rubble of his personal commitment to the party, this was what had survived.

The 1980s was a critical time in the evolution of Samuel's political and historical thought. Whilst it did not constitute a retreat from his political values, it was, nonetheless, a period of self-reflection. At a 1989 conference, 'Out of Apathy: Voices of the New Left Thirty Years On' convened by the Oxford Socialist Society, he made the astonishing concession that he had not wanted to live in a 'socialist society' for some thirty years. As for his political convictions, he explained that he had come to view socialism as a metaphor for principles of 'collectivity, solidarity and opposition' rather than in any more specific terms.[110]

The decade following HW 13 brought further significant changes. There were tensions amongst and between both the student body and the management at Ruskin College. Attempts to balance Ruskin's legacy of critical independent education with a hostile Conservative political climate and unpromising economic situation became increasingly difficult. Nationally, high levels of unemployment placed pressure on further education to be a means of accessing employment (rather than fermenting discontent). Social critique became a luxury few could afford. The HW, meanwhile, left its Ruskin base and became itinerant, touring

---

109 Ibid., 201–2.
110 Raphael Samuel, 'Then and Now: A Re-evaluation of the New Left', in Robin Archer et al., eds, *Out of Apathy: Voices of the New Left Thirty Years On* (London: Verso, 1989), 149.

the country. Its principal constituency shifted from universities, adult education and worker students towards polytechnic colleges, community arts centres and local museums.[111]

Samuel was no longer the central organising figure behind Workshop meetings, although he remained involved, calling Workshops on issues that specifically concerned him. *HWJ*, too, continued to carve out its own path distinct from the HW, increasingly adopting the character of an academic journal in fact if not in name. This was later reinforced by its transition to the Oxford University Press in 1990 following a disagreement with their original publishers.[112]

The nature of his relationship to the post-1979 HW movement and journal is suggested by his style of writing about it in the *History Workshop: A Collectanea*, a commemorative volume published on the 25th anniversary of the HW in 1991. His editorials on 'Ruskin Historians' and the early Workshop are full of detail, anecdote, warmth and humour. By contrast the later editorial 'History Workshop 14–25' is sparse in detail, less than two pages in length, and whilst this could have been a simple case of not knowing as much about them as he had done the Ruskin Workshops the tone he used was also cooler, although not unkind:

> The atmosphere at the provincial workshops is inconceivably more relaxed – partly perhaps because there is more room to move in, less overcrowding. There are no simmering resentments at outsiders coming in ... [T]here are no newspapers sellers at the door canvassing for recruits, no theatre of the platform and the floor ...[113]

These attributes were not bad things, but when contrasted to his affectionate accounts of the discomforts and passions in the early Workshop, it seemed he missed the old fighting spirit.

---

111 Raphael Samuel, 'History Workshop 14–25', in *History Workshop: A Collectanea 1967–1991*, 14–25.
112 Samuel, 'History Workshop Journal', in *History Workshop: A Collectanea 1967–1991*, 109. See also Barbara Taylor, 'History Workshop Journal', *Making History: The Changing Face of the Profession in Britain*, The Institute of Historical Research, www.history.ac.uk/makinghistory/resources/articles/HWJ.html (accessed May 2014).
113 Samuel, 'History Workshop 14–25', 146.

Samuel's descriptions of the journal were diplomatic but critical. He acknowledged that the relationship between HW and the journal had quickly bifurcated, each pursuing its own path with little organic connection existing between the two. Considering the *HWJ* as it appeared to him in 1991, his phrasing was revealing:

> The *Journal* is prospering and has what at least to the editors seems a challenging programme of work. It still calls itself a journal of 'socialist historians,' though from 1981 onwards … this was qualified and undermined by the addition of the word 'feminist' to the masthead.[114]

The scepticism in this comment is clear, but it is more difficult to interpret its implications. It could be read as the view of an old Marxist unwilling to embrace new forms of cultural politics, such as feminism, and clinging steadfastly to an outdated notion of socialism. On the other hand, perhaps what he really regretted was the lack of a unifying term:

> It is a curious fact that as the Journal has become … less movement orientated it has become *more* political. Socialism, in the early issues of the Journal, was an adjective rather than a noun. It stood for a diffuse identity rather than a specific platform or line.[115]

It was his 'diffuse identity', and all the openness it entailed, that had motivated the original HW movement.

Samuel's historical work and interests increasingly took on a London focus. He was closely involved with the London History Workshop Centre (1981) and in preparations for the Festival of London. The group worked on a major project, 'Exploring Living Memory', but, in a by now familiar story, their experiences of attempting to work with the Labour-led local council proved frustrating.[116] Other activities yielded more pleasant results. Following a Workshop on 'Romance Fiction' held at Ruskin College in May 1984, he formed the Popular Literature Group which met at his London home in Elder Street to read and discuss popular literature as a cultural artefact.[117] It was through this reading group that he met Alison Light, a literary scholar and critic, whom he married in 1987.[118]

---

114 Ibid., 108.
115 Ibid., iv.
116 Mary Chamberlain and Raphael Samuel, 'Festival of London History', in *History Workshop: A Collectanea 1967–1991*, 163–64.
117 Alison Light and Raphael Samuel, 'Popular Literature Group', in *History Workshop: A Collectanea 1967–1991*, 52–53.
118 Alison Light, oral communication with author, February 2014, Oxford.

HW 13 was significant because of the extent to which it had symbolised the fission and fractures that had long been simmering between political generations, positions and agendas. The debates about the relationship between history and theory had forced the most direct indication yet of Samuel's view of 'people's history' and the contribution of the critical intellectual. Underpinning all of his responses was a deep conviction that the intellectual had first and foremost to work on the ground: to seek, or create, spaces for dialogue, to forge connections and provide guidance. It was this instinct that underpinned his energetic but highly controversial engagement with the national past and popular memory.

6
Stranger Memories of Who We Really Are: History, the Nation and the Historian

Raphael Samuel (third from right, back row), Ruskin staff and students during a field trip to Ironbridge, 1994
Raphael Samuel Archive, Bishopsgate Institute, London, courtesy of Alison Light and the Raphael Samuel Estate.

Patrick Wright was perplexed. What on earth was Raphael Samuel up to? Wright had just sat down to review Samuel's *Theatres of Memory* and was unimpressed.[1] Samuel had always 'played up' to the role of the people's historian, appearing at times perilously close to abandoning his responsibilities as a critical intellectual. His latest offering brought to mind something of those zealous young intellectuals of the 1960s who had gone off to work in factories or on collective farms, driven by some combination of romantic zeal and middle-class guilt. But this book of his, surely, was too much![2]

For a start, it was inconsistent with his earlier views. Only a few years ago, Samuel had been one of the sternest critics of the heritage industry and its promiscuous play with the past. One had only to recollect some of his writings where he had strongly criticised the 'gentrification' of his home turf in Spitalfields, East London.[3] He had been utterly confounded at the anachronistic attempts to recreate a fictitious Georgian glamour in what had been the old weavers' quarter. And now, here he was, celebrating retro-chic and other such liberties with the past, going so far as to suggest that *professional* historians had something to *learn* from it. This was not only inconsistent, it was foolhardy. As an intellectual and educator, surely Samuel had a responsibility to reject it, to put the record straight, to say firmly to people who did not know any better that *it was not like that*. Wright was particularly stung by Samuel's response to Wright's own book, a careful meditation on the links between heritage, memory, psychologies of nostalgia and the role of history.[4] And yet here he was, painted as a killjoy and boisterously clubbed over the head in Samuel's folkish-fairground approach to history. Just what exactly was Samuel trying to achieve?

Whilst the 1980s was an inauspicious time for the political left, for Samuel it was another period of reinvention. Whereas many of his colleagues and comrades felt socialism to be a demoralised and fractured force, further strained by the decade's aggressive invocations of patriotism, he seemed to relish a renewal of the battle of ideas. He read the flourishing of history in the popular sphere as a potential opportunity rather than a dismal

---

1   Raphael Samuel, *Theatres of Memory: Past and Present in Contemporary Culture* (London: Verso, 1994).
2   Patrick Wright, 'Review of Theatres of Memory', *The Guardian*, 5 February 1995.
3   Raphael Samuel, 'A Plaque on All Your Houses', *The Guardian*, 17 October 1987; Raphael Samuel, 'The Pathos of Spitalfields', *The Spectator*, 20 May 1989.
4   Patrick Wright, *On Living in an Old Country: The National Past in Contemporary Britain* (London: Verso, 1985).

calamity. This chapter examines the controversial position he assumed in the debates surrounding British national history. It also engages with *Theatres of Memory* (1994), the only sole-authored monograph published during his lifetime, which, it suggests, was both a response to the times *and* a reassertion of his preexisting priorities and principles.

An outbreak of nostalgia?

At the start of the 1980s, Britain seemed a country in decline. Internationally, the once almighty epicentre of empire was now greatly reduced to the status of a small-island member of the European Economic Community, increasingly peripheral on the international economic and political stage. Domestically, the economic slump of the 1970s, the embittered state of British industry besieged by strikes, and high levels of unemployment had resulted in a nation disillusioned and unsure of itself.[5]

For Conservative Prime Minister Margaret Thatcher, the reason for this decline lay in history and the throttling of British entrepreneurial spirit; choked between upper-class paternalism, leftist expansions of state control and the denigration of an intellectual and cultural elite, the capitalist middle classes had been squeezed out. This interpretation, as James Raven observed, was not unique to Thatcher but had been given substance by historians from both the right *and* left of the political spectrum.[6] On the one hand, historian Martin J. Weiner could endorse this from a neoliberal perspective but, on the other, Perry Anderson could also propose a similar explanation for the 'incompleteness' of Britain's capitalist revolution.[7]

For Thatcher, if the fault lay in history so must the remedy. Her response to this was to adopt a bewildering position, simultaneously iconoclastic and deferential towards the past. More than any other British prime minister, she attacked the pillars of the establishment in a 'neo-populist' confrontation with hereditary privilege: deregulating the City of London

---

5 For overviews of this period see: Mark Garnett, *From Anger to Apathy: The British Experience since 1975* (London: Jonathan Cape, 2007); Richard Vinen, *Thatcher's Britain: The Politics and Social Upheaval of the Thatcher Era* (London: Simon & Schuster, 2009); Andy McSmith, *No Such Thing as Society* (London: Constable, 2010).
6 James Raven, 'Viewpoint: British History and the Enterprise Culture', *Past and Present* (*P&P*), 123 (1989), 178–204.
7 Martin J. Weiner, *English Culture and the Decline of the Industrial Spirit 1850–1980* (Cambridge: Cambridge University Press, 1981); Perry Anderson, 'Origins of the Present Crisis', *New Left Review* (*NLR*), I/23, Jan–Feb (1964), 26–53.

and attacking the Higher Civil Service, the Church of England, the House of Lords, the universities, the Bar and the Tory Party itself. She re-invented liberal *laissez-faire* economic policy, pushing back the role of the state and allowing market forces to assume a leading role.

At the same time, Thatcher invoked a return to 'Victorian values', extolling the 'virtues' of that era which she identified as thrift, industry, self-help and mutual aid, and making these the platform upon which she fought the 1983 election. Britain *would* become the prosperous nation of shopkeepers whose industry had built the greatest empire of the modern era. At first things did not augur well; the economic measures she imposed on entering office were deemed as harsh and she was deeply unpopular amongst her own party. In 1981 *The Times* was moved to declare her the most unpopular prime minister since polls began.[8] In the 1983 election, however, not only was Thatcher re-elected but with an increased parliamentary majority. Something had clearly changed.

The change in attitude owed a debt to the Falklands War (2 April–14 June 1982). As the crisis unfolded, Thatcher had stepped effortlessly into the role of the resolute war leader, naturally inviting comparisons (particularly for gifted cartoonists) to Elizabeth I, Victoria, even Britannia herself. In both political rhetoric and in the popular press, the conflict was framed with constant reference to national pride, patriotism and British greatness.

Thatcher demonstrated the same singleness of purpose in her response to the resurgence of the Cold War. The division between the Western European nations allied behind NATO and those nations behind the Soviet Union's iron curtain in the East had drawn a geographical and ideological dividing line across the continent since the establishment of the Warsaw Pact in 1955. During the 1980s hostilities resurfaced with renewed fears, on both sides, of the nuclear threat posed by the other. Whereas her predecessor, Labour Prime Minister James Callaghan, had not felt the threat to be urgent, Thatcher felt differently. Within a week of gaining office, the British Prime Minister was advising the German Chancellor (Helmut Schmidt) of the need for a greater nuclear capacity in Western Europe.[9]

---

8   *The Times*, 9 October 1981.
9   McSmith, *No Such Thing as Society*, 44.

Though Thatcher was not the first politician to draw upon a vision of the national past to justify their politics, what was more striking was the extent to which it appeared to capture public imagination. Not only did Conservative victory in the 1983 election suggest public support, it was reinforced by the increasing popularity of the national past in popular culture. If British manufacturing languished in the doldrums, the 'heritage industry' flourished. History filled the contents of television listings, commanded large box-office takings at the cinema, prompted the mushrooming of multiple museums and public exhibitions, drove the boom in the antiques trade and saw thousands flocking to National Trust properties to peer into the inner chambers of the social elite and picnic on their lawns. The appetite for the English past appeared insatiable.[10]

This was further compounded by an ineffective opposition. As Clive Christie argued, the Labour Party's response to the Falklands War was divided, reflective of deeper divisions and ongoing disputes amongst the membership about what the party stood for.[11] The protracted industrial disputes in the late 1970s had done much to damage the party's traditional relationship with the labour movement. Its failure to respond effectively to economic decline had similarly discouraged the electorate. The crisis reached a peak in the disastrous 1983 election campaign. Led by Michael Foot, representing the 'old socialists', on a politically brave platform of unilateral disarmament, the party received its lowest share of vote since its official formation in 1918.

Left intellectuals and historians, meanwhile, recognised that the motivation behind the Falklands War followed no economic rationale but plumbed instead an 'ugly nationalist sentiment which will cloud our political and

---

10 The *National Heritage Act (1983)* was a critical piece of legislation in changing the way in which historical buildings and sites could be managed. It was also responsible for establishing English Heritage (the Historic Buildings and Monuments Commission). John Delafons, *Politics and Preservation: A Policy History of the Built Heritage 1882–1996* (London: D & FN Spon, 1997). Other indications of history's popularity include the surge in National Trust membership figures, from 1 million in 1980 to 2 million by 1990: National Trust, 'Our History', www.nationaltrust.org.uk/what-we-do/who-we-are/our-history/ (accessed May 2014). History was also prominent in film, television and literature. Margaret Butler claimed that British cinema was 'rescued from oblivion by costume drama'. Margaret Butler, 'Costume Drama', BFI Screen Online, www.screenonline.org.uk/film/id/570755/ (accessed May 2014). See also: Peter Mandler, *The Fall and Rise of the Stately Home* (New Haven: Yale University Press, 1997); David Cannadine, 'Conservation: The National Trust and the National Heritage', in *In Churchill's Shadow: Confronting the Past in Modern Britain* (London: Penguin Press, 2002); Alex Murray, 'The Heritage Industry and Historiographic Metafiction: Historical Representations in the 1980s', in Emily Horton, Philip Tew and Leigh Wilson, eds, *The 1980s: A Decade of Contemporary British Fiction* (London: Bloomsbury Academic, 2014), 125–50. The most extensive survey and analysis of history in British popular culture was undertaken by Samuel: Samuel, *Theatres of Memory*.
11 Clive Christie, 'The British Left and the Falklands War', Political Quarterly 55:3 (1984): 288–307.

cultured life'.[12] Appeals to the splendours and glories of nation provided a spectacle that was fuelled by a manipulation of fears and desires, and crafted for the purposes of consolidating Thatcher's neo-populist politics.[13] On the growth and proliferation of history in the public sphere, art historian Robert Hewison's *The Heritage Industry: Britain in a Climate of Decline* (1987) launched an early critique of its intellectual cynicism, viewing it as clear evidence of a lack of strong cultural leadership.[14]

The analysis flew freely but, as Eric Hobsbawm pointed out, this nationalism had been *tapped* not manufactured by the Tories, corresponding to deep-rooted emotions of humiliation. The left's reticence to engage with the appeal of national identity in any great depth had rendered it remote and ineffective.[15] Hobsbawm's own efforts to address this issue, as coeditor of *The Invention of Traditions* (1983), cast an iconoclastic eye over the historical roots of the British national myths, puncturing many of its favourite conceits and revealing the extent to which so many appeals made in the name of great tradition were in fact no older than the late nineteenth and early twentieth centuries.[16] Elsewhere, Wright took a more serious approach to the appeal of the national in social psychology. His study *On Living in an Old Country* (1985) probed the internal dynamics of nostalgia in relation to Britain's loss of global dominance, arguing that nostalgia articulated the confusion and trauma fostered by the violent pace at which old ways and means of living had given way to aggressive modernisation.[17]

In disrupting some of the claims made in the name of the national past, books like *The Invention of Traditions* and *On Living in an Old Country* had greater appeal than much of the more overtly politicised writing.

---

12   E.P. Thompson, *The Times*, 29 April 1982, 12.
13   Stuart Hall, 'The Great Moving Right Show', *Marxism Today*, January 1979, 14–22. See also: Stuart Hall, *The Hard Road to Renewal: Thatcherism and the Crisis of the Left* (London: Verso, 1988); Anthony Barnett, 'Iron Britannia', *NLR*, I/134, Jul–Aug (1982), 5–96.
14   Robert Hewison, *The Heritage Industry: Britain in a Climate of Decline* (London: Methuen, 1983). See also: Paul Reas and Stuart Cosgrove, *Flogging a Dead Horse: Heritage Culture and Its Role in Post-Industrial Britain* (Manchester: Cornerhouse, 1993).
15   Eric Hobsbawm, 'Falklands Fallout', *Marxism Today*, 14 January 1983. See also: Clive Christie, 'The British Left and the Falklands War', *Political Quarterly*, 55, 3 (1984), 288–307.
16   Hugh Trevor-Roper, 'The Invention of Tradition: The Highland Tradition of Scotland', in Eric Hobsbawm and Terence Ranger, eds, *The Invention of Tradition* (Cambridge: Cambridge University Press, 1983). See also David Cannadine, 'The Past in the Present', in Lesley Smith, ed., *The Making of Britain: Echoes of Greatness* (London: Macmillan, 1988); Cannadine, 'Brideshead Revered', *London Review of Books*, 31 March 1983.
17   Wright, *On Living in an Old Country*.

While they unravelled or exposed, however, they offered little by way of a compelling alternative. Within history as a profession, the appetite for big stories (grand narratives) appeared greatly diminished. In an influential article in *Past and Present* (*P&P*), David Cannadine contended that the fracturing of the major political ideological positions (socialist, conservative, liberal) had prompted a breakdown in the 'consensus' which, according to Cannadine, had characterised the discipline during the 1950s and 1960s. There was no longer a common framework, a shared set of big questions or agreed definitions, to which historians, arguing from their respective political positions, all made reference.

The result, Cannadine argued, was the fragmentation of the discipline into a multitude of specialisms, with research carried out on more and more concentrated periods of time. The ferocity of the recent epistemological debates had further undermined confidence in the validity of history as a form of knowledge. So, whilst history on the ground and in the market boomed, history in the academy retreated further within the safety of the seminar room and library. He concluded with a call for historians to assert a more active presence in public and political debate.[18]

Cannadine's appeal was significant because it recognised that what was at stake was *not* only a scholarly battle but a political one. The rules of engagement and mode of thinking were, therefore, different from those of the academic historian. Such a battle was *exactly* the territory sought and occupied by Samuel who, after the travails of interminable epistemological debate, relished the challenge with gusto. In 1983 Samuel called a Workshop to confront 'Victorian values' head-on, the papers from which were published in a *New Statesman* supplement on 'Victorian Values'.[19] His own contribution, 'Soft Focus Nostalgia', followed Hobsbawm in juxtaposing the industriousness and enterprise invoked by Thatcher with the exploitation endured by the workforce that had made it possible. Like Hall and Wright, he reflected on the appeal of 'Victorian Values' which, he suggested, lay in the seductive aesthetics of the images chosen, the reassuring sense of solidity and stability that they invoked in what were highly uncertain times. The brevity of the article allowed him little time to elaborate on these insights.

---

18 David Cannadine, 'Viewpoint British History: Past, Present – and Future?', *P&P*, 116 (1987), 169–91.
19 'Victorian Values: Special Supplement', *New Statesman*, 27 May 1987.

For all Samuel's distaste for the neo-Tory version of the national past, personal abhorrence was also blended with fascination. He could not but be aware of the way in which Thatcher had successfully appropriated the language of the libertarian left for her own political purposes.[20] Later, he would go as far as to describe her as the most 'philosophically interesting Prime Minister' of his lifetime.[21] The invocation of individual responsibility, independence and autonomy chimed with the same spirit of self-help and independence that could be discerned in Young's studies of community life in Bethnal Green, in Thompson's self-creating English working class or his own recognition of the important role played by small-scale enterprise in Headington Quarry. Most importantly, it was *popular*, not just amongst the aspiring lower-middle classes but, critically, amongst members of the working class. It was not enough to suggest that the entire country had been skilfully manipulated or was suffering from a collective postcolonial breakdown: there was something more urgent, more profound about appeals to the national past.

The 1984 HW on patriotism was another major engagement with the issue, called to confront and combat the 'jingoism' of the Falklands War.[22] According to Samuel's earliest letter to the HW collective, the prompt came from an article written by Christopher Hill appearing in *The Guardian*:[23]

> I found Christopher Hill's splendid article in The Guardian quite intimidating at first: how on earth could we match up to, be worthy of the place he had outlined for an expanded HW as intervening in a major way in the issues raised, from the Conservative side ... Thinking about it, it seemed to me the article contained the answer and we should make its spoken and unspoken problematic PATRIOTISM and NATIONAL IDENTITY.[24]

---

20   Raphael Samuel, 'A Dotted Line to Thatcherism', in Robin Archer et al., eds, *Out of Apathy: Voices of the New Left Thirty Years On* (London: Verso, 1989), 131.
21   Raphael Samuel, 'The History Woman', *The Times*, 4 July 1991; Samuel, 'Mrs Thatcher and Victorian Values', *Island Stories: Unravelling Britain* (London: Verso, 1998), 330–48. See also Brian Harrison, 'Mrs Thatcher and the Intellectuals', *Twentieth Century British History*, 5, 2 (1994), 206–45.
22   Raphael Samuel, 'Preface', in Samuel, ed., *Patriotism: The Making and Unmaking of British National Identity:* Vol. I, *History and Politics* (New York: Routledge, Chapman and Hall, 1989), i.
23   Christopher Hill, 'History is a Matter of Taking Liberties', *The Guardian*, 30 July 1983.
24   Raphael Samuel, Letter to History Workshop Collective August 1983, RS 4: History Workshop Events/Patriotism, 293, Raphael Samuel Archive (RSA), Bishopsgate Institute, London.

This initial objective was quickly superseded by the reality of the conference, which revealed the extent of division and diversity amongst the broadly constituted left, on the subjects of nation, national identity and patriotism.[25] Samuel's notes reviewing the conference were untroubled by this; on the contrary they expressed his general delight with the event:

> The week-end had a veritable feast of excellent, considered and accessible papers and will make a fine (and money-raising) book for the Centre; and it was, I think, thoroughly enjoyed by numbers of the participants.

His only reservation was over 'the absence of a more central feminist component of the Workshop', but he felt that was as much to do with the state of feminist history in Britain as it was with the HW itself.[26]

In the book collection that finally emerged from the HW (some five years later), national identity was viewed from a myriad of different perspectives and methodological approaches: the theoretical and the historical, the physical and the psychological, the religious, the gendered and the racial. Samuel's preface boldly defined the collection's common objective as an:

> escape from unitary or essentialist notions of all kinds; not only Tory ones of a supposedly transcendental national being, but also Gramscian notions of hegemony (that currently fashionable version of Marxism which emphasises the tutelary powers of the privileged); Weberian notions of social domination (rule by bureaucracies of elites); and sociological theories of social control.[27]

His own contributions combined long-standing interests with the fruits of more recent work with his partner Alison Light. 'An Irish Religion' revisited early research into the experience of Irish migrant workers in nineteenth-century Britain. 'Doing the Lambeth Walk' explored the depiction and portrayal of class politics in the contemporary stage musical 'Me and My Girl', and 'Dockland Dickens' charted the different interpretive registers applied to the work of Charles Dickens.[28] His opening editorial, 'Exciting to be English', was a characteristically breathless

---

25 Samuel, 'Preface', in *Patriotism:* Vol. I, x–xvii.
26 Raphael Samuel, 'Letter to History Workshop Collective', RS 4: History Workshop Events/ Patriotism, 294, RSA.
27 Samuel, 'Preface', in *Patriotism:* Vol. I, xvii.
28 Raphael Samuel, 'An Irish Religion', in Samuel, ed., *Patriotism: The Making and Unmaking of British National Identity:* Vol. II, *Minorities and Outsiders*; Raphael Samuel and Alison Light, 'Doing the Lambeth Walk', in Samuel, ed., *Patriotism: The Making and Unmaking of British National Identity:* Vol. III, *National Fictions*; Raphael Samuel, 'Docklands Dickens', in *Patriotism:* Vol. III.

historical survey of the rise, fall and rise again of patriotism. Whilst still cleaving to a conventional 'leftist' position (evident in comments such as: 'the more cosmopolitan capitalism becomes the more it seems to wear a homespun look; the more nomadic its operations the more it advertises its local affiliations'), the tone of the writing was curious rather than hostile conceding the attraction and 'vitality of the national idea.'[29]

The Workshop on patriotism had not produced an alternative left-wing narrative of the nation to oppose the Tory one. It had not used history as a means of analysing relationships of domination and social control or processes of manipulation and indoctrination. At best, if taken as an overall collection, it was a demonstration that the notion of patriotism was neither self-contained nor stable as a category of thought but always belonged as part of wider imaginative frameworks.[30] Critics, such as Cannadine, found this eclecticism ambiguous and frustrating. Unsatisfied with Samuel's editorial explanation, which he described curtly as a masterclass in 'free association', he found the collection incoherent, an ad hoc assemblage of different variations on the theme of patriotism, none of which had been fully explored.[31] This view was echoed by historian Miles Taylor for whom the collection lacked a clear historiographical overview of patriotism (again targeting the ebullient introduction and its author), further proof of the political left's uneasy and ambiguous relationship with the concept.[32]

Nevertheless, the fact that Samuel recognised *excitement*, as opposed to melancholia, manipulation or mindlessness, as an important factor in the appeal of patriotism had significance. Furthermore, the fact that he was far from being downcast by diversity on the left all suggest that his modus operandi in this particular battle of ideas differed from his contemporaries. It was certainly more optimistic and, arguably, more strategic. The chance to develop a more substantial theorisation for his ideas came through the sixth international oral history conference on 'Myth and History', held at St John's College, Oxford, in 1987. A book collection, comprised of some of the conference papers, was later published in the HW series as *The Myths We Live By* (1991).

---

29 Raphael Samuel, 'Exciting to be English', in *Patriotism:* Vol. I, lx.
30 Raphael Samuel, 'Preface', in *Patriotism:* Vol. I, xvii.
31 David Cannadine, 'Patriotism', in *History in Our Time* (New Haven: Yale University Press, 1998), 89–95.
32 Miles Taylor, 'Patriotism, History and the Left in Britain', *Twentieth Century British History*, 33, 4 (1990), 971–87.

Whilst not making a direct contribution to the book collection, Samuel, together with coeditor Paul Thompson, wrote the editorial introduction to the book, identifying the central theme and problematic as 'the universality of myth as a constituent of human experience' and advancing the argument that '[Myth] lies behind any historical evidence'; which was not to say that they were 'working with memories of a false past' but that the facts of the past were inevitably, necessarily, given structure and, therefore, meaning by their connection with larger frameworks of *belief* or hypotheses about the past.

Importantly, the editors argued, this process was not a specialised one. It occurred in everyday life, continually taking place amongst communities ('imagined' or actual), within families and by individuals, all drawing upon mythic frameworks, reinterpreted and adapted, in order to make sense of their own experiences and connect them in relation to others. Exploring the relationship between myth and history, the two editors concluded, offered not only clues to the past but the processes in which the 'past' was created. They pressed the need to formulate 'a better understanding of a continuing struggle over the past, which goes forward, always with uncertain outcome, into the future'.[33] So, in the year that Cannadine had written his lament for the big stories of history, Samuel was further discovering, with delight, the creativity inherent in the profusion of possible histories that rushed to fill the void.

History, the nation and the schools

Given Thatcher's recognition of history as a critical tool in the restoration of Britain's national fortunes (both morally *and* economically), it was little surprise that history should figure prominently in Conservative plans for a national curriculum. In the 1980s, Britain had one of the most decentralised and autonomous education systems in Europe.[34] British teachers enjoyed considerable freedom in both the content and style of what they taught. Since the 1960s, a strong 'progressivism' had come to dominate pedagogical practices. In history this often involved

---

33 Raphael Samuel and Paul Thompson, 'Introduction', in Samuel and Thompson, eds, *The Myths We Live By* (London: Routledge, 1991), 21.
34 Ross E. Dunn, 'The Making of a National Curriculum: The British Case', *History Teacher*, 33, 3 (2000). For an overview of education in postwar Britain, see: Ken Jones, *Education in Britain: 1944 to the Present* (Cambridge: Polity Press, 2003).

thematic project work, more sensitive to social issues such as class, gender and race than to strict chronologies. For Thatcher, and others working in education, such an ad hoc approach to education was creating a younger generation uncompetitive for the tough demands of the emerging world of commerce and work.

The *Education Reform Act (1988)* was an attempt to address this 'problem'. The government proposed that the British education system be entirely overhauled and replaced with a government-approved national curriculum for all basic subjects including history. This was not a sudden development. The Conservative Government naturally favoured an emphasis on 'British' history and national culture, a view shared amongst some teachers and educationalists favouring 'traditional' values. Others, identifying with progressivist approaches, found any such suggestion of a return to 'facts and dates' teaching styles or 'drum and trumpet' forms of history unbalanced.

A National Curriculum History Working Group, chaired by Commander Saunders Watson (the aristocratic owner of Rockingham Castle, Northamptonshire), was set up to draft a curriculum. Caught between multiple contending camps and interest groups, their eventual report (published in April 1990) was a doomed document, destined to satisfy no one. Certainly, many of the participants felt the venture impeded from the start by political pressure and avid media attention.[35] Ultimately, it would take a further six years before any sort of 'agreement' was reached.

The imposition of a history curriculum into the nation's schools raised the stakes in the battle for the nation's past considerably.[36] Samuel was the first to sound the alarm, calling a forum on the subject published in *History Today* in 1984.[37] In fact, no other British historian became so involved and vocal in these debates. He followed them intently, writing multiple articles which appeared in the national press and, of course, organising a series of Workshops to address the topic, culminating with a number of 'teach-ins' held at Ruskin College, the first two addressing the immediate

---

35 Gareth Elwyn Jones, 'The Debate Over the National Curriculum for History in England and Wales, 1989–90: The Role of the Press', *Curriculum Journal*, 11, 3 (2000), 299–322; Robert Guyver, 'History's Doomsday Book', *History Workshop Journal (HWJ)*, 30 (1990), 100–8.

36 Keith Crawford, 'A History of the Right: The Battle for Control of National Curriculum History 1989–1994', *British Journal of Educational Studies*, 43, 4 (1995), 433–56; Vivienne Little, 'A National Curriculum in History: A Very Contentious Issue', *British Journal of Educational Studies*, 38, 4 (1990), 319–34.

37 Raphael Samuel, 'Forum: What is History?', *History Today*, 34, May (1984), 6–9.

'national curriculum question' (June 1989 and May 1990) in response to the working group's report. A third (June 1991), on 'The Future of English', covered the prehistory of the teaching of English as well as providing a historical perspective on contemporary issues such as the teaching of English in schools.[38]

Unlike the patriotism workshop, the 'History, the Nation and the Schools' series was not intended as a means of posing a left-wing alternative but as an opportunity to debate the teaching of history and, more specifically, the teaching of national past. Samuel personally approached figures far removed from the HW's usual constituency including teachers and academics associated with the right (such as Robert Skidelsky, Jonathan Clark, Norman Stone), not only inviting them to participate but entering into protracted correspondence with some of them.[39] His efforts went further still, involving members of the working party and the Chief Inspector of Schools R.H. Hennessey.[40] He was, however, unable to entice the Labour Party into the debates.[41]

Up until that point, the HW had been experiencing a more understated existence travelling around the country. The 'History, the Nation and the Schools' Workshops recaptured some of the old ambition and ferocity of the early days, although attendance remained in the hundreds rather than the thousands, and attendees were typically academics and educational professionals rather than hot-blooded unionists and anarchists. Nevertheless, the questions raised about national history and national education, combined with the lively media interest in the sessions, renewed some sense of political urgency.[42] These Workshops also presented a rare

---

38 Alison Light and Raphael Samuel, 'Report Back', *HWJ*, 32 (1991).
39 Examples of this correspondence can be found in Samuel 038/History, the Nation and the Schools, RSA.
40 Alice Prochaska, 'The History Working Group: Reflections and Diary', *HWJ*, 30 (1990), 80–90.
41 Raphael Samuel, 'Educating Labour', *New Statesman and Society*, 6 April 1990.
42 Ken Jones, a senior figure in the National Union of Teachers, remembers being warned against speaking to the media camped outside the Workshop. Oral communication with author, December 2012, London, transcript held in author's private collection.

conjunction of the HW with the *History Workshop Journal* (*HWJ*), which published several of the papers from the HW meetings as well as carrying numerous readers' letters on the subject.[43]

The intensity of the debates and the extremism of some of the opinions on offer, both from the left and the right, gave an unfortunate sense of pantomime to the proceedings. Speaking as a proponent for the 'traditional' history, R.H.C. Davies was quoted as telling one of the Workshops: 'I don't have any time for all this multi-cultural history … I have trouble with these foreign names'. Stone asserted that it was: 'the responsibility of school teachers to ram home the national culture'.[44] To the left of the spectrum, writer Gemma Moss assaulted the lines of scholarly propriety by suggesting that 'there seems to be a view that Jackie Collins is degrading and Shakespeare morally uplifting: they're different that's all. There's no reason why Mills and Boon shouldn't be taught alongside Jane Eyre'. Another participant said more bluntly: 'English is a white middle-class scene. Texts like Conrad's *Heart of Darkness* are racist'.[45] The ensuing headlines suggest some of the fun journalists had in creating their own villains and heroes out of the proceedings. 'Raised Voices in a Very British Battle', quipped the *Times Educational Supplement*.[46] 'Toppling the English Citadel' sneered *The Daily Telegraph* before proceeding on a critique-cum-demolition of the English professor, Marxist and Workshop participant, Terry Eagleton.[47]

At the Workshops themselves, the 'new historians' 'won' easily (they had the best arguments and the funniest jokes) but this was unsurprising as they were on their home turf and playing, for the most part, to their 'home crowd', their internal differences allayed for the sake of a common enemy whose extremities were easily ridiculed. There was, however, a sense that all this drama, as intensely as it was contested, had a slightly tired feel of

---

43   Papers published in the *HWJ* from the workshops included: Janet L. Nelson, 'A Place for Medieval History in the National Curriculum?', *HWJ*, 29 (1990), 103–6; Sylvia L. Callicott, 'What History Should We Teach in Primary Schools?, *HWJ*, 29 (1990), 107–10; Shula Marks, 'History, the Nation and Empire: Sniping from the Periphery', *HWJ*, 29 (1990), 111–19; Angela V. John, 'Sitting on the Severn Bridge: Wales and British History', *HWJ*, 30 (1990), 91–100; Paul Gaolen, 'Only Connect…', *HWJ*, 30 (1990), 109–13; Paul Gilroy, 'Nationalism, History and Ethnic Absolutism', *HWJ*, 30 (1990), 114–19; Stephen Yeo, 'The More it Changes, the More it Stays the Same?', *HWJ*, 30 (1990), 120–28. See also: 'Reader's Letters', *HWJ*, 30 (1990).
44   Roger West, 'History, the Nation and the Schools: Ruskin College, Oxford, 3 June 1989', *HWJ*, 29 (1990), 196–98.
45   John Clare, 'Toppling the English Citadel', *The Daily Telegraph*, 20 June 1991.
46   Ian Nash, 'Raised Voices in a Very British Battle', *The Times Educational Supplement*, 25 June 1990.
47   Clare, 'Toppling the English Citadel'.

a well-trodden 'set piece' between the 'left' and the Tories. As Roger West remarked in his report back for the *HWJ* following the first Workshop meeting, both the extreme right and the extreme left were minorities. The curriculum would be based on a 'wishy washy liberal compromise' and it was this, West suggested, that would have been more useful and informative to debate.[48]

In fact, some of the papers did reflect on what a contemporary national history curriculum might look like. In the second Ruskin 'teach-in', a stream on Four Nations History proposed Britain be approached in terms of the relationships between its component nations, Scotland, Ireland, England and Wales, or even through other geographic or cultural demarcations: North and South, East and West, lowlands and highlands, town and country.[49] Another stream reflected on 'The British Empire' as a potential framework, having the immediate benefit of situating Britain within a global context and allowing room for exploring the transformative impact of cultural encounter and exchange.[50]

Samuel was also inclined towards a more complex engagement with the questions raised by the history curriculum debates. Practical experiences of teaching adult students for almost 30 years, along with growing frustration at the disconnection between intellectuals and the popular movement had sharpened his scepticism towards the extreme or doctrinaire. The patriotism workshop had demonstrated the sheer diversity of perspectives, as well as the depth of emotion, on the national question amongst the political left. *The Myths We Live By* had further emphasised the critical importance of large stories, myths, in actively making meaning of experience and the need, therefore, to approach such matters sensitively and with a degree of self-reflectivity. To substitute one set of beliefs with another was not education but indoctrination. Equally, to demolish all beliefs as false was little more than nihilism that silenced further discussion.

---

48   West, 'History, the Nation and the Schools', 197.
49   Speakers included: Hugh Kearney, Angela Clark and Jonathan Clark, RS 7: History Workshop Events/History, the Nation and the Schools recall conference, 74, RSA. See also Hugh Kearney, *The British Isles: A History of Four Nations* (Cambridge: Cambridge University Press, 1989); Jonathan Clark, 'National Identity, State Formation and Patriotism: The Role of History in the Public Eye', *HWJ*, 29 (1990), 95–102. A similar argument had been proposed by J.G.A. Pocock, 'British History: A Plea for a New Subject', *Journal of Modern History*, 47 (1975), 601–21.
50   Speakers included: Polly O'Hanlon, Shula Marks, Stuart Hall, RS 7: History Workshop Events/History, the Nation and the Schools recall conference, 74, RSA.

Building on these insights, his position paper 'Grand Narratives', delivered at the first 'teach-in', argued that despite pessimism amongst the profession following the perceived break-up of overarching political ideologies – 'liberalism, constitutionalism, socialism, imperialism' (which he was not convinced had actually taken place) – there was no reason to assume history would cease to pursue large questions over long trajectories but these would assume quite a different appearance.[51] Giving the example of feminism, he argued:

> It gives gender, as a subject and as a problematic, the centrality which Marxists have given to class. It asks for, and builds on, a history addressed to the private sphere rather than the world of public affairs, and interprets the second in the light of the first rather than the other way round.

In a second paper, 'The Case for National History', given the following year, he advanced his reasons for supporting the presence of national history on the curriculum, saying 'history, whether we like it or not, is a national question and it has always occupied a national space', and going on to add that:

> If British history is restored to the school curriculum, it should be for pedagogic reasons – because it is the country they know best (they are not obliged to love it) whose language (even if they are bi-lingual) they speak, whose literature they read, whose famous events are dramatized on TV or burlesqued by the stand-up comic.[52]

To this end, history was part of a social conversation in which everyone was unavoidably implicated. It was, therefore, important to be able to follow and understand what was being said if one was to participate effectively.

Samuel's articles, which appeared with remarkable frequency in the national press, elaborated on these themes. Writing for the mainstream media was very different from doing so for left-wing journals. It prompted greater deliberation over the choice of words. One worried note to Stephen Bates (at the time, editor for *The Guardian*'s education section) combined defiance: 'I am leaving in Neo-Piagetian it doesn't implicate you editorially ... it ought to be possible to mention the name of the

---

51 Raphael Samuel, 'Grand Narratives', *HWJ*, 29 (1990), 125.
52 Raphael Samuel, 'The Case for National History', Samuel 028/History, the Nation and the Schools, RSA.

Freud of child development theory in pages devoted to education' with a touch of anxiety 'you have the liberty to cut out Neo-Piagetian if you can't stomach it'.[53]

So, perhaps exercising a greater delicacy and care to come across as reasonable than he might have done otherwise, Samuel's contributions contained words of critique for all sides of the political spectrum. Of a 'traditional' history based around big events and leaders: 'a history of carriage folk which ignored the horses' hooves, or a narrative of battles which only had eyes for the general staff, would be as airless as a bunker'.[54] On the other hand, a history piously stripped of its colourful individuals was equally lacklustre:

> If heroes and heroines are myth … they are nevertheless a necessary fantasy. We all need, at some stage in life, mentors. We all seek out people to believe in, patterns to follow, examples to take up.[55]

On the subject of teaching methods, he acknowledged that it was the right, not the left, who had led the return to a subject-based teaching of history and conceded that 'progressive' history could risk too great an immersion in minutiae at the expense of larger questions. At the same time, the skills-based approach it advocated, 'the critical reading of documents and original materials', were the fundamental tools of the historian's craft.[56] Furthermore, its appeals to direct physical encounters and sensory experience were a vital means for rousing a sense of connection to the past.

At the core of his arguments was the view that the teaching of history should not lament the breakdown of consensus nor aspire to restore it, that it should neither pursue one particular version of the past nor one dominant method of teaching it. Far from being a symptom of decline, conflict was the lifeblood of history: 'history is a house of many mansions and its narratives change over time'.[57] The teaching of history needed to embrace such conflict because it was through the jostling and struggling of contending views and interpretations that ideas were challenged and changed.

---

53 Raphael Samuel, 'Letter to Stephen Bates', Samuel 038/ History, the Nation and the Schools, RSA.
54 Raphael Samuel, 'Heroes below the Hooves of History', *The Independent*, 31 August 1989.
55 Raphael Samuel, 'The People with Stars in Their Eyes', *The Guardian*, 23 September 1995.
56 Raphael Samuel, 'The Return of History', *London Review of Books*, 14 June 1990.
57 Raphael Samuel, 'A Bit of Conflict is Exactly What History Needs', *The Independent*, 27 March 1990; Raphael Samuel, 'History's Battle for a New Past', *The Guardian*, 21 January 1989.

At times, his position seemed discordant with many of his comrades and colleagues of the left. Notably, it received fulsome support from a most unexpected quarter, the Cambridge historian Professor Geoffrey Elton, a staunch supporter of Winston Churchill and Margaret Thatcher. Despite the apparent ideological chasm, or even abyss, between the two men, Elton found much to praise in Samuel's work which he expressed in a letter dated 20 May 1990, shortly after receiving copies of the papers given at the second Workshop:

> Do I detect a note of surprise on your part in finding the two of us so very widely agreed? My own sense that there are unbridged gullies about was restored by Stephen Yeo's address which to me seemed to embody all the doctrinaire convictions of the so-called left, especially the obligatory genuflections before the deities of the Pantheon – Christopher Hill, Raymond Williams and E.P. Thompson & Co. You talk much better sense because you are concerned about History rather than EDUCATION, that sad intrusion in teaching and learning ... Now I find myself very much at one with you about the real role of history in education ... I do think the dividing line lies between those to whom history ... is an important element in the make-up of all the people, both in providing a three-dimensional setting to life's experience and in offering a particular (critical and imaginative) training of the mind, irrespective of content, and on the other those who wish to use it to promote particular social or political ends.[58]

Elton concurred with Samuel about the transference of emphasis from a politics conveyed through the specific subject and object of history to the practice of history-making itself. On one point, however, he misread his unlikely 'ally'. Samuel did not (could not) see the 'real role of history in education' as something that was *possible* to separate or even distinguish from politics. This was not politics as a tribal 'war of position' amongst creeds or factions, but as an ongoing process (a whole way of struggle) of negotiating and renegotiating social self-identity. As one of Samuel's articles concluded:

> If history is an arena for the projection of ideal selves, it can also be the means of undoing and questioning them, offering more disturbing accounts of who we are and where we come from than simple identification would suggest.[59]

---

58   Geoffrey Elton, Letter to Raphael Samuel, Samuel 038/History, the Nation and the Schools, RSA.
59   Samuel, 'The Return of History'.

It was against the backdrop of these debates about national identity, popular memory, history and education that Samuel came to write his own 'more disturbing' account: *Theatres of Memory: Past and Present in Contemporary Culture* (1994).

Theatres of Memory

In a tribute to Samuel published shortly after his death, Stuart Hall said of *Theatres of Memory*:

> Of course, in one sense he had been preparing to write such a book ever since he first recognised the social history of working-class life as his true vocation in the early 1960s. In another sense, the book, ... was the product of a kind of expansion of sympathies, an opening up of himself to the 'play' of the sheer abundant, tumultuous variety of the popular, of which the early Raphael would not have been capable.[60]

As Hall suggested, the book, whilst no simplistic 'history as autobiography', bore many of the 'enthusiasms' collected over the course of his life. Unsurprisingly, reviews of the book reflected the sort of conflicting opinions that its author engendered. Writer and biographer Fiona MacCarthy praised its humanity and creativity, seeing Samuel in the same tradition as Hill and E.P. Thompson.[61] Clark was also receptive, expressing particular pleasure at the book's critical stance towards elements of the political left. Keith Thomas offered more cautious praise whilst still noting some of the book's more eccentric qualities.[62]

Other responses were cooler. Wright, whose own book was subject to cheerful pillory in *Theatres of Memory* (depicted as one of the prompts for po-faced academics to denigrate heritage in the name of cultural studies), suspected that Samuel's abrupt shift towards a militant support of popular history-making was the gratification of a personal vanity in his aspiration towards the role of the 'people's historian'.[63] Richard Hoggart, recently retired from the assistant directorship of the United Nations Educational, Scientific and Cultural Organization (UNESCO), disliked what he took

---

60 Stuart Hall, 'Raphael Samuel: 1934–1996', *NLR*, I/221, Jan–Feb (1997), 126.
61 Fiona MacCarthy, 'Treading Softly on Our Dreams: Review of Raphael Samuel *Theatres of Memory*', *The Observer*, 12 February 1995.
62 Keith Thomas, 'Retrochic', *London Review of Books*, 20 April 1995, 7–8.
63 Samuel, *Theatres of Memory*, 263; Wright, 'Review of Theatres of Memory'.

to be the book's apparent refusal to judge 'good' from 'bad' forms of heritage. For Hoggart, *Theatres of Memory* was the work of a confused Marxist and the product of his various quarrels which, he suggested, were with the left, with professional historians but, above all, with himself.[64]

Historian Stefan Collini, writing a few years after the book's publication, provided a more measured assessment of this tension. Whilst not denying the book's imaginative qualities, he saw Samuel's rejection of a privileged role for the trained historian as a restriction on his own capacity to make effective social criticism. Like Wright, he also hinted that this was a slightly disingenuous posture to assume given that some of the book's best passages were clearly the work of a historian who had himself undergone a thorough historical training.[65]

The critics, in particular Wright and Collini, raised an important point concerning the contending, sometimes clashing, agendas within the book. *Theatres of Memory* was inherently protean, containing multiple strands, any one of which might have formed the basis of a single monograph. Such a study, however, was not the main objective of *Theatres of Memory*. Arguably, the book covered three overlapping areas, all of which corresponded to those most persistent in Samuel's own intellectual identity and background. It was at once a historical study, a political polemic and an educational philosophy, the arguments from which were inextricably entwined with one another, yet retaining their distinctive features and implications.

On one level, *Theatres of Memory* was a history of popular-history-making in postwar England. As such it followed a recurrent theme in Samuel's overall body of work, the 'Nineteenth Century Cromwell' project for example, or the 'People's History' editorial and most recently the 'Exciting to be English' essay. Set out in its pages was an ethnographic survey of the forms and uses of history in contemporary popular culture combined with a shrewd analysis of the ways in which they were negotiated with the wider conditions of their times. Particular impulses or inclinations, he noted, were both 'top-down' and 'bottom-up' in their origins. For example:

---

64 Richard Hoggart, 'Review: Theatres of Memory', *Political Quarterly*, 66, 3 (1995), 215–16.
65 Stefan Collini, 'Speaking with Authority: The Historian as Social Critic', in *English Pasts: Essays in History and Culture* (Oxford: Oxford University Press, 1999), 95–102.

6. STRANGER MEMORIES OF WHO WE REALLY ARE

> The revival of brick, possibly, owes more to sociological changes than it does to aesthetics. It is the business recolonization of the inner city which has turned warehouses into hot properties … Likewise it is the formation of new housing classes – 'gentrifiers' in the inner city, long-distance commuters on greenfield sites in the countryside.[66]

Equally:

> Andy Thornton's, for instance – a husband and wife team who set up as architectural salvage merchants in 1975 – now find themselves manufacturers of replica ware for hotel groups and brewery chains right across the country, as well as for the theme parks and open-air museums: among their clients, as well as McDonald's … are the House of Lords, the National Museum of Photography and Eurodisney.[67]

The historical argument of the book was that in this postwar world the past had ceased to be viewed as the prelude to an inevitable present. Rather than a linear march through time, it lingered in places and moments, no longer seeking explanation but the shock of encounter and the thrill of enchantment. The past had become a plaything, a product and production.[68] Far from undermining the discipline the result was, potentially, democratic; an expanding, as opposed to contracting, historical culture.[69]

The book's political philosophy was asserted from the outset:

> It is the argument of *Theatres of Memory* … that memory, so far from being merely a passive receptacle or storage system, an image bank of the past, is rather an active, shaping force; that it is dynamic … It is also my argument that memory is historically conditioned changing colour and shape according to the emergencies of the moment … Like history, memory is inherently revisionist and never more chameleon than when it appears to stay the same.[70]

---

66 Samuel, *Theatres of Memory*, 128.
67 Ibid., 102.
68 Never one to be pinned down, elsewhere in the book Samuel flipped his own argument on its head suggesting that if one looked outside of 'official' history texts and included novels, plays, nursery rhymes, place names, material culture and so on, this sort of playful memory work was not a new, 'post-modern', development, but business as usual.
69 See for example: Cannadine, 'Viewpoint British History: Past, Present – and Future?'; Raphael Samuel, 'Unofficial Knowledge', in *Theatres of Memory*, 3–50.
70 Samuel, 'Unofficial Knowledge', 3–50, ix–x.

The recognition of memory as a product of both individual psychology *and* social conditioning reasserted Samuel's fidelity to the socialist humanism of the first New Left but also showed a more sophisticated understanding of pluralism and complexity.

His final chapter, 'Who Calls So Loud: Dickens on Stage and Screen', showcased his credentials as a cultural analyst, probing the intellectual work being done during that most passive of activities, watching a screen ('There is no reason to think that people are more passive when looking at old photographs, or film footage ...')![71] In a disarmingly anecdotal style, belying the seriousness of the analysis, he recounted how his own interpretive responses were shaped against an array of material factors including technological medium (book, film, television, stage), time (a Christmas-time cinema outing), location (the windswept Hebrides as opposed to London in the festive season) and emotional contexts (the first Dickens film seen as a child, a Dickens novel read on honeymoon, later seen as a film). His account reflected upon the fusion of new information (the experiences gathered through adulthood) with existing impressions (the lingering ghosts of childhood), and the subtle negotiations that this prompted. By the time he reached his closing scene, there was little doubt that even when sat before a moving image, memory was hard at work, contesting every frame.[72]

As part of his case for memory work as a valid form of history-making, *Theatres of Memory* contained a lively polemical attack on those who he considered denied its vibrancy. The culprits, familiar villains on the Samuelian stage, included professional historians, cultural critics and sociologists. The conceits of professional historians, those who would claim a privileged position over the study of history, were ruthlessly parodied, the equally 'theatrical' nature of the academic world exposed:

> The enclosed character of the discipline is nowhere more apparent than in the pages of the learned journals, where young Turks, idolizing and demonizing by turn, topple elders from their pedestals, and Oedipal conflicts are fought out ... Academic rivals engage in gladitorial combat, now circling one another warily, now moving in for the kill. In seminars such conflicts service the function of blood sports and are followed with bated breath.[73]

---

71 Ibid., 271.
72 Ibid., 413–28.
73 Ibid., 4.

As a result, much valuable research work went unacknowledged, biographers were not counted, antiquarians were deemed a 'different species', local historians were scorned for their parochialism and oral historians deemed guilty of *naive* empiricism. What this amounted to, Samuel continued, was 'the unspoken assumption that knowledge filters downwards' and the preservation of a hierarchy in which the professional enjoyed the top position, enthusiasts a lowly second and, condemned to the periphery, 'the commentators and communicators who will present garbled accounts of scholarly controversy to the general public' and who 'might exist on another planet for the attention they receive in the tearoom circles at the Institute of Historical Research'.[74]

And yet, this hierarchical structure was founded on an illusion of authenticity that was entirely misplaced:

> Professional historians are poorly placed to condescend to retrochic since … it is one of the currencies in which we deal. We too put the past in quotation marks, as a way of marking our distance from it, and often as a way of extracting some quaint comic effect. … In any event, our work is always an imaginative reconstruction of the past, never – for all the elaboration of our footnotage-mimesis.[75]

Or, later:

> Are we not guilty ourselves of turning knowledge into an object of desire? And is it not the effect, if not the intention, of our activity as historians to domesticate the past and rob it of its terrors by bringing it within the realm of the knowable?[76]

Similarly, the cultural critics, both left and right, who saw the 'heritage industry' as a crass assault on the past and further evidence of a wider moral and intellectual decline, failed to acknowledge the substantial quantities of significant, original historical research that it involved:

> Another sphere where heritage could be said to have a definite edge over academic history … is in the history of the environment. Here it is showing signs of re-uniting natural history with archaeological inquiry …[77]

---

74 Ibid., 4–5.
75 Ibid., 114.
76 Ibid., 271.
77 Ibid., 277.

Or, with its ear positioned 'closer to the ground', its shrewd understanding of how the 'collective unconscious' experienced and made sense of the contemporary world:

> In the spirit of the age – the here-and-now – it is centrally concerned not with politics or economics, the subjects of yesteryear's grand narratives ... but essentially with that great preoccupation of the 'Me' generation: lifestyles. It privileges the private over the public sphere ... when it seeks to reconstruct grand narrative it is through the medium of the history of the self.[78]

As for the sociologists who attributed the 'heritage disease' to the triumph of an aggressive Conservative cultural hegemony, the unfolding cultural logic of late capitalism, or the fulfilling culture of national decline, their eagle-eyed perspective overlooked what a closer one revealed to be more complex:

> So far as being the medium through which a Conservative hegemony of the national past becomes hegemonic, one could see its advent as part of a sea-change in attitudes which has left any unified view of the national past – liberal, radical, or Conservative – in tatters. Culturally it is pluralist.[79]

Furthermore, the lack of concern for authenticity was, in some cases, a deliberate and self-conscious part of its aesthetic politics:

> It is deficient in what the Victorians called high seriousness, drawing much of its pleasure from the play of the incongruous or the bizarre. Its tastes are cavalier and eclectic, syncretizing ancient and modern and accommodating a promiscuous mix of different styles ... It approaches its work in the spirit of the beachcomber, or the snapper-up of unconsidered trifles, rather than that of the antiquarian or the connoisseur collecting gems, treasuring relics and worshipping at time-hallowed shrines.[80]

Moreover, Samuel pressed, its detractors neglected the politically radical components in its expansive repertoire of instincts:

> One way of attempting to account for the popularity of heritage ... is as an attempt to *escape* from class. Instead of heredity it offers a sense of place, rather as environmentalism offers the activist and the reformist an alternative to the worn-out routines of party politics.[81]

---

78   Ibid., 196–97.
79   Ibid., 281.
80   Ibid., 112.
81   Ibid., 246.

6. STRANGER MEMORIES OF WHO WE REALLY ARE

As McCarthy noted in her review, the book's populism followed in the tradition occupied by figures like Hill and Thompson.[82] But in an important way it also departed from the two men by being dramatically more expansive and receptive in its definition of 'the people' and the wide range of their imaginative activities.

It was in this openness that his critics claimed he teetered dangerously on the brink of relativity, of accommodating too much, discriminating too little and undermining his own powers of critique. Symptomatic of this, as Bill Schwarz noted in his otherwise positive foreword to the second edition of the book (released in 2012), was the ambiguity surrounding the *difference* between memory work and history that seemed at many points to dissolve altogether in the impassioned defence of the popular.[83] The key issue at stake was how to reconcile plurality with the 'trained scepticism' critical to historians' craft.

Here, the educational philosophy of *Theatres of Memory* came into effect. Characteristically, this was not clearly set out in the book although the concluding paragraphs gave some intimation of its nature. Repeating his welcome of an expanding historical culture and the exciting challenges it presented to individual and collective identities, Samuel urged historians not to attempt to return to history as a single master narrative, or retreat to 'the cloistered seclusion of a library carrel' but to engage with it.[84] The manner and form of this engagement went unstated and unspecified, but in another sense the book performed the role he was proposing for the historian in an age of plurality.

Clues about the nature of this role could be discerned in the sheer liveliness of the writing, the energy with which the smallest of details – in the most mundane (or profane) of places ('Jemima Puddleduck has been annexed for potty training, a grimacing figure on nursery toilet rolls') – were illuminated, made to sparkle with hidden promise.[85] They were also present in the playful mockery of 'scholarly seriousness', in which trips to the supermarket yielded as much treasure as those to the archive (for example, note 68 in 'Retrochic' reads: 'Notes on a visit to Sainsbury's, Islington, 21 September 1993') and *Foxe's Book of Martyrs* lay cheek by

---

82 McCarthy, 'Treading Softly on Our Dreams'.
83 Schwarz, 'Foreword'.
84 Samuel, *Theatres of Memory,* 444.
85 Ibid., 93, 107.

jowl with *The Eagle* comic in the footnotes.[86] Or, again, in the book's self-identification as an 'open text', to 'be read by different readers in different ways for different purposes', a gleeful relinquishing of authorial claims to sovereignty over meaning and use.[87]

Above all, this role was showcased in his 'teacher-ly' notes, the points at which he strayed from argument and analysis to discuss potential avenues of research. On the use of photographs, for example, he advised:

> Formal analysis, in terms of composition, lighting and frame – the grammar of photography – could tell us something about what the camera is up to … Record linkage, illuminating the visible by the evidence of things unseen, and focusing on what the frame excludes, might help us piece together the original contexts.[88]

He went on to suggest that 'school photographs, if they were illumined by comparative analysis might equally be serviceable for the study of corporate loyalties and pedagogic ideals', or the field of 'bodily theatrics' generously enlarged if it took account of the 'fantastic wealth of imagery in which notions of masculinity and femininity … are refracted through notions of family and community, youth and age, culture and class'.[89] Elsewhere, the 'return to brick' in architectural design might prompt a discussion on 'double-coding', in which meanings referenced both past and present simultaneously.[90] A friendlier stance towards heritage could 'begin to educate us in the language of looks, initiate us into the study of colour coding, familiarize us with period palettes'.[91] Through these and dozens more insights like them, *Theatres of Memory*, as a text, revealed its basic purpose: to issue an open invitation to think and rethink about the past.

In the making of such an invitation, it is possible to venture a reply to the book's critics. Whilst not all forms of history-making provided equally 'good' (authentic) accounts of the past, they all had the *potential* to provide an insight or perspective into both the past *and* the present. The value of history as a form of knowledge (and also its main point of distinction from memory) was not as an object in itself, but as a conscious process

---

86   Ibid., 117, 47.
87   Ibid., x.
88   Ibid., 330.
89   Ibid., 332–33.
90   Ibid., 130.
91   Ibid., 274.

of critical inquiry. The role of the historian was, therefore, to facilitate the making of such an inquiry, to provide it with guidance, probing at memory's silences. This drive to galvanise participation and create spaces for different voices in a shared conversation had been the 'simple truth' behind the History Workshop.[92] It had been the enduring motivation of the long-term adult educator, the source of residual hope for the New Left activist, the main function of the party organiser and the underpinning political and intellectual values of the youthful Popular Front communist.

Samuel intended to continue the project marked out in *Theatres of Memory* with *Island Stories: Unravelling Britain* (1998), the second of his intended trilogy on the multiple notions of nation and the role of place as an optic in historical analysis. He had had a second volume ready for publication but in the two years following the publication of *Theatres of Memory* up to his death in December 1996 he had substantially reworked it, writing whole new essays that reflected the continual shifts in his interests and insights. Whilst there is, of course, no way of knowing what the book would ultimately have looked like had he lived to finish it, his wife Alison and his close friends Gareth Stedman Jones and Sally Alexander compiled the collection in tribute to both the ideas and issues motivating his current interests but also to those ideas that had underpinned Samuel's historical work over the course of his life.[93]

The new essays in the book, many of them unfinished and unedited, showcased Samuel's capacity for imaginative historiographical surveying. One addressed some of the many 'genealogies' of the term nation. Another considered the different variations on the notion of British. In 'Four Nations History' he sketched out both the uses and the restrictions of the four nations approach to history, which had been become increasingly popular following the intensive debates over the writing and teaching of British national history. 'Empire Stories' provided a powerful example of his capacity to transform even the most minute and quotidian of subject matter (such as the popular availability of exotic fruits, such as bananas) into a connection with wide analytical frameworks such as empire or the idea of 'modernity'.[94]

---

92   Raphael Samuel, 'Editorial Introduction', in Samuel, ed., *History Workshop: A Collectanea 1967–1991* (Oxford: History Workshop 25, 1991), iv.
93   Sally Alexander, Alison Light and Gareth Stedman Jones, 'Editors Preface', in Raphael Samuel, *Island Stories: Unravelling Britain* (London: Verso, 1998).
94   A lengthy extract from Elizabeth Gaskell's novel *Cranford* (1851) is used to open 'Empire Stories: The Imperial and the Domestic', in *Island Stories*, 74–75.

There was a review of Asa Briggs's history of broadcasting, which saw Samuel, in the familiar guise of the people's historian, probing the 'silences' in Briggs's account. What of regional broadcasting? What of the technologies involved in children's broadcasting? What of that omnipresent, all-knowing figure; the BBC secretary? Buoyantly, he concluded by congratulating Briggs for having written such an 'open text' that others could use as the platform for their own inquiries.[95] Further pieces paid homage to the enthusiasm for popular history and heritage that had characterised *Theatres of Memory*. Tourist attractions such as the Lost Gardens of Heligan and the Tower of London, both destinations for an afternoon outing, were potential portals for historical inquiry. How could the gardens reveal something of the impact of the empire on the study of natural history? How could the tower provide a portal into the practical realities and imaginative lives of generations past? There was an entire section devoted to the question of history teaching in British schools, the subject that had so preoccupied Samuel during the 1980s. Another section on the political uses of history challenged the Tory notion of 'Victorian values', the invocation of R.H. Tawney by the short-lived Social Democratic Party and Labour MP Tony Benn's account of the Labour Party's ancestral roots.

One of the essays, 'Country Visiting: A Memoir', gave another tantalising glimpse into what might have formed the subject matter of the intended third book, *Memory Work*. In *Theatres of Memory*, Samuel had envisaged it as a study into the intimate processes in which an individual comes to construct and formulate memory, intending to argue that: 'subjectivity, like history itself is socially constructed, a creature or child of its time'.[96] He had already sketched this out in significant sections of his 'Lost World' essays, alluding to the intimate ways in which belief is constructed and, as discussed above, in his closing chapter in *Theatres of Memory* had explored the dialogue between internal and external factors in the formation of interpretation.[97] In the essay included in *Island Stories*, he advanced this theme. Using the memories of his mother, Minna,

---

95 Ibid., 191. It is uncertain whether Briggs, after 30 years and five volumes worth of work on this project, entirely welcomed being credited as the author of an 'open text'.
96 Samuel, *Theatres of Memory*, xi.
97 See in particular 'Family Communism', in Raphael Samuel, *The Lost World of British Communism* (London: Verso, 2006), 57–59.

and his own recollections of their experiences and relationship to the British countryside, he set out to further demonstrate how perceptions were framed in negotiation to both wider contexts and personal histories.

Keeping up a brisk pace, the essay explored the intricate connections that united personal motivations behind the perception of the countryside, such as the desire for activity or enchantment, with the political philosophies with which they became entangled. He brushed on the role played by artists, writers, photographers and filmmakers in the creation of symbolic narratives of place and the consequent development of rural tourism and infrastructure, such as the Youth Hostels Association or organised rail tours, designed to facilitate access to and use of the countryside. All these factors working in dialogue at different levels provided the available resources with which to think and construct a viewpoint.

Within this process, the individual perspective was both framed but also framing, selecting from the information available to it the elements most familiar, most reconciliatory with its existing experiences and impulses. The potency of this framing was only fully revealed when the perspective was disrupted, an experience Samuel provided a personal example of in the essay: 'Five years ago, walking in the Cévennes, it struck me that I had been seeing the same scenery all my life, even though it was in different places and under different names'.[98] His point here was that the way we view the world becomes so embedded and normalised that the tell-tale signs of construction, the seams at the sides, are not easily apparent. But, as his comment intimated, moments come when the discrepancies between what we perceive and our means of explaining them grow too wide. This sense of the limitations of our existing knowledge is the spark required for a process of inquiry, a need for new information with which to resolve the disturbance: the search for new histories.

'Country Visiting' gave no clues about the result of his investigations into his residual ideas of the countryside. The essay had been left unfinished, subject to a further inquiry, to writing and rewriting. Perhaps this incomplete, in-progress, personal-memoir cum critical-essay is a fitting analogy for his history-making. Stemming from an experience of disruption to the way he had viewed the world – the breakdown of his

---

98   Samuel, *Island Stories*, 130.

communist belief – he had embarked on an intensive and wide-ranging investigation into the world around him, restlessly seeking out every possible angle from which to view it.

What drove this process? Was it fear of once again being subject to self-deception, to delusion? Was it hope of once again finding a sense of all-encompassing belonging? Looking over the course of his life, there were elements of both fear and hope but there was also a third possibility. Gradually, the excitement of discovery and the feeling of solidarity with those silenced and forgotten had eroded the search for a great cause. There was something defiantly liberating about *not* uncovering that single explanation but on finding instead a myriad of peculiarities and possibilities, an infinite number of lost worlds, hidden threads and stranger memories.

Afterword: The Historian's Work in Progress

Right up until his death in 1996 Samuel continued with his attempts to provoke and facilitate historical debate. He was closely involved in the conceptual development of proposals for MA courses in historiography and public history at Ruskin College.[1] Notably, these courses were as much about the idea of history as they were courses in history. In 1996, the last year of his life, he left Ruskin College, bound for the University of East London (UEL) where he assumed responsibility for a proposed Centre for East London History, a fitting homecoming for the Londoner whose natural affinity to the city, and attraction to its diverse communities and converging layers of histories, had been lifelong.[2] In the Centre, he saw another opportunity to create a space for unspoken histories to find a voice through shared discussion and debate.[3]

Samuel turned the role of the historian upside down, inverting many accepted conventions for both professional and radical history-making. Working within a postwar political and intellectual culture characterised by fragmentation, he responded by expanding his emphasis from the subject matter or theory of history to its entire mode of production. In doing so, he reimagined its social value. 'Good' history was not an unanswerable argument but a conversation with an open invitation. Critics who bewailed his inconsistencies and ambiguities did not misinterpret him but failed to recognise that striving for conceptual authority was not what motivated him as an intellectual.

---

1   Hilda Kean, 'People, Historians and Public History; De-mystifying the Process of History Making', *Public Historian*, 32, 3 (2010), 25–38.
2   Carolyn Steedman, 'Raphael Samuel 1934–1996', *Radical Philosophy*, 82, Mar–Apr (1997), 53–55.
3   Following his death, it was renamed the Raphael Samuel History Centre.

In understanding Samuel as a historian, biography provides a crucial insight, unavailable by other means. In a field dominated by 'generations' and the collisions between them, he occupied a 'nonconformist' position, making it difficult to align him to one or other political moment or tradition.[4] His ideas and practices were fluid and adaptive, evident in the various roles (organiser-activist, club chairman, adult tutor, oral historian, Workshop editor) that he assumed in different contexts. But amongst these subtle transformations, there remained a continuous thread: democracy was realised in the practice as much as in the theory.

The matter of his legacy as a historian and intellectual is difficult to assess. He deliberately worked in close dialogue with his times, with the result that much of his work has a dated feel. His 'social outsiders' were more likely to be Gypsies, Jews and the Irish rather than women, ethnic or sexual minorities.[5] Despite this, there are components of a tangible legacy. The *History Workshop Journal* (*HWJ*), of which Samuel was a key founding editor, continues and, whilst more of an academic journal in character than originally intended, still strives to occupy a critical territory in contemporary historiography.

In terms of his writing, texts such as *Theatres of Memory* feel heavy-handed and repetitive. He was tackling ideas which have subsequently become more familiar and more fluently expressed, but here again he still touched on themes that have contemporary relevance in a style that continues to offer a unique perspective on what have become more common questions of historical representation. Further evidence of his enduring significance can also be seen in a number of recent studies that have used his work as the basis for their own investigations into the politics of heritage, memory and the role of the historian.[6]

Samuel's legacy also contains elements that are hard to measure. His main stock-in-trade was inspiration and the provision of spaces to experiment. The History Workshop (HW) movement (in conjunction with other spaces and endeavours such as the Social History Group and the Centre

---

4   Ken Jones, 'Raphael Samuel: Against Conformity', *Changing English: Studies in Culture and Education*, 5, 1 (1998), 17–26.
5   Lynne Segal, 'Lost Worlds: Political Memoirs of the Left in Britain', *Radical Philosophy*, 121, Sept–Oct (2003), 6–23.
6   Laurajane Smith, *The Uses of Heritage* (New York: Routledge, 2006); Katherine Hodgkin and Susannah Radstone, eds, *Memory, History, Nation: Contested Pasts* (New Brunswick: Transaction Publishers, 2006); Jorma Kalela, *Making History: The Historian and the Uses of the Past* (Basingstoke: Palgrave Macmillan, 2012).

for Social History) all helped to facilitate the development of cultural history in Britain. Within this, the HW in particular contributed to the development of a British feminist history.

The HW and the *HWJ* provided a crucial 'nursery' for the early work of a number of prominent British historians.[7] Samuel's work as a tutor was also directly influential for a generation of historians such as Sally Alexander, Alun Howkins and Paul Martin, all of whom were his former students.[8] Equally, there were countless others who benefited not only from his approach to history but also from his compassion and support. Some of these became prominent, holding high-profile public offices; others are not so widely known, but play significant roles in politics, social and community work, and educational and heritage work.

Samuel's most enduring significance, however, was the attitudinal response he offered to plurality in history-making. Instead of lamenting the fragmentation of conceptual categories, he shifted focus onto how they could be brought into dialogue with one another. Assessing an attitudinal change requires an adjustment in what we acknowledge as intellectual work. Samuel suggests the need to read texts for their performative points as much as their content or intellectual affiliations, to see the skill in organising a journal, project or event as much as that required for turning out well-written prose. Moreover, he demands a recognition of the work involved in guiding without (directly) imposing authority and the resourcefulness needed to 'bring with you' people whose social, cultural and intellectual positioning is far removed from your own, to make them feel valued and encouraged to carry on.

This raises a question of how we treat the ethical dimension of intellectual work and where this figures in our frameworks of critical judgement. When lacking a neat unfolding development of published work, professional titles and accolades, how do we 'see', if we 'see' at all, the historian who opts to make the democratisation of history-making, rather than publication, their primary professional objective?

---

7   Including amongst others: Sheila Rowbotham, Professor of History, University of Manchester; Gareth Stedman Jones, Professor of the History of Ideas, Queen Mary University of London; Carolyn Steedman, Emeritus Professor of History, University of Warwick; and Barbara Taylor, Professor of History, Queen Mary University of London (all correct as of April 2017).
8   Sally Alexander, Professor of Modern History, Goldsmiths University of London; Alun Howkins, Emeritus Professor of Social History, University of Sussex; Paul Martin, Associate Tutor of Museum Studies, University of Leicester (all correct as of April 2017).

The historian recast in this way is far less glamorous than the scholarly expert or the politicised intellectual (although perhaps more useful to those who benefit from it). Whilst a more modest role, it is no less difficult. It requires a magpie's eye for hidden treasure and a gadfly's glee in provocation.[9] It demands endless patience, gritty endurance and extraordinary feats of imagination. It draws on an archive hidden in plain sight, on streets, in bodies and voices, and offers a past that is always in progress, the work of a vast ensemble cast. This was the role of the people's historian that Raphael Samuel adopted, adapted and came to personify.

---

9   Samuel's magpie qualities were frequently noted by commentators: '[T]hat great cornucopia of popular life and customs', Stuart Hall, 'Raphael Samuel: 1934–1996', *New Left Review*, I/221, Jan–Feb (1997), 126; '[A] show case for Samuel's quite astonishing historical and cultural range …', Stefan Collini, 'Speaking with Authority: The Historian As Social Critic', in *English Pasts: Essays in History and Culture* (Oxford: Oxford University Press, 1999), 95. I am grateful to Lawrence Goldman for suggesting the term 'gadfly' in relation to Samuel's general intellectual persona.

Select Bibliography

Archival and private collections

Brian Harrison, 'Interview with Raphael Samuel', 20 October 1979, 19 Elder Street, London, transcripts held in author's private collection.

Brian Harrison, 'Interview with Raphael Samuel', 18 September 1987, 19 Elder Street, London, transcripts held in author's private collection.

Brian Harrison, 'Interview with Raphael Samuel', 23 October 1987, 19 Elder Street, London, transcripts held in author's private collection.

Raphael Samuel Papers, Raphael Samuel Archive (RSA), Bishopsgate Institute, London.

Ruskin College Papers, RSA, Bishopsgate Institute, London.

Oral and written communications

Recordings and transcripts currently held in author's private collection. These will be deposited in the Raphael Samuel Archive, Bishopsgate Institute, London, in due course.

I am grateful to the following for discussing my research with me:

- Sally Alexander, January 2012, London.
- Jonathan Clark, May 2013, email communication.
- Paul Connell, March 2012, email communication.
- Anna Davin, January 2012, London.
- David Douglass, December 2012, Newcastle.
- David Goodway, May 2012, Yorkshire.

- Stuart Hall, May 2012, Hampstead, London.
- Brian Harrison, January 2012, Oxford.
- Alun Howkins, May 2012, Diss, Norfolk.
- Alun Howkins, October 2013, email communication.
- Ken Jones, December 2011, Goldsmiths College, London.
- Hilda Kean, December 2011, Bishopsgate Institute, London.
- Alison Light, January 2012, February 2014, Oxford.
- Ian Manborde, January 2012, email communication.
- Paul Martin, January 2012, email communication.
- Gareth Stedman Jones, December 2011, University of Cambridge, Cambridge.
- Carolyn Steedman, May 2013, University of Warwick, Coventry.
- Barbara Taylor, December 2012, Bishopsgate Institute, London.

Raphael Samuel works cited (when named as single author or editor)

Samuel, Raphael, 'The New Fabians', *Oxford Left*, Trinity Term (1953), 17–21.

——, 'Socialism and the Middle Class', *Oxford Left*, Hilary Term (1954), 24–27.

——, 'The Mind of British Imperialism' *Oxford Left*, Michaelmas Term (1954), 40–48.

——, 'Class and Classlessness', *Universities and Left Review*, 6 (1959), 44–51.

——, 'The Boss as Hero', *Universities and Left Review*, 7 (1959), 26–31.

——, 'The Deference Voter', *New Left Review*, I/1, Jan–Feb (1960), 9–13.

——, 'Dr Abrams and the End of Politics', *New Left Review*, I/5, Sep–Oct (1960), 1–8.

——, 'Bastard Capitalism', in E.P. Thompson, ed., *Out of Apathy* (London: New Left Books, 1960).

——, 'The Perils of the Transcript', *Oral History*, 1, 2 (1971), 19–22.

——, 'Headington Quarry: Recording a Labouring Community', *Oral History*, 1, 4 (1972), 107–22.

——, 'Comers and Goers', in H.J. Dyos and Michael Wolff, eds, *The Victorian City: Images and Realities* (London: Routledge, 1973), 123–60.

——, ed., *Village Life and Labour* (London: Routledge & Kegan Paul, 1975).

——, 'Local History and Oral History', *History Workshop Journal*, 1 (1976), 191–208.

——, 'The Workshop of the World: Steam Power and Hand Technology in Mid-Victorian Britain', *History Workshop Journal*, 3 (1977), 6–72.

——, 'On the Methods of the History Workshop: A Reply', *History Workshop Journal*, 9 (1980), 162–76.

——, 'British Marxist Historians 1880–1980', *New Left Review*, I/120, Mar–Apr (1980), 21–96.

——, ed., *People's History and Socialist Theory* (London: Routledge & Kegan Paul, 1981).

——, 'Soft Focus Nostalgia', *New Statesman*, 27 (1983).

——, 'Cry God May for Maggie, England and St George', *New Statesman*, 27 (1983).

——, 'Religion and Politics: The Legacy of R.H. Tawney', *The Guardian*, 29 March 1984.

——, 'Forum: What is History?', *History Today*, 34, May (1984).

——, 'Ancestor Worship', *The Guardian*, 4 October 1984.

——, 'What is Social History?', *History Today*, 35, March (1985).

——, 'The Vision Splendid', *New Socialist*, 27, May (1985).

——, 'Enter the Proletarian Giant', *New Socialist*, 29, July (1985).

——, 'Utopian Sociology', *New Society*, 2 October 1987.

——, 'History that's Over', *The Guardian*, 9 October 1987.

——, 'A Plaque on All Your Houses', *The Guardian,* 17 October 1987.

——, 'Jews and Socialism: The End of a Beautiful Friendship?', *The Jewish Quarterly*, 35, 2 (1988), 7–20.

——, 'Born Again Socialism', in Robin Archer et al., eds, *Out of Apathy: Voices of the New Left Thirty Years On* (London: Verso, 1989).

——, 'A Dotted Line to Thatcherism', in Robin Archer et al., eds, *Out of Apathy: Voices of the New Left Thirty Years On* (London: Verso, 1989).

——, 'Then and Now: A Re-evaluation of the New Left', in Robin Archer et al., eds, *Out of Apathy: Voices of the New Left Thirty Years On* (London: Verso, 1989).

——, 'History's Battle for a New Past', *The Guardian,* 21 January 1989.

——, ed., *Patriotism: The Making and Unmaking of British National Identity,* 3 vols (London: Routledge, 1989).

——, 'Philosophy Teaching by Example: Past and Present in Raymond Williams', *History Workshop Journal*, 27 (1989), 141–53.

——, 'The Pathos of Spitalfields', *The Spectator*, 20 May 1989.

——, 'Heroes below the Hooves of History', *The Independent,* 31 August 1989.

——, 'Grand Narratives', *History Workshop Journal,* 29 (1990).

——, 'A Bit of Conflict is Exactly What History Needs', *The Independent,* 27 March 1990.

——, 'Educating Labour', *New Statesman and Society*, 6 April 1990.

——, 'One in the Eye – 1066 and All That', *The Times Educational Supplement*, May 1990.

——, 'The Return of History', *London Review of Books,* 14 June 1990.

——, ed., *History Workshop: A Collectanea 1967–1991* (Oxford: History Workshop 25, 1991).

——, 'The History Woman', *The Times,* 4 July 1991.

——, 'Reading the Signs I', *History Workshop Journal,* 32 (1991), 82–109.

——, 'Fact Grubbers and Mind Readers: Reading the Signs II', *History Workshop Journal*, 33 (1991), 220–51.

——, *Theatres of Memory: Past and Present in Contemporary Culture* (London: Verso, 1994).

——, 'The People with Stars in Their Eyes', *The Guardian*, 23 September 1995.

——, *Island Stories: Unravelling Britain* (London: Verso, 1998).

——, *The Lost World of British Communism* (London: Verso, 2006).

Books and articles

Abelove, Henry, Betsy Blackmar, Peter Dimock and Jonathan Schneer, eds, *Visions of History* (Manchester: Manchester University Press, 1983).

Abrams, Mark and Richard Rose, *Must Labour Lose?* (Harmondsworth: Penguin, 1961).

Abramsky, Chimen, 'Raphael Samuel', *The Jewish Chronicle*, 17 January 1997.

Abramsky, Sasha, *The House of Twenty Thousand Books* (London: Halden Publishers, 2014).

Addison, Paul, *Churchill on the Home Front: 1900–1955* (London: Jonathan Cape, 1992).

——, and Harriet Jones, eds, *A Companion to Contemporary Britain 1939–2000* (Oxford: Blackwell, 2005).

Akhtar, Miriam and Steve Humphries, *The Fifties and Sixties: A Lifestyle Revolution* (London: Boxtree, 2001).

Alexander, Sally and Anna Davin, 'Feminist History', *History Workshop Journal*, 1 (1976), 4–6.

Althusser, Louis, 'Ideologies and Ideological State Apparatuses: Notes Towards an Investigation', *La Pensee*, 151 (1970).

Amis, Kingsley, *Socialism and the Intellectuals* (London: Fabian Tracts 304, 1957).

——, 'I Don't Like to be Old', *The Spectator*, 28 March 1958, 22.

Anderson, Perry, 'The Left in the Fifties', *New Left Review*, I/29, Jan–Feb (1965), 3–18.

——, 'Origins of the Present Crisis', *New Left Review*, I/23, Jan–Feb (1964), 26–53.

——, 'Socialism and Pseudo-Empiricism', *New Left Review*, I/35, Jan–Feb (1966), 2–42.

——, 'Components of the National Culture', *New Left Review*, I/50, Jul–Aug (1968), 3–57.

——, *Considerations of Western Marxism* (London: New Left Books, 1976).

——, *Arguments within English Marxism* (London: Verso, 1980).

——, 'A Culture in Contraflow I', *New Left Review*, I/180, Mar–Apr (1990), 41–78.

——, 'A Culture in Contraflow II', *New Left Review*, I/182, Jul–Aug (1990), 85–137.

——, 'Diary', *London Review of Books*, 21 October 1993.

Andrews, Geoff, *End Games and New Times: The Final Years of British Communism 1964–1991* (London: Lawrence and Wishart, 2004).

Archer, Robin, Diemut Bubeck, Hanjo Glock, Lesley Jacobs, Seth Moglen, Adam Stenhouse and Daniel Weinstock, eds, *Out of Apathy: Voices of the New Left Thirty Years On* (London: Verso, 1989).

Arensburg, Conrad and Solon Kimball, *Family and Community in Ireland* (Cambridge: Harvard University Press, 1948).

Ascherson, Neil, 'Profile: The Age of Hobsbawm', *The Independent on Sunday*, 2 October 1994.

Atwood, Sara E., *Ruskin's Educational Ideals* (Surrey: Ashgate Publishing Ltd, 2011).

Bailey, Michael, Ben Clarke and John. K. Walton, *Understanding Richard Hoggart: A Pedagogy of Hope* (Chichester: Wiley-Blackwell, 2012).

Bailey, Roderick, 'Thompson (William) Frank (1920–1944)', *Oxford Dictionary of National Biography* (Oxford: Oxford University Press, 2004).

Banner, James M. Jr and John Gillis, eds, *Becoming Historians* (Chicago: Chicago University Press, 2009).

Barker, Martin, ed., *The Video Nasties: Freedom and Censorship in the Media* (London: The Works, 1984).

Barnes, Philip, *A Companion to Post War British Theatre* (Totowa, NJ: Barnes and Noble, 1986).

Barnett, Anthony, 'Iron Britannia', *New Left Review*, I/134, Jul–Aug (1982), 5–96.

Bauman, Zygmunt, *Legislators and Interpreters: On Modernity, Postmodernity and Intellectuals* (Cambridge: Polity Press, 1989).

Beer, Samuel, *Britain against Itself: The Political Contradictions of Collectivism* (New York: Norton, 1982).

Benson, John, *The Rise of Consumer Society in Britain 1880–1980* (London: Longman, 1994).

Blaazer, David, *The Popular Front and the Progressive Tradition: Socialists, Liberals and the Quest for Unity 1884–1939* (Cambridge: Cambridge University Press, 1992).

Black, Lawrence, *The Political Culture of the Left in Affluent Britain 1951–64: Old Labour, New Britain?* (London: Palgrave Macmillan, 2003).

Blackburn, Robin, 'Raphael Samuel: The Politics of Thick Description', *New Left Review*, I/221, Jan–Feb (1997), 133–38.

Blackledge, Paul, *Perry Anderson, Marxism and the New Left* (London: Merlin, 2004).

Blain, Douglas, 'Raphael Samuel', *The Spitalfields Trust Newsletter*, December 1996.

Blake, William with David V. Erdman, ed., *The Complete Poetry and Prose of William Blake* (Berkeley and Los Angeles: University of California, 2008).

Bolton, Paul, 'Education Historical Statistics', *Social and General Statistics*, House of Commons Library, 27 November 2012.

Branson, Noreen, *History of the Communist Party of Great Britain 1931–1951* (London: Lawrence and Wishart, 1997).

Briggs, Asa, *Michael Young: Social Entrepreneur* (New York: Palgrave Macmillan Ltd, 2001).

Briggs, Robin, 'Hill, (John Edward) Christopher (1912–2003)', *Oxford Dictionary of National Biography* (Oxford: Oxford University Press, 2007).

Brooks, Ron, *King Alfred School and the Progressive Movement 1889–1998* (Cardiff: University of Wales Press, 1998).

Burrows, John, *The Crisis of Reason: European Thought 1848–1914* (New Haven: Yale University Press, 2000).

Calder, Angus, *The Myth of the Blitz* (London: Pimlico, 1992).

Callicott, Sylvia L., 'What History Should We Teach in Primary Schools?', *History Workshop Journal*, 29 (1990), 107–110.

Cannadine, David, 'Brideshead Revered', *London Review of Books*, 31 March 1983.

——, 'Viewpoint British History: Past, Present – and Future?', *Past and Present*, 116 (1987), 169–91.

——, 'The Past in the Present', in Lesley Smith, ed., *The Making of Britain: Echoes of Greatness* (London: Macmillan, 1988).

——, *The Pleasures of the Past* (New York: WW Norton & Company Inc., 1989).

——, *History in Our Time* (New Haven: Yale University Press, 1998).

——, *Class in Britain* (London: Penguin, 2000).

———, *In Churchill's Shadow: Confronting the Past in Modern Britain* (London: Penguin Press, 2002).

Certeau, Michel de, *The Practice of Everyday Life* (Berkeley and Los Angeles: University of California Press, 1988).

Cesarani, David, 'Who Speaks for British Jews?', *New Statesman*, 28 May 2012, 23–27.

Childs, David, *Britain since 1945: A Political History* (London: Routledge, 2001).

Christie, Clive, 'The British Left and the Falklands War', *Political Quarterly*, 55, 3 (1984): 288–307.

Chun, Lin, *The First British New Left* (Edinburgh: Edinburgh University Press, 1993).

Clare, John, 'Toppling the English Citadel', *The Daily Telegraph*, 20 June 1991.

Clark, Elizabeth A., *History, Theory, Text: Historians and the Linguistic Turn* (Cambridge, MA: Harvard University Press, 2004).

Clark, Jonathan, 'National Identity, State Formation and Patriotism: The Role of History in the Public Eye', *History Workshop Journal*, 29 (1990), 95–102.

———, 'History as the Art of Memory', *The Times*, 23 February 1995.

Clark, Jonathan and Margot Heinemann, eds, *Culture and Crisis in Britain in the Thirties* (London: Lawrence and Wishart, 1979).

Clarke, Simon, 'Socialist Humanism and the Critique of Economism', *History Workshop Journal*, 8 (1979), 138–56.

Cole, G.D.H., 'What Workers' Education Means?', *Highway*, October 1952.

Collini, Stefan, *English Pasts: Essays in History and Culture* (Oxford: Oxford University Press, 1999).

Conradi, Peter, *A Very English Hero: The Making of Frank Thompson* (London: Bloomsbury, 2012).

Corfield, Penelope J. 'E. P. Thompson, the Historian: An Appreciation', *NLR*, I/201, Sept–Oct (1993), 10.

Crawford, Keith, 'A History of the Right: The Battle for Control of National Curriculum History 1989–1994', *British Journal of Educational Studies*, 43, 4 (1995), 433–56.

Croft, Andy, 'Authors Take Sides: Writers in the Communist Party 1920–1956', in Kevin Morgan, Nina Fishman and Geoff Andrews, eds, *Opening the Books: New Perspectives in the History of British Communism* (London: Pluto Press, 1995).

——, 'Walthamstow, Little Gidding & Middlesborough: E.P. Thompson, Adult Education and Literature', *Socialist History*, 8 (1995), 22–48.

——, ed., *A Weapon in the Struggle: The Cultural History of the Communist Party in Britain* (London: Pluto Press, 1998).

Crosby, Nigel, *Anti Fascism in Britain* (London: Macmillan Press Ltd, 2000).

Davies, Ioan, 'British Cultural Marxism', *International Journal of Politics, Culture and Society*, 4, 3 (1991): 323–43.

Davin, Anna, 'Imperialism and Motherhood', *History Workshop Journal*, 5 (1978), 9–66.

——, 'The Only Problem Was Time', *History Workshop Journal*, 50 (2000), 239–45.

Davis, Madeleine, 'Reappraising Socialist Humanism', *Journal of Political Ideologies*, 18, 1 (2013), 57–81.

Delafons, John, *Politics and Preservation: A Policy History of the Built Heritage 1882–1996* (London: D & FN Spon, 1997).

Dench, Geoff, Tony Flower and Kate Gavron, eds, *Young At Eighty: The Prolific Public Life of Michael Young* (Manchester: Carcanet Press, 1995).

Diski, Jenny, *The Sixties* (London: Profile, 2009).

Dunn, Ross E., 'The Making of a National Curriculum: The British Case', *History Teacher*, 33, 3 (2000).

Dutt, Rajani Palme, 'Intellectuals and Communism', *Communist Review*, September (1932), 421–30.

Dworkin, Dennis, *Cultural Marxism in Postwar Britain: History, the New Left, and the Origins of Cultural Studies* (Durham and London: Duke University Press, 1997).

Dyos, H.J. et al., 'The Interview in Social History Part 1: General Discussion', *Oral History*, 1, 4 (1972), 126–46.

Eaden, James and David Renton, *The Communist Party of Great Britain since 1920* (London: Palgrave Macmillan, 2002).

Eley, Geoff, *Forging Democracy: The History of the Left in Europe 1850–2000* (New York: Oxford University Press, 2000).

———, *A Crooked Line: From Cultural History to the History of Society* (Michigan: University of Michigan Press, 2005).

———, and Keith Nield, *The Future of Class in History: What's Left of the Social?* (Michigan: University of Michigan, 2007).

Elliot, Gregory, *Perry Anderson: The Merciless Laboratory of History* (Minneapolis: University of Minnesota Press, 1998).

Feldman, David and Jon Lawrence, eds, *Structures and Transformations in Modern British History: Essays for Gareth Stedman Jones* (Cambridge: Cambridge University Press, 2011).

Fieldhouse, Roger, 'The 1908 Report: Antidote to Class Struggle?', in Geoff Andrews, Hilda Kean and Jane Thompson, eds, *Ruskin College: Contesting Knowledge, Dissenting Politics* (London: Lawrence and Wishart, 1999), 35–58.

Fine, Gary and Philip Manning, 'Erving Goffman', in George Ritzer, ed., *The Blackwell Companion to Major Contemporary Social Theorists* (Malden: Blackwell Publishing Ltd, 2003).

Ford, Boris, ed., *Modern Britain: The Cambridge Cultural History* (Cambridge: Cambridge University Press, 1992).

Fyrth, Jim, ed., *Britain, Fascism and the Popular Front* (London: Lawrence and Wishart, 1985).

Gaolen, Paul, 'Only Connect…', *History Workshop Journal*, 30 (1990), 109–13.

Garnett, Mark, *From Anger to Apathy: The British Experience since 1975* (London: Jonathan Cape, 2007).

Gentry, Kynan, 'Ruskin, Radicalism and Raphael Samuel: Politics, Pedagogy and the Origins of the History Workshop', *History Workshop Journal*, 76 (2013), 187–211.

Gilroy, Paul, 'Nationalism, History and Ethnic Absolutism', *History Workshop Journal*, 30 (1990), 114–19.

Glennerster, Howard, 'Townsend, Peter Brereton (1928–2009)', *Oxford Dictionary of National Biography* (Oxford: Oxford University Press, 2004).

Goffman, Erving, *Asylums: Essays on the Social Situation of Mental Patients and Other Inmates* (Harmondsworth: Penguin Books, 1961).

Goldman, Lawrence, *Dons and Workers: Oxford and Adult Education since 1850* (Oxford: Clarendon Press, 1995).

Green, James R., *Taking History to Heart: The Power of the Past in Building Social Movements* (Boston: University of Massachusetts Press, 2000).

Green, Jonathan, *All Dressed Up: The Sixties and the Counterculture* (London: Pimlico, 1998).

Guyver, Robert, 'History's Doomsday Book', *History Workshop Journal*, 30 (1990), 100–8.

Hall, Catherine, 'The Tale of Samuel and Jemima: Gender and Working Class Culture in Early Nineteenth Century England', in Harvey Kaye and Keith McClelland, eds, *E. P. Thompson: Critical Perspectives* (Philadelphia: Temple University Press, 1990), 78–102.

Hall, Stuart, 'A Sense of Classlessness', *Universities and Left Review*, 5 (1958), 26–31.

——, 'The Great Moving Right Show', *Marxism Today*, January 1979, 14–22.

——, *The Hard Road to Renewal: Thatcherism and the Crisis of the Left* (London: Verso, 1988).

——, 'Raphael Samuel: 1934–1996', *New Left Review*, I/221, Jan–Feb (1997), 119–27.

——, 'The Life and Times of the First New Left', *New Left Review*, 61, Jan–Feb (2010), 177–95.

——, Alun Howkins, Sally Alexander and John Walsh, 'Raphael Samuel 1934–1996', *History Workshop Journal*, 43 (1997).

——, 'Richard Hoggart, *The Uses of Literacy* and the Cultural Turn', in Sue Owen, ed., *Richard Hoggart and Cultural Studies* (London: Palgrave Macmillan, 2008).

Halsey, A.H., 'Young, Michael Dunlop, Baron Young of Dartington (1915–2002)', *Oxford Dictionary of National Biography* (Oxford: Oxford University Press, 2006).

——, and Josephine Webb, eds, *Twentieth-Century British Social Trends* (Basingstoke: Macmillan, 2000).

Hamilton, Scott, *The Crisis of Theory: E.P. Thompson, the New Left and Post War British Politics* (Manchester: Manchester University Press, 2012).

Harding, Arthur and Raphael Samuel, *East End Underworld: Chapters in the Life of Arthur Harding* (London: Routledge, 1981).

Harris, Jose, 'The Arts and Social Sciences 1939–1970', in Brian Harrison, ed., *A History of Oxford University*, Vol. VIII: *The Twentieth Century* (Oxford: Oxford University Press, 1995), 217–49.

Harrison, Brian, 'History at the Universities 1968: A Commentary', *History*, 53 (1968), 357–80.

——, 'Oxford and the Labour Movement', *Twentieth Century British History*, 2, 3 (1991), 226–71.

——, 'Mrs Thatcher and the Intellectuals', *Twentieth Century British History*, 5, 2 (1994), 206–45.

Harrison, J.F.C., *Learning and Living 1790–1960: A Study in the History of the English Adult Education Movement* (London: Routledge and Kegan Paul, 1961).

Hay, Douglas, Peter Linebaugh, John G. Rule, E.P. Thompson and Cal Winslow, eds, *Albion's Fatal Tree: Crime and Society in Eighteenth Century England* (Harmondsworth: Penguin, 1977).

Hebdige, Dick, *Hiding in the Light: On Images and Things* (Routledge: London 1988).

Heinemann, Margot, '1956 and the Communist Party', *The Socialist Register*, 13 (1976).

Hennessey, Peter, *Never Again: Britain 1945–51* (London: Cape, 1992).

——, *Having It So Good: Britain in the Fifties* (London: Penguin, 2007).

Hewison, Robert, *The Heritage Industry: Britain in a Climate of Decline* (London: Methuen, 1983).

——, *Culture and Consensus: England, Art and Politics since 1940* (London: Methuen, 1995).

Hill, Christopher, *The English Revolution, 1640* (London: Lawrence and Wishart, 1940).

——, 'The Norman Yoke', in John Saville, ed., *Democracy and the Labour Movement: Essays in Honour of Dona Torr* (London: Lawrence and Wishart, 1954).

——, *The World Turned Upside Down: Radical Ideas During the English Revolution* (Harmondsworth: Penguin Books, 1975).

——, 'History is a Matter of Taking Liberties', *The Guardian*, 30 July 1983.

——, 'A First Class Performer', *History Workshop Journal*, 42 (1996), 207–9.

——, Rodney Hilton and Eric Hobsbawm, '*Past and Present*: Origins and Early Years', *Past and Present*, 100 (1983), 3–14.

Hindess, Barry and Paul Hirst, *Pre-Capitalist Modes of Production* (London: Routledge and Kegan Paul, 1975).

Hinton, James, *The Mass Observers: A History 1937–1949* (Oxford: Oxford University Press, 2013).

Hobsbawm, Eric, 'Where Are British Historians Going?', *Marxist Quarterly*, II/1 (1955).

——, 'The Historians' Group of the Communist Party', in Maurice Cornforth, ed., *Rebels and Their Causes: Essays in Honour of A.L. Morton* (London: Lawrence and Wishart, 1978).

——, 'The Forward March of Labour Halted?', *Marxism Today*, September 1978.

——, 'Falklands Fallout', *Marxism Today*, 14 January 1983.

——, *On History* (London: Wiedenfield and Nicholson, 1997).

——, *Interesting Times: A Twentieth Century Life* (London: Abacus, 2002).

——, and Terence Ranger, eds, *The Invention of Tradition* (Cambridge: Cambridge University Press, 1983).

Hodgkin, Katherine and Susannah Radstone, *Memory, History, Nation: Contested Pasts* (New Brunswick: Transaction Publishers, 2006).

Hoggart, Richard, *The Uses of Literacy: Aspects of Working-class Life, with Special References to Publications and Entertainments* (London: Chatto and Windus, 1957).

——, 'Review: Theatres of Memory', *Political Quarterly*, 66, 3 (1995), 215–16.

Holdsworth, Nadine, *Joan Littlewood's Theatre* (Cambridge: Cambridge University Press, 2011).

Hott, Terry, 'Interview with E. P. Thompson', *The Leveller*, 22 January 1978, 22.

Howe, Antony, 'The Past is Ours: Political Usage of English History by the British Communist Party and the Role of Dona Torr in the Creation of Its Historians' Group 1930–56', PhD thesis, University of Sydney, 2004.

Howkins, Alun, 'The People's Historian', *Red Pepper*, February 1997.

Hughes, H.D., 'History Workshop', *History Workshop Journal*, 11 (1981), 199–201.

Hutton, Ronald, *Debates in Stuart History* (London: Palgrave Macmillan, 2004).

Iggers, George G., *Historiography in the Twentieth Century: From Scientific Objectivity to the Postmodern Challenge* (Hanover: Wesleyan University Press, 2005).

——, and Edward Q. Wang, eds, *A Global History of Modern Historiography* (London: Routledge, 2013).

Jeffreys, Kevin, *Retreat from New Jerusalem: British Politics 1951–64* (New York: St Martin's Press, 1997).

Jennings, B., 'Revolting Students: The Ruskin College Dispute 1908–9', *Studies in Adult Education*, 9, 1 (1977), 1–16.

John, Angela V., 'Sitting on the Severn Bridge: Wales and British History', *History Workshop Journal*, 30 (1990), 91–100.

Johnson, Richard, 'Edward Thompson, Eugene Genovese, and Socialist-Humanist History', *History Workshop Journal*, 6 (1978), 79–100.

Jones, Gareth Elwyn, 'The Debate over the National Curriculum for History in England and Wales, 1989–90: The Role of the Press', *Curriculum Journal*, 11, 3 (2000), 299–322.

Jones, Ken, 'Raphael Samuel: Against Conformity', *Changing English: Studies in Culture and Education*, 5, 1 (1998), 17–26.

——, *Education in Britain: 1944 to the Present* (Cambridge: Polity Press, 2003).

Jones, Mervyn, 'The Man from Labour', *New Left Review,* I/1, Jan–Feb (1960), 14–17.

——, 'Raphael Samuel', *The Times*, 11 December 1996.

Judt, Tony, 'A Clown in Regal Purple: Social History and the Historians', *History Workshop Journal*, 7 (1979), 66–94.

——, with Timothy Snyder, *Rethinking the Twentieth Century* (London: William Heinemann, 2012).

Kalela, Jorma, *Making History: The Historian and the Uses of the Past* (Basingstoke: Palgrave Macmillan, 2012).

Kaye, Harvey, *The British Marxist Historians* (Cambridge: Polity Press, 1984).

——, *The Education of Desire: Marxists and the Writing of History* (London: Routledge, 1992).

——, and Keith McClelland, eds, *E.P. Thompson: Critical Perspectives* (Philadelphia: Temple University Press, 1990).

Kean, Hilda, 'Public History and Raphael Samuel: A Forgotten Radical Pedagogy?', *Public History Review*, 11 (2004), 51–62.

——, 'People, Historians and Public History; De-mystifying the Process of History Making', *Public Historian*, 32, 3 (2010), 25–38.

Kearney, Hugh, *The British Isles: A History of Four Nations* (Cambridge: Cambridge University Press, 1989).

Kenny, Michael, *The First New Left: British Intellectuals After Stalin* (London: Lawrence and Wishart, 1995).

Kerr, Peter, *Postwar British Politics: From Conflict to Consensus* (London: Routledge, 2005).

Kettle, Martin, 'The Experience of History', *New Society*, 6 December 1979.

Kiernan, V.G., 'Torr, Dona Ruth Anne (1883–1957)', *Oxford Dictionary of National Biography* (Oxford: Oxford University Press, 2004).

Klimke, Martin and Joachim Scharloth, eds, *1968 in Europe: A History of Protest and Activism 1956–1977* (London: Palgrave Macmillan, 2008).

Kynaston, David, *Family Britain 1951–1957* (London: Bloomsbury, 2009).

——, *Modernity Britain: Opening the Box 1957–59* (London: Bloomsbury, 2013).

Lago, Mary, *India's Prisoner: A Biography of Edward John Thompson 1886–1946* (Colombia: University of Missouri Press, 2001).

Laity, Paul, ed., *Left Book Club Anthology* (London: Victor Gollancz, 2001).

Lambert, Peter and Phillipp R. Schofield, eds, *Making History: An Introduction to the History and Practices of a Discipline* (Abingdon: Routledge, 2004).

Lawrence, Jon, 'Social-Science Encounters and the Negotiation of Difference in 1960s England', *History Workshop Journal*, 77 (2014), 215–39.

Laybourn, Kevin, *Marxism in Britain: Dissent, Decline and Re-emergence 1945–c2000* (London: Taylor and Routledge, 2006).

Leach, Robert, *Theatre Workshop: Joan Littlewood and the Making of Modern British Theatre* (Exeter: University of Exeter Press, 2006).

Lefebvre, George with R.R. Palmer, tr., *The Coming of the French Revolution, 1789* (Princeton: Princeton University Press, 1947).

Lessing, Doris, *Walking In the Shade: Volume Two of My Autobiography* (New York: Harper Collins, 1997).

Levin, Bernard, *The Pendulum Years: Britain and the Sixties* (London: Jonathan Cape, 1970).

Light, Alison and Raphael Samuel, 'Report Back', *History Workshop Journal*, 32 (1991).

——, 'A Biographical Note on the Text', in Raphael Samuel, *Island Stories: Unravelling Britain* (London: Verso, 1998).

——, 'Preface', in Raphael Samuel, *The Lost World of British Communism* (London: Verso, 2006).

Linebaugh, Peter, 'From the Upper West Side to Wick Episcopi', *New Left Review*, I/201, Sep–Oct (1994), 18–33.

Linehan, Thomas, *Communism in Great Britain: From Cradle to Grave 1920–1939* (Manchester: Manchester University Press, 2007).

Little, Vivienne, 'A National Curriculum in History: A Very Contentious Issue', *British Journal of Educational Studies*, 38, 4 (1990), 319–34.

Littlewood, Joan, *Joan's Book: Joan Littlewood's Peculiar History as She Tells It* (London: Methuen, 1994).

Löwy, Michael and Robert Sayre, with Catherine Porter, tr., *Romanticism against the Tide of Modernity* (Durham: Duke University Press, 2001).

MacCarthy, Fiona, 'Treading Softly on Our Dreams', *The Observer*, 12 February 1995.

MacLachlan, Alastair, *The Rise and Fall of Revolutionary England: An Essay on the Fabrication of Seventeenth Century History* (London: Macmillan, 1996).

Mandler, Peter, *The Fall and Rise of the Stately Home* (New Haven: Yale University Press, 1997).

Marks, Shula, 'History, the Nation and Empire: Sniping from the Periphery', *History Workshop Journal*, 29 (1990), 111–19.

Marris, Peter, 'Knowledge and Persuasion: Research at the ICS', in Geoff Dench, Tony Flower and Kate Gavron, eds, *Young at Eighty: The Prolific Public Life of Michael Young* (Manchester: Carcanet Press, 1995).

Martin, Paul, 'Look, See, Hear', in Geoff Andrews, Hilda Kean and Jane Thompson, eds, *Ruskin College: Contesting Knowledge, Dissenting Politics* (London: Lawrence and Wishart, 1999).

Marwick, Arthur, *The Sixties: Cultural Revolution in Britain, France, Italy and the United States 1958–1974* (Oxford: Oxford University Press, 1998).

Mason, Tim, 'The Teaching and Study of History', *Isis*, 31 May 1961, 20–21.

——, 'Reform of the History Syllabus', *Isis*, 5 December 1962, 15.

——, 'The History Syllabus: The End of the Road?', *Isis*, 13 March 1963.

——, 'Nineteenth Century Cromwell', *Past and Present*, 40 (1968), 187–91.

Matthews, Wade, *The New Left, National Identity, and the Break-up of Britain* (Leiden and Boston: BRILL, 2013).

May, Alex, 'Keal, Minna (1909–1999)', *Oxford Dictionary of National Biography* (Oxford: Oxford University Press, 2004).

McClelland, Keith, 'Towards a Socialist History: Some Comments on Richard Johnson, "Edward Thompson, Eugene Genovese, and Socialist-Humanist History"', *History Workshop Journal*, 7 (1979), 101–15.

McCrindle, Jean, 'The Hungarian Uprising and a Young British Communist', *History Workshop Journal*, 62 (2006), 194–199.

McEwan, Malcolm, 'The Day the Party Had to Stop', *The Socialist Register*, 13 (1976).

McIntyre, Stuart, *A Proletarian Science: Marxism in Britain 1917–1933* (London: Lawrence and Wishart, 1986).

McKenna, Frank, 'Victorian Railway Workers', *History Workshop Journal*, 1 (1976), 9–25, 26–73.

McSmith, Andy, *No Such Thing as Society* (London: Constable, 2010).

Medvedev, Zhores A. and Roy A. Medvedev, *The Unknown Stalin* (London: I.B. Tauris, 2006).

Miliband, Ralph, 'The Sickness of Labourism', *New Left Review*, I/1, Jan–Feb (1960), 5–9.

Miner, Horace, *The Primitive City of Timbuctoo* (Princeton: Princeton University Press, 1955).

Monk, Ray, 'Life without Theory: Biography as an Exemplar of Philosophical Understanding', *Poetics Today*, 28, 3 (2007), 527–70.

Morgan, Kenneth, *Britain since 1945: The People's Peace* (Oxford: Oxford University Press, 2001).

Morgan, Kevin, *Against Fascism and War* (Manchester: Manchester University Press, 1989).

——, Nina Fishman and Geoff Andrews, eds, *Opening the Books: New Perspectives in the History of British Communism* (London: Pluto Press, 1995).

Morton, A.L., *A People's History of England* (London: Gollancz, 1938).

Murray, Alex, 'The Heritage Industry and Historiographic Metafiction: Historical Representations in the 1980s', in Emily Horton, Philip Tew and Leigh Wilson, eds, *The 1980s: A Decade of Contemporary British Fiction* (London: Bloomsbury Academic, 2014), 125–50.

Nairn, Tom, 'The British Political Elite', *New Left Review*, I/24, Mar–Apr (1964), 19–25.

——, 'The English Working Class', *New Left Review*, I/24, Mar–Apr (1964), 43–57.

Nash, Ian, 'Raised Voices in a Very British Battle', *The Times Educational Supplement*, 25 June 1990.

Nelson, Janet L., 'A Place for Medieval History in the National Curriculum?', *History Workshop Journal*, 29 (1990), 103–6.

Newens, Stan, 'The Genesis of *East End Underworld*: Chapters in the Life of Arthur Harding by Raphael Samuel', *History Workshop Journal*, 64 (2007), 347–54.

Noakes, Lucy, *War and the British: Gender, Memory and National Identity* (London: I.B. Tauris, 1998).

Nore, Ellen, *Charles A. Beard, An Intellectual Biography* (Carbondale: Southern Illinois University Press, 1983).

Obelkevich, Jim, 'New Developments in History in the 1950s and 1960s', *Contemporary British History*, 14, 4 (2000), 125–42.

Orwell, George, *Inside the Whale and Other Essays* (London: Penguin, 1957).

Osgerby, Bill, 'Youth Culture', in Paul Addison and Harriet Jones, eds, *A Companion to Contemporary Britain* (Oxford: Blackwell, 2005).

Ovenden, Keith, *A Fighting Withdrawal: The Life of Dan Davin, Writer, Soldier, Publisher* (Oxford: University of Oxford Press, 1996).

Owen, Sue, ed., *Richard Hoggart and Cultural Studies* (London: Palgrave Macmillan, 2008).

Palmer, Bryan, *E. P. Thompson: Objections and Oppositions* (London: Verso, 1994).

Pascal, Blaise, *Pensees and Other Writings* (Oxford: Oxford University Press, 1995).

Pearson, Geoffrey, 'Falling Standards: A Short, Sharp History of Moral Decline', in Martin Barker, ed., *The Video Nasties: Freedom and Censorship in the Media* (London: The Works, 1984).

Perkins, Harold, *The Rise of the Professional Society* (New York and London: Routledge, 1989).

Pocock, J.G.A., 'British History: A Plea for a New Subject', *Journal of Modern History*, 47 (1975), 601–21.

Pollins, Harold, *The History of Ruskin College* (Oxford: Ruskin College Library Publication, no. 3, 1984).

Pollitt, Harry, 'The Road to British Socialism', in *Looking Ahead* (London: Communist Party of Great Britain, 1947).

Prescott, John, 'Genuine Love for Others', *The Guardian*, 11 December 1996.

Prochaska, Alice, 'The History Working Group: Reflections and Diary', *History Workshop Journal*, 30 (1990), 80–90.

Purdie, Bob, '"Long Haired Intellectuals and Busy Bodies": Ruskin, Student Radicalism, and Civil Rights in Northern Ireland', in Geoff Andrews, Hilda Kean and Jane Thompson, eds, *Ruskin College: Contesting Knowledge, Dissenting Politics* (London: Lawrence and Wishart, 1999).

Radstone, Susannah and Katherine Hodgkin, *Memory, History, Nation: Contested Pasts* (New Brunswick: Transaction Publishers, 2006).

Ranciere, Jacques, *The Intellectual and His People: Staging the People Volume 2* (London: Verso, 2012).

Rapaport-Albert, Ada, 'Chimen Abramsky Obituary', *The Guardian*, 19 March 2010.

——, 'Professor Chimen Abramsky: Historian', *The Times,* 19 March 2010.

Raven, James, 'Viewpoint: British History and the Enterprise Culture', *Past and Present*, 123 (1989), 178–204.

Reas, Paul and Stuart Cosgrove, *Flogging a Dead Horse: Heritage Culture and Its Role in Post Industrial Britain* (Manchester: Cornerhouse, 1993).

Ree, Jonathan, 'A Theatre of Arrogance', *Times Higher Educational Supplement*, 5 June 1995.

Renton, David, 'The History Woman', *Socialist Review*, 224 (1998).

Rettie, John, 'How Khrushchev Leaked His Secret Speech to the World', *History Workshop Journal*, 62 (2006), 182–93.

Robbins, (Lord), *The Robbins Report: Higher Education* (London: Her Majesty's Stationery Office, 1963).

Rose, Jonathan, *The Intellectual Life of the British Working Classes* (New Haven: Yale University Press, 2001).

Rosen, Andrew, *The Transformation of British Life 1950–2000: A Social History* (Manchester: Manchester University Press, 2003).

Rowbotham, Sheila, 'Remembering 1967', in Raphael Samuel, ed., *History Workshop: A Collectanea 1967–1991* (Oxford: History Workshop 25, 1991).

——, 'The Personal and the Political: Interview with Dorothy Thompson', *New Left Review*, I/200, Jul–Aug (1993), 87–100.

——, 'Some Memories of Raphael', *New Left Review*, I/221, Jan–Feb (1997), 128–32.

——, *Promises of a Dream: Remembering the Sixties* (London: Penguin, 2000).

——, Lynne Segal and Hilary Wainwright, *Beyond the Fragments: Feminism and the Making of Socialism* (London: Merlin Press, 1979).

Rule, John, 'Thompson, Edward Palmer (1924–1993)', *Oxford Dictionary of National Biography* (Oxford: Oxford University Press, 2004).

——, and Robert Malcolmson, eds, *Protest and Survival: The Historical Experience – Essays for E. P. Thompson* (London: Merlin Press, 1993).

Salvatore, Nick, 'Biography and Social History: An Intimate Relationship', *Labour History*, 87 (2004), 189–92.

Samuel, Raphael, Barbara Bloomfield and Guy Boanas, eds, *The Enemy Within: Pit Villages and the Miners' Strike of 1984–5* (London: Routledge and Kegan Paul, 1986).

——, Ewan MacColl and Stuart Cosgrove, eds, *Theatres of the Left 1880–1935: Workers' Theatre Movements in Britain and America* (London: Routledge and Kegan Paul, 1985).

——, and Gareth Stedman Jones, 'Sociology and History', *History Workshop Journal*, 1 (1976), 6–8.

——, and Gareth Stedman Jones, eds, *Culture, Ideology and Politics* (London: Routledge and Kegan Paul, 1982).

——, and Charles Taylor, 'A Left Notebook', *Universities and Left Review*, 1, 2 (1957), 79–80.

——, and Paul Thompson, eds, *The Myths We Live By* (London: Routledge, 1990).

Sandbrook, Dominic, *Never Had It So Good* (London: Abacas, 2006).

——, *White Heat: A History of Britain in the Swinging Sixties* (London: Little Brown, 2006).

Saville, John, ed., *Democracy and the Labour Movement: Essays in Honour of Dona Torr* (London: Lawrence and Wishart, 1954).

——, 'The Twentieth Congress and the British Communist Party', *The Socialist Register*, 13 (1976).

——, 'Edward Thompson, the Communist Party and 1956', *The Socialist Register*, 30 (1994).

——, *Memoirs from the Left* (London: Merlin, 2003).

——, and E.P. Thompson, 'Why We Are Publishing', *The Reasoner*, 1 (1956), 1–3.

——, and E.P. Thompson, 'Editorial', *The New Reasoner*, 1, Summer (1957), 1.

Schiffrin, Deborah, 'Jewish Argument as Sociability', *Language and Society*, 13, 3 (1984), 311–35.

Schwarz, Bill, 'Review: British Marxist Historians', *Times Higher Educational Supplement*, 11 September 1987.

——, '"The People" in History: The Communist Party Historians Group 1946–1956', in Richard Johnson, Gregor McLennan, Bill Schwarz and David Sutton, eds, *Making Histories: Studies in History-Writing and Politics* (Minneapolis: University of Minnesota, 1982).

——, History on the Move: Reflections on History Workshop', *Radical History Review*, 57 (2002), 202–20.

——, 'Keeper of Our Shared Memory', *The Guardian*, 10 December 1996.

——, 'Foreword', in Raphael Samuel, *Theatres of Memory: The Past in Contemporary Culture* (London: Verso, 2012).

Scott-Brown, Sophie, 'The Art of the Organiser: Raphael Samuel and the Origins of the History Workshop', *History of Education: The Journal of the History of Education*, 45, 3 (2016), 372–90, www.tandfonline.com/doi/full/10.1080/0046760X.2015.1103907, 15 December 2015.

Searby, Peter, with John Rule and Robert Malcolmson, 'Edward Thompson as a Teacher: Yorkshire and Warwick', in John Rule and Robert Malcolmson, eds, *Protest and Survival: The Historical Experience – Essays for E. P. Thompson* (London: Merlin Press, 1993).

Segal, Lynne, 'Lost Worlds: Political Memoirs of the Left in Britain', *Radical Philosophy*, 121, Sept/Oct (2003), 6–23.

Selbourne, David, 'On the Methods of the History Workshop', *History Workshop Journal*, 9 (1980), 150–61.

——, 'The Last Comrade', *The Observer*, 15 December 1996.

Sharma, Aradhana and Akhil Gupta, eds, *The Anthropology of the State* (Malden: Blackwell, 2006), 86–111.

Sinfield, Alan, *Literature, Politics and Culture in Postwar Britain* (Los Angeles and Berkeley: University of California Press, 1989).

Smith, Laurajane, *The Uses of Heritage* (New York: Routledge, 2006).

Smith, Lesley ed., *The Making of Britain: Echoes of Greatness* (London: Macmillan, 1988).

Smithson, Sue, *Community Adventure: The Story of Long Dene School* (London: New European Publications, 1999).

Stedman Jones, Gareth, 'The Pathology of English History', *New Left Review*, I/46, Nov–Dec (1967), 29–43.

——, *Outcast London: A Study of the Relationship between Classes in Victorian Society* (Oxford: Clarendon Press, 1971).

——, *Languages of Class: Studies in English Working Class History 1832–1982* (Cambridge: Cambridge University Press, 1971).

——, 'Obituary: Raphael Samuel', *The Independent*, 11 December 1996.

——, 'History and Theory', *historein* [Athens], 3 (2001), 103–24.

——, 'Samuel, Raphael Elkan (1934–1996)', *Oxford Dictionary of National Biography* (Oxford: Oxford University Press, 2004).

Steedman, Carolyn, 'Raphael Samuel (1934–1996)', *Radical Philosophy*, 82 (1997).

Steele, Tom, *The Emergence of Cultural Studies 1945–65: Cultural Politics, Adult Education and the English Question* (London: Lawrence and Wishart, 1997).

Tawney, R.H., *Religion and Rise of Capitalism* (London: J. Murray, 1936).

Taylor, Charles, 'Marxism and Humanism', *New Reasoner*, 2 (1957), 92–98.

——, 'Socialism and the Intellectuals – Three', *Universities and Left Review*, 1, 2 (1957), 18–19.

——, 'Alienation and Community', *Universities and Left Review*, 5 (1958), 11–18.

Taylor, Miles, 'Patriotism, History and the Left in Britain', *Twentieth Century British History*, 33, 4 (1990), 971–87.

Thomas, Keith, 'Should Historians be Anthropologists?', *Oxford Magazine*, 1 June 1961.

——, 'History and Anthropology', *Past and Present*, 24 (1963), 3–24.

——, 'The Tools and the Job', *The Times Literary Supplement*, 7 April 1966.

——, *Religion and the Decline of Magic: Studies in Popular Belief in Sixteenth and Seventeenth Century England* (London: Weidenfeld and Nicolson, 1971).

——, 'Retrochic', *London Review of Books*, 20 April 1995.

——, 'Diary', *London Review of Books,* 10 June 2010.

Thompson, Dorothy, 'On the Trail of the First New Left', *New Left Review*, I/215, Jan–Feb (1996), 93–100.

——, 'Introduction', *The Essential E. P. Thompson* (New York: The New Press, 2001).

Thompson, E.P., *William Morris: Romantic to Revolutionary* (London: Lawrence and Wishart, 1955).

——, 'Socialist Humanism: An Epistle to the Philistines Part I/II', *New Reasoner*, 1 (1957), 105–143.

——, 'Socialism and the Intellectuals', *Universities and Left Review*, 1, 1 (1957), 31–36.

——, 'Commitment in Politics', *Universities and Left Review*, 6 (1959), 50–55.

——, 'The Long Revolution I', *New Left Review*, I/9, May–Jun (1961), 24–33.

——, 'The Long Revolution II', *New Left Review*, I/10, Jul–Aug (1961), 34–39.

——, *The Making of the English Working Class* (London: Victor Gollancz, 1963).

——, 'The Peculiarities of the English', *The Socialist Register*, 2 (1965), 311–362.

——, 'History From Below', *The Times Literary Supplement*, 7 April 1966.

——, 'Time, Work-Discipline and Industrial Capitalism', *Past and Present*, 38 (1967), 56–97.

——, 'The Moral Economy of the English Crowd in the Eighteenth Century', *Past and Present*, 50 (1971), 76–136.

———, *Whigs and Hunters: The Origin of the Black Act* (New York: Pantheon Books, 1975).

———, *William Morris: Romantic to Revolutionary* (New York: Pantheon Books, 1977).

———, *The Poverty of Theory: Or an Orrery of Errors* (London: Merlin Press, 1978)

———, *Writing by Candlelight* (London: Merlin, 1980).

———, *The Heavy Dancers* (New York: Pantheon Books, 1985).

———, *Customs in Common* (London: Merlin Press, 1991).

———, *Witness against the Beast: William Blake and the Moral Law* (New York: New Press, 1993).

———, *Beyond the Frontier* (Stanford: Stanford University Press, 1997).

———, ed., *The Railway: An Adventure on Construction* (London: British-Yugoslav Association, 1948).

———, ed., *Out of Apathy* (London: Stevens, 1960).

Thompson, Frank, *There is a Spirit in Europe: A Memoir of Frank Thompson*, collected by E.P. Thompson and T.J. Thompson (London: Golancz, 1947).

Thompson, Paul, *The Work of William Morris* (London: Heinemann, 1967).

———, *The Edwardians: The Remaking of British Society* (London: Weidenfield and Nicholson, 1975).

———, *Voices of the Past* (Oxford: Oxford University Press, 1978).

The Times, 'Professor Chimen Abramsky: Historian', 19 March 2010.

Tomlinson, Jim, *The Politics of Decline: Understanding Post War Britain* (Abingdon: Routledge, 2014).

Torr, Dona, ed., *History in the Making* (London: Lawrence and Wishart, 1948).

Townsend, Peter, 'Peter Marris', *The Guardian*, 5 July 2007.

Trevor-Roper, Hugh, 'The Invention of Tradition: The Highland Tradition of Scotland', in Eric Hobsbawm and Terence Ranger, eds, *The Invention of Tradition* (Cambridge: Cambridge University Press, 1983).

Veldman, Meredith, *Fantasy, the Bomb and the Greening of Britain* (Cambridge: Cambridge University Press, 1994).

Vinen, Richard, *Thatcher's Britain: The Politics and Social Upheaval of the Thatcher Era* (London: Simon & Schuster, 2009).

Walzer, Michael, *The Company of Critics* (New York: Basic Books, 2002).

Ward, Colin, *Anarchy in Action* (London: George Allen and Unwin Ltd, 1973).

——, ed., *A Decade of Anarchy 1961–1970: Selections from the Monthly Journal Anarchy* (London: Freedom Press, 1987).

——, 'Fringe Benefits', *New Society*, 17 November 1989.

——, *Anarchism: A Very Short Introduction* (Oxford: Oxford University Press, 2004).

——, ed., *Anarchy: A Journal of Desire Armed 1961–1970*, National Library of Australia.

Webb, W.L., 'A Thoroughly English Dissident', *Radical History Review*, 58 (1994), 160–164.

Weber, Max with T. Parsons, tr., and R.H. Tawney, *The Protestant Ethic and the Spirit of Capitalism* (London: Allen and Unwin, 1930).

Webster, Wendy, *Imagining Home: Gender, 'Race' and National Identity 1945–64* (London: Routledge, 1998).

Weeks, Jeffrey, 'Foucault for Historians', *HWJ*, 14 (1982), 106–19.

Weiner, Martin J., *English Culture and the Decline of the Industrial Spirit 1850–1980* (Cambridge: Cambridge University Press, 1981).

West, Roger, 'History, the Nation and the Schools: Ruskin College, Oxford, 3 June 1989', *History Workshop Journal*, 29 (1990), 196–98.

Westwood, Sallie and J.E. Thomas, eds, *The Politics of Adult Education* (Leicester: National Institute of Adult Continuing Education, 1991).

White, John J., *Bertolt Brecht's Dramatic Theory* (New York: Boydell and Brewer Inc., 2004).

Williams, Raymond, 'The Uses of Literacy: Working Class Culture', *Universities and Left Review*, 1, 2 (1957), 29–32.

——, *Culture and Society 1780–1950* (London: Chatto and Windus, 1958).

——, 'Culture is Ordinary', in Norman Mackenzie, ed., *Convictions* (London: MacGibbon and Gee, 1958).

——, *The Long Revolution* (London: Chatto and Windus, 1961).

——, *Politics and Letters: Interviews with New Left Review* (London: New Left Books, 1979).

Willmott, Peter, *Adolescent Boys of East London* (London: Routledge & K. Paul, 1966).

Wood, Neal, *Communism and British Intellectuals* (London: Gollancz, 1959).

Worley, Matthew, *Class against Class: The Communist Party in Britain between the Wars* (London: I.B. Taurus, 2002).

Wright, Patrick, *On Living in an Old Country: The National Past in Contemporary Britain* (London: Verso, 1985).

——, 'Review of Theatres of Memory', *The Guardian*, 5 February 1995.

Yeo, Stephen, 'The More it Changes, the More it Stays the Same?', *HWJ*, 30 (1990), 120–28.

Young, Michael, 'Willmott, Peter (1923–2000)', *Oxford Dictionary of National Biography* (Oxford: Oxford University Press, 2004).

——, and Peter Willmott, *Family and Kinship in East London* (London: Routledge and Kegan Paul, 1957).

SELECT BIBLIOGRAPHY

Audio-visual sources and websites[1]

Abramsky, Sasha, 'The House of Twenty Thousand Books', YouTube, 6 June 2014, www.youtube.com/watch?v=h37Gf-awf0E&feature=youtu.be.

Berlin, Mike, 'The Partisan Café', BBC Radio 4, 4 December 2008.

Bishopsgate Library's channel, 'Raphael Samuel on history from below, 1990', YouTube, 5 January 2012, www.youtube.com/watch?v=w96_Nf-RJHs.

Butler, Margaret, 'Costume Drama', BFI Screen Online, www.screenonline.org.uk/film/id/570755/.

Conway, Paul, 'Minna Keal 1909–1999', April 2000, www.musicweb-international.com/keal/.

Dreier, Peter, '*The House of Twenty Thousand Books* by Sasha Abramsky', Huffington Post, 8 June 2014, www.huffingtonpost.com/peter-dreier/the-house-of-twenty-thousand-books_b_5467086.html.

Education in England, The Robbins Report (1963), www.educationengland.org.uk/documents/robbins/robbins1963.html.

Edwardian Online, 'Paul Thompson', UK Data Service, www.ukdataservice.ac.uk/use-data/guides/dataset/family-life.

National Trust, 'Our History', www.nationaltrust.org.uk/lists/our-history-1945-2000.

Smith, Graham, 'The Making of Oral History', *Making History: The Changing Face of the Profession in Britain*, The Institute of Historical Research, www.history.ac.uk/makinghistory/resources/articles/oral_history.html.

Stedman Jones, Gareth, 'History and Theory: An English Story', *historein* [Athens], 3 (2001), 103–24, ejournals.epublishing.ekt.gr/index.php/historein/article/viewFile/2193/2033.pdf.

Taylor, Barbara, 'History Workshop Journal', *Making History: The Changing Face of the Profession in Britain*, The Institute of Historical Research, www.history.ac.uk/makinghistory/resources/articles/HWJ.html.

---

1 All websites checked as of April 2017.

www.ingramcontent.com/pod-product-compliance
Lightning Source LLC
Chambersburg PA
CBHW061251230426
43664CB00025B/2927